Talking Law
Vol II

The Podcast Diaries

SALLY PENNI

DEDICATION

Thank you to my lovely children Jack, Will and Madeleine,
and of course to my husband.

CONTENTS

ACKNOWLEDGMENTS AND DEDICATIONS

Thank you to all the NHS staff and keyworkers who risked their lives to save many lives.

This book is dedicated to the loving memory of all those whom we loved so dearly and lost in 2020.

In life they taught me so much. Their deaths were a shock and have had a profound effect on me; more than I ever thought. Funny thing about grief, you never know when it will strike you.

Especially dedicated to these amazing people:

John Broadley, 1951 - 2020
Jamie Aarvold, 1946 - 2020
Denise Johnson, 1967 - 2020
Allen Coleman, a farmer, father and husband

John

To JB, John Broadley, colleague, friend, mentor. Much loved in death as he was in life.

JB was a barrister for 35years at Cobden House Chambers Manchester. John was the eldest of 4. Three brothers Paul and Tony and sister Helen. He leaves 3 sons, one grandchild and a wife. He will be much loved by all who knew him and his many wonderful stories. He was a formidable barrister who understood the human condition. He was funny, articulate, kind and great company. He taught me so much. He was an example of all that was good about the Bar and being a Barrister. Above all he was my friend. I shall miss him dearly.

Jamie

James Hilary Aarvold was the most extraordinary man.

He was the son of Sir Carl Aarvold, the former Recorder of London and the former Common Sergeant of London who sat at the Old Bailey. Jamie was not in the law. He worked in insurance. He did admire lawyers. Certainly he had a lot of time for my work. Jamie was a father, pops, a brother, husband, friend, counsel and friend to me.

Thank you for being You and a great leader of the 'outlaws' in-laws.

Thank you for always having a sense of humour and teaching me how to be a decent human being.

Jamie leaves his brilliant wife Jilly, Zander, Pippin, Benji, Eliza, Joe Fish, Poppy, Molly, Tom.

Denise

Denise Johnson aged 53 was a black singer with various bands. Glorious voice and most wonderful person. A legend and Mrs Manchester who left us unexpectedly too early.

Allen

Allen Coleman was a farmer from Hampshire.

He leaves two sons and 4 grandchildren. He spent many wonderful years in Cornwall with his beloved Pat, the love of his life. He acquired from Pat S-J three extra children, Ali, Peter, Robbie, and eight grandchildren, Lily, James, Archie, Anna, Max, Jack, Will, Madeleine.

I enjoyed our many chats.

Geoff Stanley-Jones, 1948-1998

Not lost in 2020 but 20 years ago.
Gone but remembered and never forgotten. So loved.
Grandpa Geoffrey.

Edith Yawa Akumah,

A midwife well known and respected. She adopted numerous orphaned children. She was a great believer in Education and loved reading. The eldest of 5, Emile, Victoria, Blay, and Pauline. She leaves Doris, Denis, Dickson and their respective children.

And in loving memory of all those who you have loved and lost.

INTRODUCTION

My Talking Law podcast has over 27K listeners and downloads. It occurred to me though that if my granny was alive, she just might like to read it rather than listen. To this end here is the transcript of all the episodes of the Podcast with additional chapters. My guests were chosen for their inspirational stories. Their bon traditional routes to the Bar. I like to think of them as ordinary people with extraordinary stories about life, wellbeing and an interest in the law. Please don't ask me if I have a favourite, I don't. Each story is powerful and inspirational if you are in the law or not.

In this book I have added some extra chapters on the subject matters that I often ask my guests about, including wellbeing, resilience, financial wellbeing. Diversity in legal profession is covered in book one Talking Law volume I. these books are. A series of books a in a trilogy.

During the writing of this book several things happened. A global pandemic- covid19, mental health awareness week, black lives matter and school diversity week (pride parade weekend did not happen). These things meant barristers and lawyers like myself had to work from home in a lockdown for 12 week. Laws were passed to stop people going out and spreading the virus. The virus originated from China. In the UK over 43K people died. The virus disproportionately killed black and minorities and the elderly in care comes. It was a worrying time.

I will deal with each of these separately and briefly.

Covid 19

During the pandemic, lawyers worked, home-schooled their children, so became, we all became, teachers, cooks, cleaners, counsellors, mentors. The evidence showed that women bore the brunt of the work. 1950s housewives were reborn. The survey came from the Fawcett Society.

During Covid 19 the courts closed. The only good thing was I could interview some of my guests but remotely. It did make me wonder if we could all survive with simply the technology. I reread Richard Susskind's book on technology. He is the Chair of the society of technology. The courts are closed. There is talk of doing away with Jury trials in criminal cases in England and Wales because of the backlog due to Covid 19. A fundamental change in law. A subject beyond the pages of this book.

BLM Black Lives Matter

Also during Covid, we saw protest of black lives Matter a movement started in the USA after the death of Rodney King some 20 years ago. The movement regained life this time after George Floyd killed by the people who should have protected him, US police officers officers. Extraordinary, black and white people felt strongly against the treatment of Floyd that they risked their own lives to protest against racial injustice in the UK and USA. It sparked a global protest using the hashtag #blm #black lives matter. It caused all aspects of business, law, and society to look at what they can do about systematic racism. To consider the difference between Equality and equity. What positive action we can all take beyond being not racist.

Many of us shared the racism and the casual racism we suffer when we go to work in court. Being mistaken for defendant or the client, being asked to interpret for black defendants in the dock as I was the only black counsel in the case. It was not just the law, in society as a whole we share our incidents of racism including the editor of Vogue UK, Edward Enninful OBE, a black man, shared how he was racially profiled.

The effect of BLM

What will the BLM movement be like? Will this be like #metoo movement? How can our non BAME colleagues support and become allies for change?

In the law it means organisations such as, the Inns, CPS, Bar council, the circuits, and as well as our tv and radio broadcasters, festival holders to look at the performers and attenders. For example, the CPS can look at how many CPS prosecutors there are. They must also look at how many category 4 prosecutors there are. This is the highest categories who can prosecute the most serious cases. This is important as there are few Treasury counsel who are black and BAME. As the recruitment of QCs and Judges from the Bar it is important that the decision makers reflect these people. Equally black lawyers are often considered to be in less prestigious sets. In the old days in ghetto type chambers. Good lawyers but this has often been the reference. It is not true.

BLM and the Inns of court

The Inns of court must look at the make up of Hall and look at how they appoint Benchers. Look at more diverse range of benchers, under 40s and under 50s. Look at appointment processes. Review them. Do an audit of the number of BAME Benchers, women and BAME. Consider more links of the inns less London based and involve the circuits more.

The Circuits

Each region of the UK that Barristers practice in is split into a circuit. Each circuit needs to look at why it is the practitioners are not representative of the areas of high BAME demographics they serve. Some of this is historic. However, each circuit can consider having have an E and D and I officer. Conduct an audit of their Black and BAME members. Some of this can be Bar Council led. The circuits can ask them what else they would like to see. Perhaps even a buddy system. A complaints process on each circuit. Each circuit should Appoint a liaison Judge who can deal with complaints of racism and sexism from the Bar and solicitors. The Judicial office already has diversity judges and have done a tremendous amount of work on diversity, but this would an extra useful measure. Circuit leaders can step in to represent barristers who face racism and the designated judge can deal with the offending judge or judges. Local area law societies must look at the judicial office holders. The Bar council and the Law Society should look at its office holders.

For my part, I think the JAC are doing their best to recruit more diverse judges. I am not yet a judge but there is time. I am hopeful. The number of BAME entrants is higher however retention of women is still low.

Intersectionality

Intersectionality is so important. As a woman who set up an organisation with members consisting of men and women, I must acknowledge the fact that there is intersectionality between certain characteristics

For example black women lawyers are 73 per cent less likely to become partners than their white male counterparts. Black women suffer a double deficit, a double transection they are treated worst of all the groups. We must be aware of this.

In my view, the future is bright, in the words of Reverend Wilson who marched with Martin Luther King in the Civil Rights movement, and attended the George Floyd funeral, the people protesting in the BLM movement are not only the black people like in the 60s but rather whit, Asian, Hispanic and all. I believe in building allies with our colleagues and friends. Helping people to understand the plight of Black and minority lawyers at the Bar and solicitors.

I saw a placard held by a blonde lady on TV in a protest in London, wearing a mask that said, I am not black, but I stand with you. She had written it. You may not be black, reading this but you can stand with me. Acknowledge the issues and be an ally. The future is bright. Young people will not stand for inequality. As I stand as an ally for all that is fair and just you can be too. Positive discrimination is unlawful. Positive action is okay. There is a clear distinction. Most minority lawyers do not support quotas.

So what can ordinary people do beyond being allies? What can they do beyond not being racist? We can be positively anti-racist. We can Call It Out when it occurs because silence is complicit. Have compassion. We all have compassion for there is finite resource. Ensure you have a supportive network, you have self-compassion or you will burn out

I have also listed the number of webinars and support we gave during Covid 19 to lawyers, students and beyond.

Finally: the profits from sale of this book will go to 3 chosen charities: Billable hours founded by Sean Jones QC, the NHS and RMCH.

1 THE PODCAST INTERVIEWS

Here is a transcript of the Podcast interviews.
They are up to the time of writing.

Hello and welcome to Talking Law, from Women in the Law and Business UK. I'm Sally Penni, a Barrister at Kenworthy's Chambers in Manchester. I am also the Joint Vice Chair of the Association of Women Barristers and the founder of Women in the Law and Business UK, an organisation which is passionate about supporting the next leaders in law and encouraging career progression through personal development. On each episode of Talking Law you'll get to hear from a leading advocate in the legal professions. Someone who has very much walked the walk and talks the talk and has something to say about the profession we have all chosen. These interviews include the following:

• *Gina Miller, activist and businesswoman. Gina's cases over the last couple of years have led to her being considered a role model to many of us, both inside and outside of the law, especially her passion for the importance of the rule of law.*

• *The Secret Barrister, a phenomenon on Twitter and the author of a best-selling book. Of course, nobody knows the true identity of the Secret Barrister — no, not even me! They were kind enough to answer a series of questions for Talking Law — the Podcast voiced by an actor.*

• *Stephanie Boyce, Deputy Vice President of the Law Society of England and Wales. An experienced general counsel, Stephanie is set to become the Vice President of The Law Society this year and President in 2021 — the first ever black woman to hold that post.*

- *Sean Jones QC. Widely recognised as one of the leading employment lawyers in the UK, Sean has built a leading practice focused on complex and high-profile cases. He acts for both claimants and defendants in claims covering the wide range of employment, commercial employment and sport-related disputes.*

- *Joanna Hardy. Joanna is widely regarded as one of the UK's leading junior criminal barristers, practising from Red Lion Chambers in the central London. She is ranked in both the 2019 and 2020 editions of the Legal 500, as well as the Evening Standard's Progress 1000, a list of the most influential people in London.*

- *Chris Daw QC. After being called to the Bar in 1993, Chris built his reputation acting in high-profile trials dealing with serious organised crime and commercial fraud. He was appointed Queen's Counsel in 2013 and now acts in a broader range of matters, whilst maintaining a substantial criminal practice.*

- *Brie Stevens-Hoare QC. Brie is a highly experienced property barrister, dealing with all aspects of property litigation, and she recently won Barrister of the Year at the Modern Law Awards and Chambers UK's Real Estate Silk of the Year Award.*

Gina Miller

This month on the Podcast you'll meet activist and businesswoman, Gina Miller. Gina's cases over the last couple of years have led to her being considered a role model to many of us in the law and outside of the law, especially her passion for the importance of the rule of law. I started our conversation by asking her if she saw herself as a role model.

No, and it's so many things that I don't wake up and think. I don't think I'm going to be an inspiration, a role model, brave, courageous, all these sorts of things, I just wake up and think I'm going to do the best I can do today - that tends to be my thoughts - and try and bring some sort of humanity and kindness in places where we seem to have lost them, and those are about my only thoughts as I wake up. And then it's, the second thought tends to be, well, to gear myself up knowing that there'll be some abuse coming from some direction that day, because when you stand up – and I found over 30 years of campaigning that when you are making a difference there are those who feel threatened by it and will therefore seek to silence you, or to diminish your voice - and it's then getting my mindset, my head and my heart in the right place to know I'm doing what I do because I believe it's right and I won't let others define my voice or who I am, where I am and what I'm doing, which they often will try to do, especially if you have a voice that's making a difference.

Absolutely. I mean, we know you because of the Brexit case – and I hate using that term – or the Brexit cases, but really you have spent your career, your life, fighting for the importance of the rule of law and the importance of the rule of law, and I just wondered where does that sort of motivation originate?

I think it's both nature and nurture. I think, you know, I was born this girl or a woman who always has or had growing up – and even now – a very strong sense of justice. I hate bad things being done to people, innocent people, so a strong sense of justice, it's something that I think I was just born with. And then that was honed by my father, growing up with somebody who was very politically aware but also very socially minded, very much a social justice campaigner through his entire life, so having him as my father from a very early age, talking to me about the importance of the rule of law was formative. And then when I came to the UK and started studying, I also fell in love with history, and when you bring those things together, I think you can see history repeating itself quite often. And what I realised is that the law and Judges – the rule of law and Judges – they're sort of almost a playbook that happens throughout history at times of populism, at times of the rise of autocracy, dictatorship, that one of the things used in the toolbox is to diminish the rule of law and the place of lawyers and Judges. Because the rule of law, democracy, human rights, are all interlinked and are fundamentally about protecting people, and so if you want to diminish rights, equality – actually, and also accountability – what those people who want to be in power do is they try to demolish those who practice the law or defend the law, and it's not something new, it's happened every 100 years or so, so I'm very alert to that. I'm very alert to how important the rule of law is, and the practitioners in the rule of law are to the civility of our society.

Yes. I mean, do you wish you'd been a lawyer?

Well, I studied. I always wanted to be a lawyer. I mean, I always wanted to follow in my father's footsteps, and it was sort of almost ready-made for me to go back and take on his practice. But once I'd grown up in England, this was my home. And I wanted to, and I studied law and I was about to take my finals …

Yes, I read that!

… and I, you know, it was, it's the only thing I ever dreamt of being. You know, I was going to be the first black barrister who was going to the Courts. I was going to be the, you know, the one who sent words into the Courtroom as if they were soldiers into battle, that was going to be me, and, you know, the intellectual, if you like, game of debating and fighting for people's rights is something I always wanted to do. So, for me, it was a huge tragedy. It was almost a mourning for me when I couldn't do my finals, and I was faced with this terrible, terrible dilemma in that I could've, because I was attacked on campus and I was brutally attacked, sexually attacked, and I couldn't take my finals, and the university at the time, because I was on course for a First, offered to sort of bury the incident by awarding me my degree, and my dilemma was, could I accept that? And I think, my sense of justice, I just couldn't.

Yes

I couldn't bring myself to take something that I hadn't earned, so I said no, and always thought I would go back to the law. So, the ironies of finding myself in the Supreme Court twice –

Twice, yes!

But also, you know, there's bitter sweetness in life, and unbeknown to my university, because it's all changed, they awarded me an Honorary Degree of Law on the month – 30 years later to the month – that I should have actually got my degree.

Wow!

They didn't know it, and I said that in my speech when I accepted my Honorary Degree, and it brought tears to so many people in the audience.

Oh my gosh!

But to me that was one of the most emotional times, apart from having my three children, was actually getting that Honorary Degree.

Oh my gosh! That is emotional.

It was, hugely.

Wow! And of course, they didn't know.

They had no idea.

No. Because of course many would have just accepted, you know, the degree and gone off, and I think that's a testament to who you are.

I just, I just think you have to earn what you get, and it's happened throughout my life and I just have to be comfortable and be able to be comfortable with who I am and what I have, and do I deserve it? So, that's just something that is me.

Yes. Can I ask you then about some of your legal cases, the two we know well of, but the Brexit case, the first Brexit case, and the second really, why did you bring them?

Because I was frightened. The first case I was very concerned that if it had gone through and the Royal Prerogative had been used on the domestic plain, that would completely change the power that sits in our Prime Minister and the Executive, because that would mean that you could use it on the domestic plain to change individual rights – the way we live, work, exist, would be at the behest of a Prime Minister and Executive without parliamentary scrutiny, without primary legislation, so it's a fundamental shifting of power. And I couldn't understand why the opposition and why other people weren't speaking up about this because it seemed to me such an obvious outcome of the actions the Prime Minister was going to take. And the only conclusion that I could come to in my mind was firstly that perhaps the opposition weren't aware of it; or could see themselves benefit from it if they were to come to power. And then the other thing I thought was, in a febrile environment, which it was, maybe they were just too afraid. People were afraid to speak up, and I naively thought that if I did, others would join me. I never envisaged that I was going to be the only claimant in that case.

Really?

Never! I thought – the thought of brave did strike me at that point. I thought, look, I'll put it, we'll do this, it'll be all about the black and white letter of the law, we'll keep out all the politics, all about Brexit, it'll just be about parliamentary sovereignty, people will understand that on both sides, any side of the argument, because that's what everyone's talking about, so I thought, I'll put my name to it and others would join me. So, I called academics, businesspeople, politicians, opposition – I never envisaged I was going to be on my own.

I must say, in the second case or the latter case, the prorogation case, seeing you on television when it was streamed live, as a lone figure, in blue [Laughter] was astonishing, and it was visibly a shock for the country in many ways, but in others also – the advocates of course were all men and the only woman that we could see, I know there were women solicitors from Mishcon's sitting on the second row because I think one of them assisted actually Lord Pannick - but you know that was a visibly lonely figure. Has it been a lonely figure, because you have received a huge amount of threats, abuse online and off? Has it been lonely, and how have you coped with it?

It has been lonely at times, but I think I'm a bit of a fatalist and I think of course it was going to be me, because it's almost as though 20-odd/30 years of campaigning sort of led me to this point, where I was strong enough and know myself enough and have confidence enough in what I do to not be distracted, because the abuse is horrendous. It has shown me a society that I didn't know existed in Britain, or I presumed only existed in a very small number – or amongst a very small number of people in the very, very fringes of our society. You know, the three most common are that as a woman of colour it's not my place, I should be grateful to be in the country. The second one is that I can't be intelligent enough, it must be that there are men behind me pulling my strings because I couldn't possibly be bright enough to have brought this case or have thought of it.

Nonsense!

And the third is that it can't be my money, that again it must be that I'm somehow this sort of puppet of other individuals, and all three are completely incorrect, and it is, for the majority of it, my money, my thinking, my case. But I've also noticed something change between the first case and the second case. In the first case I think there was an element of shock and surprise, and almost pride in a way though that as a woman I was standing up. By the time we came around to the second case, it was all vitriol. It was all vitriol. And to walk out of the Court, the Supreme Court, and see people standing there shouting cut my tongue out, I should be hanged, holding a noose outside, and the police doing nothing, was incredibly shocking. I mean, my team were so shocked by it and they said we don't know how you put up with it. And I, I don't know how I put up with it, but it doesn't get to me, because I think it says more about them than it does about me.

Absolutely, absolutely.

But also, I've always disliked bullies, and it's a form of bullying and silencing, but it's very targeted, and I interpreted that as saying you must be frightened of something.

Yes, probably of your intellect and your power.

But it's still carrying on now! When the battle is won — and it's very intriguing to me, because since the General Election the abuse has dialled up even more.

Really?!

And you have to think why, and I'm still pondering as to why, but it's organised, they're on social media — not that I particularly look at social media — there are many, many more bots, you can tell from how often, you know, how long they've been set up, how many followers. It's presents being sent to my office — presents I say in the loosest term — emails, it has gone to another level, and particular media have gone to a different level and are making up very elaborate stories. I mean, the day after the election there was a story that I was in Brussels with two lawyers meeting with Barnier, which is complete and utter fabrication, but they'd gone to great lengths to what I was carrying, and you have to wonder why is this happening? And I find it intriguing because it does say that they're afraid for some reason, and I don't know why because there is nothing to be afraid of, from the point of view that it's now the ball is in the Prime Minister and the Government's Court.

Yes, the case is over.

It is the case is over. They are – I mean, the only thing which I think we all have to keep an eye on and be very vigilant about is their intentions to change the constitution and rewrite the powers, and I think that is about each one of us staying vigilant and alert to that in the face of diminished opposition at the moment. But apart from that, it is they've won, and I find it very worrying, apart from the fact that it's about closing down voices, is it about closing down debate and voices. If there is an agenda which is one in which it is about diminishing rights, about rewriting what we have achieved in our society over the last four decades, then maybe they really don't want a light shone on their activities, and they know I'm quite capable of shining that light and I will not be dissuaded from doing so if it's necessary. So, it's interesting.

Yes, it is, especially it surprises me that it's gone to this level when actually the case is over and we're effectively out of Europe.

Legally there's nothing to do.

No, legally there's nothing to do, so it's a real surprise and disappointing to see that. Can I ask, in the case, one of the cases I want to ask, we saw Lord Pannick - I suppose members of the general public may never, well actually some may know Lord Pannick from the years he was writing in The Times …

Of course

… that I read when I was a student and then of course came to the Bar. What did you learn, if anything, from the legal legend that is Lord Pannick from dealing with him in the way that he dealt with the case?

One, on a personal level, is there are so many echoes of my father, because I watched my father when I was young. You know, he had defended or acted for the Grenada Government against the US invasion …

Oh right.

We had a tragedy in Guyana called the Jonestown Massacre, where again he represented the victims of the – they were made to drink a Kool Aid, if they didn't, they were shot in that disaster, in the cult that was running up there. He defended the Dominican Republic, he was an internationally renowned criminal barrister and political defender, so there were so many echoes in Lord Pannick. But the thing that really struck me is the intellect to be able to translate very complex issues into everyday accessible language is a real skill. People don't quite understand how much of an intellect it takes to be a translator …

No, they don't.

… and that's what – people tend to think that being or showing an eloquence or an intellect is about making language as complex as possible. It's actually the reverse to my mind. It's about making it accessible, and that's what he did with such flair. You know, the fact that you had millions around the world, and there are people I've had emails from around the world where people are saying, 'we were fascinated by it, not only that, we could understand'.

Yes!

Isn't that a great power to be able to make the law and complex issues understandable, and make people think that they are part of this, and it does affect them? I think that is a masterful skill.

I mean, I have to say, I am an advocacy trainer for the Inns of Court and teach barristers, and that case became a lesson in advocacy, particularly when one compares it to the other advocates in that case. Even for those of us who have been at the Bar for donkeys, actually to see that, so it's interesting from your perspective, but also so insightful.

And I have to say from, you know, being the only client and having to sign off, look at, read, every single thing in my spare time because of course in all of this I've still been running my business …

You've still been running your business!

… it was, I mean it could have been exhausting, the whole process, but everybody involved, all my legal team were just astonishing in the way they allowed me to be not just part of the process and a client but actually to be involved in the decisions that were being made. You know, it wasn't a normal client relationship, and also the fact that we had to do things so quickly, because, you know, we had to, you know, we were getting things from the Government – deadlines were unbelievable! You know, we had literally one day to file the case when Prime Minister Johnson announced the prorogation.

Wow!

I had an inkling throughout the summer because the other thing that people are not aware of is the preparation. So, for the three summers – and I mean my children, I have to say, I've promised them and my husband that this summer 2020 I may actually have a summer off, a proper summer! [Laughter] Because the last few summers I spent preparing cases. The first was the Royal Prerogative case against Mrs May, the second summer I spent all of that summer with a different legal team questioning the DUP payment, the billion pounds that were going to the DUP, and we actually were about to go to Court and then the Government sent us a letter on 27 August saying they agreed with us that it had to be primary legislation and so the payment that was supposed to happen in the October didn't happen, and it wasn't until the following March in the Supplies and Estimates Bill and the MPs rubberstamped it again. So, whilst that case didn't have to go to Court, I was preparing to go to Court on that payment.

Oh my gosh, I hadn't even – yes!

And then the third one, obviously, the prorogation case, where when the Government sent us in sort of the middle of August and the whole pre-action protocol, because we started writing – or the first letter we sent to Mr Johnson was actually on 11 July, even before he became the Premier.

Yes, that was before.

So, because we worked back and thought well, we have to start the process and so we wrote to him saying, 'if you are to become leader and you are talking about prorogation – because he was during his leadership election – then we said, you know, you do realise and we started the process that this wouldn't be legal in our view. And so, when we got a letter back in the sort of middle of August, which was a very long, very complex, very reassuring letter to me saying, "your client does not have to bring legal proceedings or approach the Courts, we are not considering prorogation …" I said to the team, this means they are.

Really?!

They had just gone too far. There were too many platitudes. You know that old saying, you know, protesteth too much …

Yes [Laughter]

… there was just something about the letter and I thought no. So, we carried on preparing.

Oh right!

And I think it's because they thought that we wouldn't be ready. So, I think they were as much surprised as everyone else that we were actually ready. And so, when the announcement was made at 10 o'clock on the Tuesday morning, we filed at 4:30 in the afternoon.

Did you?!

Yes. So, it was, yes, we were ready.

Do you know, that is some preparation! [Laughter]

We were ready!

I did wonder how it was …

The only thing we weren't ready about, and my team phoned me up, my wonderful team at Mishcon phoned me up and said, you know, we have to have a con before we do this, because the one thing we haven't been able to do is have any agreement on costs.

Oh yes.

They said, you're filing, we have no costs agreement and the Government may not agree one to try and put you off the case, what are we going to do? I said, well, we're just going to go ahead. And I think I jokingly said in the call to them, what is he going to do? Put me in prison? He could try because I'm not paying any costs! [Laughter] I said this is a public interest case and they can try! And they sort of, at times like that I think they sort of balk at me and said, you know, that's not funny. And I said, well, let's see, let's just, we'll file.

Yes. Wow! Oh my gosh.

They did eventually then after, afterwards we did agree costs, but yes at the time of filing we hadn't.

Oh my goodness! Can I ask you about some positive things? Your book came out last year, which is amazing.

Oh, thank you!

And, I really – in fact, I've forgotten to bring it to be signed, foolishly – but I wanted to ask you really why you wrote the book and how long it took you? Because it's quite personal.

Well, after the first case I was approached by quite a few publishers who were intrigued as to who I was, and it seemed as though I'd popped up from nowhere, and they were saying, you know, lots and lots of people would be really interested - and then they wanted me to write a book about the case. And I thought, how boring!

Yes, exactly.

Why is anyone really going to want to – or then a book about Brexit! Again, I thought, oh no! And I've always been very engaged with young people and I speak to a lot of Sixth Forms, a lot of Universities, law students, because I was at the Centre for Social Justice for two years and I've been a campaigner for very, very many years, so I've been speaking to young people for a long time. But something happened after Brexit. I noticed when I was going around talking to young people, especially young women, that there was a new type of fragility, a new worry about their future, about the pressure they were feeling about having to juggle careers, be successful, be good at everything. There was a new type of anxiety about having to be successful.

Yes

And somebody said to me, one woman said to me, if only there was a book that didn't make us feel worse. And I said, what do you mean about that? And they said, well, there are so many books out there about being superwomen, about being successful, and when you read them these women are so untouchable and so successful it makes you feel worse.

Yes

And I thought, well I can write a book about being honest, about failing, but about showing that it's okay to fail and pick yourself up, that real strength is about the picking yourself up not about being successful necessarily. So, I thought that's what I'm going to do. So, I approached one publisher, several publishers, and they said no, they were very sort of, you know, formulaic if you like in the book that I needed to write, and I luckily found a publisher who said you can write the book you want to write.

Wow.

And then lawyers came in again because when I did the first draft and the publishers saw it, they said, Gina, we're not sure you're going to get this through the lawyers, in two chapters in particular.

Oh, yes, yes.

And so, I had a bit of a battle and so then had to find a huge amount of evidence and so we had files about my special needs daughter but also about the chapters on domestic violence to ensure that if anyone came after me – my ex – then we had the evidence and, you know, that was – because I wanted to be – again, there was this belief that somehow I got there by magic, or it was easy, or that – women who are seen to be strong can't have failed at anything, and I wanted to say that actually strength is something that you learn through life, it doesn't necessarily happen overnight. But also, is that sometimes people can be envious of the fact that you're strong and try to break you, be it in the place of work or in relationships, the very thing that they admire about you they can feel threatened by and then systematically go about trying to break, and it's about power and ownership and all these issues, so I wanted to talk about that, and domestic violence is something – if I say that, you know, I'm a victim of domestic violence, most people think don't be silly, you know, it's silly women or stupid women or uneducated women or poor women who go through domestic violence, it can't be somebody who is together and strong as they see it.

Yes

And actually, it happens to, it can happen to anyone, male, female, anyone can be a victim of domestic violence because, as I said, it's about power and ownership, it's not about you being weak or strong.

No

And so, I very much wanted to write a message to not just young women but mainly to young people, male, female, to say it's okay to own your failures and then pick yourself up and carry on.

Yes. Can I ask you about your daughter? Earlier last year you spoke at the Women in Law Summit organised by Maddox Conferences, and I was there because I was speaking after you, and we were all so moved by your speech, but you talked there about your daughter who has special needs …

Yes, my eldest daughter, yes.

… your eldest daughter, and I just wondered if you can just share a little about that really? How did you feel - I have a son who has issues – and so, as a mother, there's always that constant you feel like a failure and you're not doing enough. How did you feel about that? You talked about that at the conference.

I think that's a time in my life when I felt the most lonely. You asked earlier about feeling lonely and isolated in this case. Actually, when I had her, she'll be 32 years old this year, but she is a child in an adult's body, so her mental age is only sort of five or six, because she was starved of oxygen at birth. But, to be a young mother, because I consciously made the decision to have her young because I wanted – I was very ambitious, I always have been, so I didn't want to step off anything, so I thought she'd grow with me.

Yes

Because I wanted to have a child or children, you know, as much as having a career. It was very much – it wasn't one or the other to me, ever. But at that time the attitude to babies, to a young baby born with special needs was to be put in an institution, and I was told, you know, all the advice from specialists, from everyone, from even her father and his family, were that she should be in a home, and to be, as a young mother, being told you have to give up your child … Even my parents, even my mother was encouraging me because she thought it would be too much of a burden on me to bring up this child, and the toll on then my marriage – and I was completely on my own, and that's when I felt most isolated because I had to fight the system, I had to fight the medical profession, I had to fight the legal profession because her father – you know, people wanted to take her away from me. And that's when I started using the law, because I started fighting for my right to keep her and for special needs children to have access to special education, but that is when I really discovered not just my own strength and my own resilience – and what more resilience than being a mother and fighting for your child, for your baby …

Absolutely, absolutely!

… you know, you will take every ounce of your strength to defend that child, and that's when I felt lonely and I had to rely on myself, and they were really, really dark times for me at that point. But, you know, I'd put her to bed and see her sleeping and, you know, that smell of your baby, and that …

Oh yes!

… I would have done anything for her, and I did.

Wow! Yes, you did, you did. I mean that is amazing. And, what about juggling motherhood?

Oh, you always feel guilty! [Laughter]

Yes, yes.

This whole idea that you don't – you do, you do. And you have to sort of – I always say when I talk to younger mothers now, I say you have to be kind to yourself. We're not very good at being kind to ourselves.

No

We sort of, we go around feeling guilty from one thing to the next and trying to be – and if you're anything like me, I'm sure that many of them will be also quite perfectionist as well.

Oh yes, yes!

So we have to sort of give ourselves a bit of space and I sort of prioritise. What I've learned to do is try and prioritise and think, okay, these are the things I'm going to do better than others, but the guilt never goes away.

No. I'm so pleased you said that!

But also, it's, it's also this whole myth of work/life balance and, you know, what is the perfect way of doing things. I just think there is no such thing. I mean, when I had my younger two who are now 14 and 12, I remember there was this Gina Ford book on – and all these babies – I think you should just burn them all, because I mean, you know, what you have to do is listen to your own voice, listen to your own heart, you know your children better than anything else, and the most important thing – I can tell you this with my children and I also speak with a lot of young children so I know how they feel about their parents who work, is they – as long as they feel loved, the two socks don't have to match …

Yes, hear, hear! [*Laughter*]

… they just want to feel that they're loved and secure, and that has nothing to do with the amount of time you spend with them. It's about how you make them feel about themselves and how close they feel to you. If they feel your love, they are loved, it's not about how much time you spend with them.

No, oh gosh that's such great, great advice! But just on the wellbeing, what do you do for wellbeing? You look great …

Oh, I've no idea, I'm not very good at anything in particular …

… let's see, even in jeans – and I'm thinking, three kids, why can't I look like that?!

I don't stop a lot. I'm very, very fortunate that I don't need a lot of sleep, so I do work a lot, and I've found a way of, you know, fitting in with them and my work and then I work at night. It's just the way I am. So, it's finding your own rhythm. But I do find time to laugh, so we play games a lot, we watch comedies and silly things, we go and spend time together, going to plays – I think, you know, plays are wonderful – but watching silly stuff. I think finding time to laugh with each other and be silly, you know, the childlike part of you is something that keeps you young.

Yes, I agree.

So, you don't have to be childish but childlike I think, and the small pleasures are really important. I don't really spend a lot of time outlaying money to go and do things. I don't, you know, there's no point in me buying a gym membership, I'll never use it, so there's no point in me buying it! [Laughter] There's no point in me trying to go to a spa or facial or anything else, I just literally will never find the time. So, you know, I say to anybody don't give me these things as presents because I'm never going to use them. So, but you know what I will do is find time to have, you know, a lovely cup of coffee or tea and listen to an audio book because I haven't got the time to always read things …

Oh yes, that's me, that's me.

… or walk, I love walking, and just finding time, and it doesn't have to be that long, but you do have to find time for yourself. I'm not very good at it, so, I'm not the one to tell others …

No, but it's …

… but I do think you need to find – because you need to look after yourself. If you're going to be a fighter, if you're going to be a campaigner, you are the tool, so you have to look after yourself, and I've learned that. I've not always been good at it, I'm only learning myself how to be better at that. But, if you want to fight on, you've got to look after yourself. That is a lesson I've learned.

Yes, that's an important one as well.

And lots of water. Water is so important.

Oh yes! I'm going to reach for some now! This year you received a lifetime achievement award from the Diversity Legal Awards, which are the only awards …

Oh, that was so lovely!

... and I missed it, sadly, because I was somewhere else. But, I wondered how that felt to receive such a – I mean, because those awards are, you know, have tough categories, loads of people nominated, and that particular one is a special award with, you know, many great people before you. How did it feel to receive that? I mean, I don't know if you receive many awards?

I don't, but it was such a surprise to me, but the evening itself was bitter sweet. The reason I say that is that it was an extraordinary thing. As you say, I don't tend to get many awards, so it was just such a surprise. So, the surprise element of it was extraordinary because I had no idea. But, the evening itself I found the room was full of so much talent, and the bitter bit of the bittersweet was, I thought, why are these individuals separate from just the professional awards? Why is there a need for a separate award?

Yes.

You know, I thought it's such a shame after all these years that we still have to have a separate award that many of the people in the room there should have been side-by-side with any category in any of the awards that happen in mainstream legal profession, in wealth management, you know, they shouldn't have been separate, so that's when I felt it was a shame. What I did find quite extraordinary and so positive was that every winner of every category – and I mean every category bar myself – when they read the accolades of those individuals, the philanthropic charitable element was in every single person's CV.

Absolutely.

Everybody who won an award that evening was giving back to their community, had started an initiative, was thinking about how do you bridge the law, the communities and society. I have been at other mainstream awards for both, as I said, wealth management, the City, the law, and I have never heard that in CVs before, and I thought this should be shouted from the rooftops.

Absolutely.

This is how people should be. They give back to the societies and the communities that afford them their success, and I want to applaud every single person in that room for being there, and everybody who won that award that evening. It was an example of how the profession should be operating.

Absolutely. And do you think that we have a profession, as a profession we have a problem with diversity? It's improving, at the entrance levels, brilliant, in gender, not so in race, but even gender, but in the senior positions we don't see the same replicated, and so those things are an example of perhaps how we can attract and retain those people who enter the law, irrespective of their gender and their race, and from different social backgrounds. Do you think that's a good way perhaps for us as a profession when you look – when you watched the prorogation case, you know, my parents phoned me to say, oh, there's a black usher. [Laughter] I said yes!

I know! It's extraordinary isn't it?!

Yes. And that is extraordinary to two professional people not in law, and the nation watching.

But, it's not just the law, it's in my world too, in the City, in that it's not in – there has been so much emphasis on entry level that that is not where the problem is.

No.

There is a problem in middle management, it's middle level. We have many – there's a lot of diversity at entry level, both across ethnic minorities, sexual orientation, whatever the diversity it.

Yes.

But something's happening that's not right. The dial's not moving at middle and senior management, and you have to ask, is that about progression? Is there still discrimination about progression? Is it that it's just too challenging to actually balance the demands on you if you are from a – if you're a mother, if you're from an ethnic minority, if you have a cultural balance because people see the law as being maybe – and also finances being, you know, more of a Caucasian cultural aggressive, you know, environment, therefore do I want to be part of that? And, you know, it's where people lie and make money, basically, you know, so there is a cultural element of that as well. But, I think there isn't enough mentoring as well, but we have to address – but all professions I think, whatever the profession, I think you have to, we have to address why is diversity meeting a sort of blockage point at middle management.

Yes

And it is across all professions. The dial is stopping there, and we have to start thinking about it because it's not about talent.

No

I am told so often we don't have the right number of people to progress, the talent isn't there, we need to mentor more talent. I'm sorry, get out there, the talent is everywhere.

Yes.

But you are not – for some reason, unconscious biases are playing in at that middle management level.

Yes, which would probably explain it. I wanted to just ask you a question that we ask all our guests – well, I ask all our guests! I don't know why I keep saying we, there's only me. [Laughter]. Do you have a favourite fictional lawyer? And then I'll ask about your favourite book. So, I'll give you an example, some people say, well, the Duchess of Sussex before she was the Duchess of Sussex, in a programme of course – I don't watch much television …

I don't either!

Oh, right, okay. Well, this is going to be no good! [Laughter]

No, no, no, I did actually watch one series – it's a friend of mine who, because she knows how intrigued I am about the law, I think I'm the only legal if you like geek who's not a lawyer is what I tell my friends. They all joke about it. But there was a programme called Silks a while ago …

Yes!

… and Martha Costello, the Silk …

Yes, Maxine Peake.

Yes, now what I loved about her, because I watched a few episodes, not all of it, but she was real …

Yes. I'll send you the box set!

But she had foibles, and she drank a bit too much, and she stayed up and worked too late, and she couldn't find the right clothes when she was pregnant, and she was sort of real. There was something real about her, and I rather liked that about her.

Yes. Well, interestingly she is Baroness Helena Kennedy who's a QC at Doughty Street, she's hers as well.

Oh, is she?!

Yes. And the funny thing about that character – I know the actress Maxine Peake because she's based in Manchester where I practise, and she was the artistic director at the Royal Exchange Theatre where I'm on the board – is that it felt real, it felt like actually the programme vaguely represented a bit of a normality.

Yes, I thought that was great. The other person I've been told – so those who tried to sort of negate my, what I do, have written, oh Gina Miller is just as scheming as that woman, that lawyer who – there was a series, and I don't know, you may know it, with, it was a President and the advisor apparently was a lawyer who was a woman. I've only seen a photograph of her. She's very beautiful, so I was like sort of very flattered, but she was a scheming sort of advisor in an American series called – it wasn't the West Wing, it was something else …

I was going to say, was it West Wing?

No, no, it wasn't West Wing. It was, she was a scheming ex-lawyer/advisor to a President. Anyway, people say, oh she's just like her. It's quite funny! [Laughter]

Oh, you're not, you're not.

It's quite funny when people think about these things. But the other thing I find very interesting is, I got asked this the other day. So, you asked about the awards …

Yes.

… So, I've had a number of people who've criticised me and said, why has Gina Miller been given this award? She's not even black.

What?!

Oh yes, it's quite interesting. One is that I don't deserve the award because I'm not black. It's a very interesting thing. Gina Miller should have won Asian Lawyer of the Year, not Black Lawyer of the Year, or whatever it was, all these sorts of things. So, there's now a nuanced discrimination coming in, which I find extraordinary.

That you're not black enough, or ….

I'm not black enough and I shouldn't call myself a woman of colour because I'm not, I'm brown. And you just think, it's extraordinary!

It's nonsense, it's nonsense!

It's absolute nonsense! But it's interesting that they're trying – divisions are being placed in places where they don't exist to try and divide and conquer, and I can feel that, but it's interesting how it's being used with a sort of – you know, you bring down a peg, bring down a peg, all the time.

Ridiculous!

It is ridiculous!

You deserve the lifetime award, and there have been people I think who've won that award for their work, irrespective of their race.

I don't think it's about that at all, but you know …

Well, you look black to me, so I've no …

Yes, [Laughter], you know I don't know what all – I always say that it's always about competency and respect and achievements. You Judge people on that. That's what you should judge people on.

I wholly agree with you, and it's nonsense to be bringing that up as an issue, quite frankly. You'll have to tell me who – off the record! You mentioned before that you listen to a lot of audibles – excellent!

Well, I've started to!

Yes, well I set up a Book Club, in fact we have a Book Club in Women of the Law, your book's coming up. But I wondered if you've got a favourite book, or a book that perhaps has changed your life?

I don't often have time to read, I have to admit, and I get slightly impatient with books, so I tend to read more pamphlets and academic papers, so I read a lot of papers and sort of try to understand what's happening in the world from as pragmatic perspective as I can, so I'll read something about anthropology, I'll read something about what's happening in technology, what's happening with AGRE foods, so I want to know what's going on in the world. But, two books that I've revisited on several occasions and really, I suppose, made an impression on me when I read them, the first one was when I was a teenager, was The Count of Monte Cristo.

Oh yes.

There is so much in that book, and if you read it again it is actually a book about human emotions and revenge, and it teaches you a lot. Not only that, it's so beautifully written but it's an extraordinary book. And the other one which I have to say quite frightening echoes in the book if we read it now, and I started reading it on the Christmas holidays, was A Tale of Two Cities.

Yes, that's another favourite.

Do you know, the character Robespierre is quite interesting against the backdrop of where we are in our history at the moment. But A Tale of Two Cities has many echoes - I think people should read it again.

Very good choices actually. I haven't read either of those for a very long time.

They're interesting books.

Yes, really interesting actually.

Because at the time of the writers, both Dickens and - you know, we were at a revolutionary time in our history, and I think we are at a revolutionary time in our history again.

Again, yes. Gosh, that's really got me thinking. [Laughter] I'll have to read it. Gina Miller, finally, can I ask you what's next? What would you like to do next? You're still running your businesses, you're a highly successful businesswoman, a mother, you've changed our history — the history books are written. I just wondered, you know, what's next? I mean, apart from planning on a summer — a legal-free summer holiday …

Well, I will go back to doing some other things, the campaigns I'd put on a backburner, because I only ever thought it'd be a year. I think like most of us we thought only a year and then, you know, two-and-a-half years later we're, here we are!

Yes.

So, I suppose that the – some ongoing will be much, much longer timelines and some will be shorter, but the one with the longer timelines - I do believe that around the Western world and modern democracies, one of the things we haven't got right is our form of economics. So, trickle-down economics has done more harm than good from my point of view. The whole pursuit of profit, the aggressive pursuit of profit, has not helped us as a society, so the idea of responsible capitalism is something that I'm going to carry on campaigning. I'd already started before, the idea that we actually should have a triple bottom line rather than just be Judged on profit, but the idea of people, profit and planet being a legal requirement for corporates and corporate governance is something I think is, it would put us in a better place as a society than just the pursuit of profit. So, that's a much longer-term and much more international campaign, but that's something I'm very interested in, in pursuing.

Yes.

The second one is – and we will visit it and carry on the conversation in the UK – is it time now for a partially codified constitution? I think it is. I think it's something that we will carry on talking about. You know, that goes hand-in-hand with the whole idea of deliberative democracy. Do we need to have something that's halfway between direct democracy and a representative democracy? And again, that is more of a global debate because other countries are experiencing what we're experiencing too. And then purely on a domestic front, I will carry on because unfortunately all the things I fought for with my daughter, the advances of respect for young people, children with special needs, because of our lack of funding we are finding or I'm hearing that a lot of those advances are being reversed and we have a lot of problems of people with young adults with special needs being locked away, being denied their human rights, being denied access to education, and then domestic violence. There is an alarming increase in violence against women.

Yes.

Young women on university campuses, in clubs. There is use of drugs against women is increasing, and a lot of this is happening sort of under the radar.

Absolutely. Gina Miller, thank you so much for talking law on the Talking Law podcast. It's been a pleasure.

It's been an absolute pleasure.

Wonderful, wonderful, to meet you, and please don't stop!

I don't have any intention of stopping anytime soon.

A huge thank you to Gina Miller for taking the time to meet with me, and a big thank you to you as well for listening to the Talking Law Podcast.

The Secret Barrister

On this episode I'm excited to bring you an interview with the Secret Barrister. A phenomenon Twitter and the author of a best-selling book, of course nobody knows the true identity of the Secret Barrister – no, not even me! They were kind enough to answer a series of questions for Talking Law, here voiced by an actor.

I'm the Secret Barrister. I'm a junior criminal barrister who's been knocking around the Courts with a very mediocre practice for the past decade or so.

So, what do you specialise in?

Crime, sex, drugs and violence mostly, the Holy Trinity!

Now, why did you go in the law in the first place?

There's no exciting answer I'm afraid, which I probably why I floundered in so many pupillage interviews. Law just seemed to be a good fit for my limited skill set pedantry, arguing and putting stuff on paper in a vaguely coherent form. I didn't go to university expecting to be practising law following my law degree. In fact, after graduating I took a somewhat roundabout route to the Bar as I tried to make up my mind. Eventually, I realised that nothing interested or excited me as much as the Criminal Bar, and then the decision was made.

And did you have any role models or mentors along the way?

Plenty, but none I can disclose without dropping fairly major clues to my identity! One of the joys of the Bar is that there's a constant source of ongoing mentoring - whenever you have a question or a problem, there is invariably somebody in Chambers or in the robing room whose expertise you can draw on. Every day is a learning day, the cliché goes, but I really believe that's true in this job. Every day I go home knowing something I didn't when I woke up that morning - even if it's as simple as "Well I won't do that again" - and the opportunity to learn from just sitting and watching the people around you is one of the underrated pleasures of the job.

Yes, I agree really. I want to move on and as you about wellbeing. Burnout is high at the Bar. We overwork, we over-stretch, we don't see enough of our kids and our family and husband, and I just wonder for you, between daily practice, writing, and you've still got a blog, what do you do for your wellbeing?

I'm probably not too good at this part. My partner would definitely say I struggle to strike the balance between work and home. Between daily practice and writing/blogging there doesn't tend to be a lot of spare time. I run when I can, which I find to be a good way of blowing off steam and clearing my mind.

Now, we love the book, The Secret Barrister book that you wrote. I just wonder, how did the book come about? It's quite unusual isn't it, to have a barrister start writing a book that becomes a number one seller in The Times?

Thank you! That's very kind. The idea for the book was actually my agent's. A few months after I started the blog, complaining about the sorry state of criminal justice, he got in touch having read some of my posts and asked if I was interested in writing a book. At first I assumed it was some sort of hoax or scam - I had visions of Mark in Peep Show being persuaded to spend his savings on "publishing" Business Secrets of the Pharaohs - but once it became clear that it was legit, I was intrigued. Together we put together a proposal, he sent it out to publishers, and we got a surprising level of interest. There were months of agonising before I committed to it, weighing up the enormous professional risks, but my brilliant other half pushed me to do it. They said it was a message that needed communicating to the public. And, though it's not good for them to hear this too often, they were right.

Now I want to ask you about diversity in the law, race, gender, social mobility. I wonder, how do you think we can improve this?

I think the law is better than it was but, given how low the baseline was, that is not saying a great deal. For me, while there is plainly a long way still to go, the fact these issues are firmly on the radar of our representative bodies is a massive breakthrough. I appreciate that there is a lot of distinction between actions and words, but convincing a profession as, ahem, "traditional" as the Bar that diversity and social mobility matter is a breakthrough.

Do you think there's a noticeable divide in the profession?

For my part, I think there is a noticeable divide in the profession, between the self-professed traditionalists stuck in the 1970s montage of Oxbridge old boys and white faces, and the modern Bar, and that second group now has more members than the first. As a result, a much broader appreciation and awareness of the importance of outreach work in schools and universities, to attract people who may wrongly assume that the Bar isn't for "people like them" by showing them the many faces of the modern Bar. Whilst I'm not complacent enough to assume that there are no problems with attitudes in the profession - there are, and we encounter them every day - I do think we have improved, and I think the key to ongoing improvement lies in ensuring that the pool of young people aspiring to come to the Bar is as wide as possible, AND that Chambers cast their nets as wide as possible.

Hear, hear, I agree with that. Now, I'm interested, I always ask this, but I wonder what's your favourite book?

Wuthering Heights. I know it's not law-related, but I'm not backing down.

It is a great book, no denying that. And do you have a favourite quote?

The classic from A Man For All Seasons between William Roper and Sir Thomas More. Well, I think it goes something like this doesn't it:

"William Roper: So now you'd give the Devil benefit of law?

Sir Thomas More: Yes. What would you do? Cut a great road through the law to get after the Devil?

William Roper: I'd cut down every law in England to do that!

Sir Thomas More: Oh? And when the last law was down, and the Devil turned round on you – where would you hide, Roper, the laws all being flat? This country's planted thick with laws from coast to coast – man's laws, not God's – and if you cut them down – and you're just the man to do it – do you really think you could stand upright in the winds that would blow then? Yes, I'd give the Devil benefit of law, for my own safety's sake."

Thank you. I want to move on to ask you about memorable cases and memorable days in Court. You've been at the Bar now for about ten years or so. Can you share with us perhaps a case that's stuck with you?

My first day on my feet. A prosecution list in the Magistrates' Court - picking up a stack of giant, disordered files at 7.30am, and having to be ready to run three consecutive trials at 09:30. Every conceivable legal and ethical problem reared its head that day - it was like an exam problem question, as if somebody was trying to test everything I'd ever learned at Bar school. I've never had a day quite like it. But eventually getting through it in one piece, leaving Court at 7pm, I realised that I could probably get through anything.

Fantastic, we all feel like that! Can I ask you, sort of, what's next?

The difficult second book is out in April 2020. It's called Fake Law and, like the first book, is aimed at trying to shine a light on the justice system for the general reader. It takes a look at the way in which our understanding of the law is distorted by the stories we are told - by the media, politicians and other special interest groups - and how as a result our rights, and our founding principles, are under threat.

I'm really looking forward to it. I've just got it actually and you very kindly have signed it for me. I want to ask you about your favourite fictional lawyer. I know lots of us at the Bar and the solicitors don't like legal dramas, but we have been influenced by some of them, you know, I often say Rumpole, or sometimes I say Atticus Finch for my very early ones, and then in my later years, you know, people like Ally McBeal because it was just hilarious, and of course Martha Costello who's one of my favourites. Who is yours?

As a teenager it was Jake Brigance from John Grisham's A Time to Kill.

Why?

The notion of a defence lawyer as the ultimate fearless conqueror in a case where they know that right is on their side was irresistible. My love for Jake has been tempered slightly with age, experience (which teaches rarely, that if ever as a lawyer, do you "know" that right is on your side) and the realisation that a lot of the stunts Jake pulled in Court would result in, at best, a discharged jury and, at worst, a hefty sanction from the BSB.

Yes, no-one wants that. Now, I want to ask you about access to justice. I'm passionate about it, but I interviewed Gina Miller, businesswoman, who brought the Brexit case, the famous prorogation case, and I wonder how important is the rule of law, especially in the context of access to justice that you write about?

It's everything. It is the foundation on which our democracy is built. Without it, civilisation collapses. And a central pillar of the rule of law is access to justice which, as Lord Reed puts it so beautifully in the Unison case (which I'll clumsily paraphrase), is meaningless if barriers are erected to prevent people from accessing the Courts. There is, as exposed in the Unison case through the Ministry of Justice's astonishing submissions, a view among many in Government that access to the Courts is only of importance to the individual parties involved, rather than a common social good. It is this ignorant view that has led to the problems in Legal Aid with which we're all so grimly familiar.

Is it hard being a regular person, not the Secret Barrister all the time, or is that the true joy of anonymity as the Secret Barrister?

It is a blessed relief to be able to practise without the attention that the Secret Barrister brings. Being able to do my day job as me, is one of the few things that keeps me sane.

Yes, that's fantastic. Can I ask you three pieces of advice and tips would you give for longevity and retention at the Bar? We know the retention, there is a retention crisis, but what three tips could you give?

1. Firstly, keep a sense of perspective. Our work is important - critically so to the people directly affected - but there is only so much we can do. We work in a broken system, and there is too much for any one person to fix. Accept your limitations, and that there will always be problems you can't solve, people you can't fix and cases you won't win.

2. Secondly, keep a sense of humour. You will crumble if you don't find a way to see the light amidst all the darkness of what we have to deal with.

3. Thirdly, surround yourself with a network of great people. Friends or family, it doesn't matter. You can't do this job as an island. You need people you can ask for help, people you can lean on and people who will pick you up when you fall.

Thank you, I agree with that. That's great advice. Now, I want to ask you please, if I may, what role do you think our male colleagues could play in the gender argument or the gender issues? I have some brilliant male colleagues in all different specialisms at the Bar and as solicitors, and they often wonder, you know, what real role they can play, and there's so much they could do. What do you think?

I think that in order to win any argument you want the broadest possible constituency behind you. Diversity of experience is key to persuading any audience; different people are persuaded by different approaches, different tone, and different arguments, born of different experiences and perspectives.

A huge thank you to the Secret Barrister for taking part in Talking Law, and do get a copy of their new book, Fake Law.

I. Stephanie Boyce

On this episode, I'm excited to bring you an interview from Stephanie Boyce, Deputy Vice President of The Law Society of England and Wales. An experienced General Counsel, Stephanie is set to become the Vice President of The Law Society later this year, and President in 2021 next year, the first ever black woman to hold that post. I started by asking Stephanie how her appointment came about.

Firstly, can I say, thank you for having me. We are recording this episode during the Coronavirus pandemic, which of course is having a huge impact on the ability of all of us to practice safely and uphold through the rule of law. But, it's important, may I say, that we stay positive, we stay strong, we stay healthy and, where we can, we stay home. So, how did I become Deputy Vice President of The Law Society? Would you believe me if I told you it took me four attempts to become Deputy Vice President?!

What?!

Yes, absolutely, four attempts! I had my first go in 2015. I had been on Counsel for about two years by that point, but such was the belief in my dream and my determination that I kept going until that dream became a reality.

Amazing. I mean, that is so fantastic to hear. Can I ask, why do you share that? You know, many people wouldn't say, for example, we've interviewed lots of Silks, well I have interviewed lots of Silks and QCs, and people don't often share the journey or the attempts, you know, why do you share that and what do you think we can all learn from it? Because it's wonderful to hear.

I share it because it's important for people to understand my journey, so people don't think I was an overnight success. Because you know, if I was an overnight success, it was the longest night ever. It's important that we recognise resilience and determination, and for me, I talk about the four attempts because the lessons for me were not just in how many times I didn't succeed. The lessons I took from the lack of success, I refined, and I built, and it propelled me forward. So, I persevered until something happened. I pushed and I pushed, and I pushed, and it's important that I tell that story so people understand that you don't just give up at the first hurdle, the first obstacle, and many, many people have said to me, I would have given up after the first attempt.

Yes

But, Sally, I can tell you, I would have kept going. And if it meant a fifth time, a sixth time, a seventh time, I would have kept going because such was the belief in my dream and the determination that I had. And long before I became Deputy Vice President, I told myself that I was Deputy Vice President.

Wow, that's so powerful. So, in essence, you know, the self-belief - we've been doing lots of webinars to deal with wellbeing and mindset - so the self-belief is really important before one could even act on it.

Absolutely. And the thing is I've always said, and absolutely believe, that not every advice that people will give you is advice that you will take. You have to know what advice to take and what advice to leave alone, leave well alone. So, there were people that told me, Stephanie, you know, go home and rest, you know, it's never going to happen in our lifetime, we're never going to see an ethnic minority person become President of The Law Society of England and Wales. And the more they kept telling me, you know, the more the naysayers kept saying, it's never going to happen, the more I kept thinking, hmm, it's going to happen, and that's absolutely what spurred me on. And the message to people, as I say, is to keep pushing and push. You persevere until something happens. That is how change comes about.

Fantastic, because you will be the first black female President of The Law Society of England and Wales. I mean, that is historical.

Absolutely, and to put it into context, when my election was announced last year, the Times newspaper reported, absolutely, that I will become the first ethnic minority President of The Law Society in 2021. So, to put it into context that in the almost 200-year history of The Law Society, you know, we've only had, I will become the sixth female to become President and, as I say, the first black person as Deputy Vice President and Vice President, as I will ascend to shortly, and then the first black person, the first ethnic minority to become President in 2021. A remarkable achievement, and I'm so honoured to serve my profession, especially during these difficult times, and immensely grateful for the support that I'm receiving and have received.

Fantastic. Well, I wonder if we can talk now about your journey in law and into our profession. I know I'm at the Bar and you're at the solicitor end, but how did you become a lawyer, because you've had quite an interesting journey, haven't you?

Well, absolutely. Growing up I saw so many injustices being perpetuated around the world and people not being able to access their legal rights, and I chose to study law. And I think that's why so many of us choose to study law is because we want to broaden our own awareness, knowledge and understanding of rights and legal issues, and together with the confidence and skills needed to deal with disputes and enable access to justice and to make a difference. So, for me, legal rights mean absolutely nothing if you don't know when those rights are being taken away, or if you don't know how to enforce those rights, hence why I got into law because I wanted, and want to make, an absolute difference.

What about the City? Can you just talk to us about the degree of roles that you've had in law?

Yes. So, essentially, I went into in-house in 2004. I had been in private practice and in fact, at that time when I qualified in 2002, other routes, other than private practice, were not really spoken about. People didn't tell you that, you know, there's an alternative other than to going into private practice and aspiring to become a partner in a private firm. I recognised very quickly - and having been made redundant twice in as many years - that the landscape was changing. The reductions in public funded work meant that I had been made redundant twice in as many years, as I said, and so, it's important for me to take a view, and I went in-house in 2004, landing my first job with the General Counsel of the Bar, and solicitor to the then Complaints Commissioner. I then went on from there to work for ACCA, the Association of Chartered Certified Accountants. I spent five years with them. I was promoted very quickly. I did a Masters there in Public Law and Global Governance with King's College University of London, and that's then propelled me into governance, taking up my first General Counsel role shortly after leaving ACCA, but not before I had worked for the Pensions Regulator. I went on to become Director of Legal Services at the Chartered Institute of Arbitrators, and then went on to take up my first GC role, I think about 2017. I then studied, and I think – unless I'm corrected - that I'm the first office holder to hold another qualification from another body. So, I'm also a Fellow of what was previously ICSA, but it's now the Chartered Governance Institute. So, a number of roles I've held with OFSTED, Pensions, Regulator, Cooperatives, I've worked podiatrists, and lastly, in my own consulting company.

Wow. So, actually quite an interesting route which, you're absolutely right, is not talked about, and indeed I know I do a lot of research on these interviews but I hadn't checked that, that you're the first person to hold a dual qualification, so to speak, which is wonderful to hear. Can I ask you, Stephanie, what is the case or a scenario that really was a game changer for you in your profession?

I think when I went to, for Bar Counsel in 2004/2005, Re; P, a barrister, was the most notable case there and, of course, you know, that case concerned whether you could be a Judge in your own course. I was the instructing solicitor, so it wasn't reported that I was the instructing solicitor on that occasion, but I got to work with some really interesting characters and see how the law was being applied. I found myself in Royal Courts of Justice in the canteen there and, if I may, Sally, just share this story, I found myself in the canteen and I was absolutely riddled with cold, but you know, was pushing on as you do. And, we'd taken a break in the case, and I found myself sat at like a breakfast bar sort of thing …

Yes

… and I realised I was sat in between two men in raincoats who were acting a bit suspicious. So, I started to look at them and think, well, what's going on here? And then I noticed that they had earpieces in …

Yes, yes, Exciting!

Yes! And I looked around and, you know, the person sat just next to me, but albeit the chap in one of the raincoats was in between us, was Cherie Blair, and I didn't know what to do with myself, you know, I just absolutely did not know what to do with myself. I thought, you know, all of a sudden I sat up straight and I didn't know whether to talk to her, approach her, whatever, but, you know, it was figures that I saw, but, you know – and even before that interaction, Mahatma, Gandhi, Nelson Mandela, you know, all those strong characters who'd immerse themselves in the law and applied the law to, you know, to effect real change, and again, you know, I know controversially at times, Margaret Thatcher. And I remember one of the first times when I was asked one of my inspiring role models and I mentioned Margaret Thatcher, and I was absolutely booed at this dinner table, and I said, let me finish, let me finish because you haven't heard why I've cited her as a role model. And for me, I make myself very clear, I do not agree with her later policies and the things which she went on to do but, for a young child, a black child growing up in rural Buckinghamshire where there weren't many role models of the same colour as me, there weren't many people of the same colour as me, and you certainly didn't see it on TV, you didn't see it in our history books at that time, but she was the Education Minister, female Education Minister, she was our first female Prime Minister, and she was a barrister, because initially I wanted to become a barrister and then subsequently changed my mind, you know, and I used to, at seven years of age, I used to do the best Margaret Thatcher impression. I can't do it anymore, so don't even ask!

Aah, I was thinking – I was going to – yes, you know, an ad hoc question, say do an impression! [Laughter]

But, you know, absolutely, she was somebody that I thought - I looked up and thought, well, if she can do it, I can do it.

Yes, so interesting, actually. And so, was she your only role model or did you have others who inspired you? I note you name, you know, some of my own heroes in Nelson Mandela and some of those people. Did you have any sort of more accessible role models, or inspirations, or mentors, or anything like that in your career?

Absolutely. In 2017 – so, my first General Counsel position was at the Society of Podiatrists. I went to work with a remarkable lady called Dr. Rosemary Gillespie, who I had mention in your book, Talking Law, yes, and Dr Gillespie - when my energy had waned and dipped, she absolutely inspired me and encouraged me and gave me the opportunity and, you know, and it was an absolute pleasure to work with her. So, she was a more tangible person, you know, rather than the rest perhaps who have earned their place in history that we talk about past and present. Also, my grandfather who fed me his hopes and dreams, but there are so many people who've inspired me into taking a leap of faith, from the man who had a dream, to the one who took a long walk to freedom, and to the woman who dedicated her life to the poor and disadvantaged. And, Sally, because of those people, you know, we are all benefactors of their, of the work of those individuals and the sacrifices they made, and I say true examples of the life of service. So, for instance, my grandfather, well, my grandparents and my parents who left the Caribbean to come to this country, the sacrifices that they made to come here and for me to have and relish in the opportunities that this country has given me.

Absolutely, absolutely. Stephanie, well, can I ask you this? I am a black woman barrister, I'm sure that people can see that if they just Google me, but the work that I've been trying to do on gender and race is really about improvement and showcasing those who exist. I wonder what your views are about diversity, social mobility in our profession, and really what can each of us do to improve it?

My view is, is that the legal profession, whether that's at the Bar, whether it's at the solicitor end, the judiciary, is that the legal profession should be open to all regardless of your background or wealth, you know, and it's my intention to leave this profession more diverse and inclusive than the one I entered. But, Sally, this has got to be a shared ambition amongst each and every one of us, and that for me means bringing men into that conversation as we advocate, as we shape, we discuss. Men are absolutely vital to that conversation. The issue of social mobility for me is another focus. As President, I will have a number of areas that I will be able to concentrate my efforts on, and social mobility for me is important. It's important, Sally, because I was told time and time again, that because of my social economical position, and let's be clear, I grew up in a single parent household on a Council estate, I was told my outlook. I was expected not to go to university, not to become - as I will become - President of The Law Society of England and Wales, but, you know, to have achieved from where I was and where I grew up and all the people who told me that you'll never make it as solicitor because, you know, you haven't gone to the right university the first time around, you don't come from the right socio-economical position, and what I say is, there are lots of initiatives out there to try and address the issue of social mobility, and I welcome all of those, but there is still much work to be done. And, especially in this country where social mobility in the last four years has been on the decline, and let's be clear, Sally, that during this current pandemic it is likely that the issue of social mobility and diversity is going to be hugely impacted, and it is vital that we continue to keep the discussion alive and that we focus attention on these issues, because whether as a black woman or a person of colour, or a male or female, gay, straight, disabled, poor, rich, whatever, we all want the same thing, and that is equality of opportunity and to be recognised for the individuals that we are

Absolutely that's so, so, well ... Stephanie, can I ask you, you're obviously very passionate about many things and you've had quite an interesting career, as I said earlier. What do you do about wellbeing? Burnout is high. I don't advocate everything I preach, I must say I probably have too many glasses of wine and not enough Yoga actually, but what do you do for relaxing and wellbeing, switch off? I note from my book, when I interviewed you, you're a keen cyclist is one of the things.

So, what I did before this pandemic is slightly different than what I'm doing now, but of course the mental health of legal professionals is an absolute growing concern, and of course, more so in this current crisis, but it's important that we find the right balance. So, before I absolutely loved cycling, and I know that currently, you know, we are able to go out for exercise, you know, once a day and, depending on who you speak to, an hour a day or however, but I haven't taken that opportunity to do so. So, what I need to do is, is that - and I haven't found myself reading terribly outside of work whilst I've been confined - but what I do is, I get, up, I try and get up the same time as I would, as if I was going into Chancery Lane. I start the day off with the Body Coach as he seeks to get the nation fit.

Oh yes, me too, gosh!

Yes, absolute lifesaver show Wicks has become. So, I do that. I do have a garden, I'm absolutely blessed that I have a garden and I do go into that and spend time. But, you know, I also take time to be very active just to speak to family because I'm not able to be with family at the moment. My little nephew who's 11 came from London before the lockdown to spend time with me because I live alone, so I'm grateful for his company, and he keeps me amused because I'm not a cook, so trying to feed the two of us has been quite interesting! But, you know, it's important that one finds time to listen to one's body and to what's going on around you. Take time to smell the flowers. So, before the pandemic, when I would go to go out and speak or whatever, I would disappear for a few moments before I went on stage or to speak, and probably you'd find me in the toilet in a safe, quiet space where I could just take some time just to breathe, just to reconnect and ground myself and just, you know, listen to my heart rates. But yes, I practice mindfulness, listening to my breathing. I haven't done much listening to classical music, cycling, as I say, I've probably been watching far too much TV in the background. I'm not moving around as much every single day, I used to do my 10,000 steps at least. Yesterday, I did 11,000 steps for the first time in over a month. Wow, I was so pleased! [Laughter]

Wow! And you're still alive and able … so that's really, really, really wonderful to hear. Stephanie, might I ask, who is your favourite fictional lawyer, and what's your favourite book?

My favourite book and my favourite film are the same, and that for me is The Colour Purple, because it reminds us to stop and smell the roses. One of the things this pandemic has done, we've had to stop and take stock, and I'm hoping that, you know, that we will come out, you know, as I say, stronger, that we will come out kinder, more compassionate, and we will take time before taking time, you know, I've got people who are rallying around me, you know, I just got a message saying, I'll drop the milk off at yours in an hour. You know, people who are really going out of their way, keen to see me stay safe for obvious reasons, but I do hope - that is my fervent hope - that we come out stronger and more compassionate as individuals and as a society and citizens of the world. So, my favourite fictional lawyer is Atticus Finch, who featured in To Kill A Mockingbird, a book I read as a child many years ago when I lived in America. And the reason he's my favourite fictional lawyer is because all of his impressiveness, his calmness and dignity in the face of such adversity, and for the following quote: "You never really understand a person until you consider things from his point of view, until you climb into his skin and walk around in it." That resonates with me so much. It resonates with me so much because I remember at times thinking, I wish I could be that person, I wish I could be that person, only to find out that actually the person that I am and the person I'm seeking to become is okay. I'm a beautiful person and I can make a difference without trying to imitate or be like anyone else.

That's so powerful. Thank you. Well, that just leaves me to ask you really what's next apart from taking your post as the President, what's next? What can we expect? You've got, is it three years you'll be in post?

No, so what will happen is, this year I will go to become Vice President, which I will hold that position for a year. Then, after the year, I will then ascend to Presidency for a year. So, what's next? I mean, we celebrated in December, 2019, which seems almost like a long time ago, Sally, we celebrated a hundred years of the Sex

Disqualification Removal Act of 1919 and, you know, we talked about the achievements within the hundred years from 1919 to 2019.

Yes

The next hundred years holds the hopes and dreams of our future generation of lawyers and, for me, you know, when we're no longer talking about gender equality, discrimination, biases, because we've achieved equality for everyone, and everyone is able to reach and achieve their full potential because they have equality of opportunity and have not been constrained because of their race, their background, gender, disability, sexuality, age, and all those other things that are perceived obstacles, that's what I would like to see and what we must all work towards achieving because this world is a beautiful place and there is room for us all.

Absolutely, and certainly our future women in the law and men in the law absolutely deserve to be part of it. Thank you so much, Stephanie, it's been wonderful chatting to you, and stay safe!

Absolutely stay safe, stay strong, stay healthy, and stay positive and stay at home as well, where you can.

A huge thank you to trailblazer, Stephanie Boyce.

Sean Jones QC

On this episode, I'm so excited to bring you an interview with Sean Jones, QC. Widely regarded as one of the leading employment lawyers in the UK, Sean has built a leading practice focused on complex and high-profile cases. He acts for both claimants and defendants in claims covering a wide range of employment, commercial law, and sports-related disputes. As we recorded our interview during lockdown for COVID-19, there are times when you might hear technology glitch a little, so please do bear with me, thank you. I started by asking Sean what inspired him to enter the law.

I've got really no good reason for going into the law side. I'd hoped to be able to say something to you along the lines of, you know, at a very early age, I was inspired to help others. And that played no, no role in me coming into the law, I'm embarrassed to say, although I developed some empathy later. A couple of things probably pushed me in that direction. The first is that I'm Roman Catholic. I was brought up in a Catholic home and it's all about the rules, everything is rules, particularly during Lent, so, you can imagine. So, from a very early age, I was arguing with my mother about whether a Jaffa cake was a cake or a biscuit, the purposes of Lent, and that sort of – you know, understanding laws and how one gets around them and where the interpretation space might be with something that was sort of culturally baked in. So, that's always fascinated me. And the other thing was just sheer stubbornness. And my, my father was a Ship's Captain, and he said I could do anything I wanted except go into the Navy or become a lawyer, so I immediately thought, well, law is it then? I'll do that as a kind of an act of rebellion. I may be the only person ever to go to the Bar as an act of parental defiance! And then when I told the school that's what I wanted to do, they said, you are not suited to the law, think about something else. I thought I'm not having that, so, it's essentially stubbornness, and at some point now, 30 years in, it's going to occur to me that choosing your entire career in order to prove other people wrong is not a very constructive way going about setting up a life, but I've enjoyed it. So, you know, even if by accident, I've made the right choice.

Yes. Why employment and media law, which I think are your main specialisms, is that right?

Yes, I don't do a great deal of media on the whole, I do sort of employment, and sport, I suppose, would be my second, second run. I really had no interest in it until I arrived in Chambers. So, Chambers did three things, public law, commercial law, which is what I was interested in, and employment law, and my first Pupil Master was a guy called Christopher Jeans QC, who's about the best employment lawyer on earth, and it really struck, me the first few cases I did with him, that I loved it and, from my point of view, it occupies a really interesting space. So, if you think about the law, it has what I call a reverse rainbow. So, at one end of the rainbow are cases which are really important, so keeping people out of jail or putting people into jail, keeping families together, taking children into care, stuff that has real social importance, which pays no money at all, you know, it's just, it's just extraordinarily ill-remunerated. Then at the other end of the rainbow, there are ships gently grazing each other in Greek ports, or arguments over whether an and is conjunctive or disjunctive in a banking agreement. That earns tons of cash! And it's just, it's a very weird career in which the more socially useful the thing you do is the less likely you are to be paid any real money for it, and employment law sits, to my mind, somewhere in between, so it's got an absolute ton of kind of personal interest. It's all about people and their relationships, and there are opportunities to make a real difference to people's lives, and yet it's not legally aided, and because it's never been legally aided the rates aren't determined by the frankly appalling way in which the Government treats people who do work of real importance for them. I just thought this looks perfect for me. I get to be nosey and well-paid.

Yes, and just talk about your seniority, really. You're a QC, you're probably one of the young QCs, clearly appointed on your brain, which is brilliant. Why did you decide to become a QC and part-time Judge?

Well, it took me two goes to get Silk, so, why did I apply? There's a set answer I could give you, which is pretty much the one I gave in the interview, which is all about, you know, taking on cases of greater interest, a bit more appellate work, being able to work with others as a team, having worked alongside juniors, all of which was true, but there's a bit of pressure on you. Certainly, in my set, taking Silk is what usually happens, and amongst my cohort it was what was generally happening. So, you reach a point where people are looking at you and saying, why have you not taken Silk? What's the problem with you? So, there is a bit of pressure from behind to kind of get on and make an application. And I would describe myself as sort of negatively ambitious. So, there are people who have a very clear, positive ambition. They say, what I want to be is Lord Chief Justice, or Master of the Rolls, or one day I'll be on the Supreme Court. These people terrify me! How do you know, that's what you want to do? But what I do know is I don't want to find myself pointed out with people saying, well, you know, he seemed to be going very well and then it all rather went to sleep and he drifted away and nothing really ultimately became of what he was doing. So, there's just a kind of pressure to keep moving like a shark, you have to keep swimming to stay alive. So, that played a rather larger part in it than I probably would have admitted during the course of my Silk interview. So far as sitting part-time is concerned, that was really a challenge to myself, so you're probably a much better person than I am, but I spent quite a lot of time thinking, oh no, not another terrible decision, and why isn't this Judge listening to what I'm saying? And it's, you know, obviously what I'm saying is correct, why can't they see it? For all the tut-tutting, you think, well, actually I've never tried being a Judge and maybe it isn't as easy as it looks, and if I'm going to spend my life moaning about a poor judicial decisions, perhaps I ought to chip in and make a few. And it really was an extraordinary difference. I hadn't really appreciated before I started to sit that as a barrister you're really a sort of glorified bookie come jockey, so people come and see you and you say your chance of success is 60% and now I will make that come true. So, you know, then you jump on the horse and ride it and try and win, but really all you're actually ever doing is trying to guess what someone else thinks, whereas we'll think in terms of the Judge. When you're a Judge, you actually have to make decisions, which is something we do surprisingly little of as an advocate, and it was a completely different thing. I thought it might just be a one step up the ladder, somewhat different, all my previous experience would be useful. But in fact, not at all. I mean, it turned out to be a different kind of job entirely. It's also a bit like when you have kids, the real you comes to the floor, you can't keep up a pretence when you have children, they kind of grind you down until the point at which your purest essence is revealed, and being a Judge is the same. So, I turned into exactly the kind of Judge I hate most [Laughter] and sometimes just sit there listening to myself being clever and, you know, interrupting with wouldn't this be a good point? I think, what are you doing? You idiot! Why are you behaving this way? It turns out that's just who I am and, you know, being a Judge revealed that to me and to everyone else, very clearly.

Yes, absolutely. Now you talked about your girls and your family. I'm obviously a woman and a black woman and the organization is Women in the Law UK, and we have loads of male members as well. I just wondered what you think about diversity in our profession and perhaps, you know, what can we all do to try and improve it?

Yes, and to point out, as I'm married to a Silk, so she, she regularly reminds me of the need for diversity in all decision-making and all areas. I think we're in a rather unique position at the Bar. I want to say one thing first because, unless you're as old as me, it's difficult to remember really how terrible it used to be. So, if I tell you a story - when I was a student, I was interning at a local firm of solicitors and I attended a murder hearing in Norwich Crown Court. And I was trapping back on the train with a Silk who we had instructed and a series of other barristers and they were talking about women coming to the Bar - and at that point there was a tiny handful of women at the Bar - and the question that was put to the Silk was have you let any women into Chambers? And that's how it was put. And his answer was, we've taken on – quote - a couple of nymphets. This is kind of early eighties, so it's really not all that long ago, but the notion that anyone would speak or even think in that sort of way now, it's so alien that it's – I think it's important to acknowledge that there's been some progress, but we are, of all professions, the one which would have the least excuse for discrimination and lack of equal opportunity, because we are all about justice. We're supposed to be all about equality. And those two things for me, and speaking as a discrimination lawyer, the key to understanding discrimination, it is unjust and stupid. So, it's unjust because, you know, whether or not your career progresses shouldn't depend on how much pigment your skin has, or whether you have a penis. Those are ridiculously stupid ideas for, you know, deciding who should and shouldn't make progress. So, it's unjust because people who, who are dealt one hand in a genetic or social lottery are prevented from achieving who they can be, completely pointlessly, and it's stupid because that's a lot of talent throw away. I mean, we've wasted centuries of intellect and ability through prejudice, so how important is it? I just don't think there is a more important thing. I mean, I think it's key to the success of the Bar that we are colour blind, sexuality blind, sex blind, that we just look for the people who have the skill, the ability and the passion to do it. And if we don't do that, then we effectively deserve to die as profession. No profession should be taking any other approach, us least of all because we're, in theory, committed to eradicating that kind of behaviour everywhere, so, we have to start at home.

What do you think, sort of, male allies can do? How can they get involved in the argument, you know, such as yourself?

Well, I think this is, this question is a bit of a trap, and the reason why I think it's a bit of a trap is because it's, it's expressly inviting me to mansplain what can be done for women's rights, to a woman! [Laughter] So, I suppose if I was a bit younger, I had all sorts of, you know, this was how we would sort out the Bar. This is, you know, if women want to progress, I'll tell them how they can progress. And, I think what's most important for men at the moment in terms of being allies is just shutting up and listening and, you know, the people who know best what needs to be done is not us. So, if we listen and act on, on the advice that we get from the female colleagues, that just seems to be that's by far and away, the better approach.

Great, great. Now, you were the founder of Billable Hours, but what is Billable Hours and how did you get involved with such a fantastic campaign if you like? Cause I've often donated

Well, firstly, thank you for your donations. I'm one of the founders, but I'll explain that as I explain how it came to be. So, the way it came to be was in the refugee crisis, the families drowning in the Mediterranean. For me, the precise moment that I became engaged in it was opening a tweet and seeing the picture of Alan Kurdi dead on the beach and weirdly struck by his shoes. I mean, a really odd thing to say, but the soles of his shoes, he had - my youngest has or had exactly the same pair of shoes, and at that moment his death became realer to me than any previous depiction of pointless, ridiculous, wasteful, suffering had been before. So, it just grabbed me, and I remember thinking, you know, something must be done. And at that point, authors of children's books had organised an online appeal using Just Giving, and what the authors were doing was matching donations. So, they'd say the first thousand pounds, I will match that, and one children's author after another stepped in to take up the next battle and keep the money coming in. Well, I remember thinking that's incredible that, you know, children's authors can do this, if only lawyers could. And, at that moment, I thought well, why can't lawyers do it? And just sort of assumed that we weren't the sort of people who do that, but thought we'd give it a try, and we were just having a conversation late at night on Twitter with two other lawyers, Adam Creme, who's now Head of Legal at Unison, and Annie Powell, who's a solicitor at Leigh Day, and we thought, well, let's just give it a go. So, set up a website and it just took off, people were really, really engaged in it. So, what we do is we say, we're a franchise, if you want to raise money, raise money, just go out and do it, and what we commit to doing from our point of view is to do two things. The first is, we gave people a hook on which to raise money. So, people would sit there - it sounds weird to say it – but people would sit there and think, how much should I give? I don't know, should I give £10, £100? And that would actually put people off donating because they couldn't work out what the right sum was. I mean, it sounds absurd but we just came up with the idea of saying, give us what you charge for one hour of your time, what we call the billable hour and the kind of the atom of the legal industry, the most basic particle, what you charge for now, just give us that. And that proved to be an extraordinarily helpful idea. It seemed a very simple one, but people immediately got it and started donating, so that was, that was fabulous. But we also decided that we would be zero infrastructure. So, at the moment we have a relationship and I don't anticipate it changing in the immediate term, with Save the Children. We said to them, what we will do is we'll raise money for the really exceptional work that you do. If there are costs to be borne, we'll bear them. So, if we need a website, we'll pay for it, if we're going to have an event, we'll make sure everyone who participates is paid, you get everything on top and we will try and make sure that we cover the costs. So far as possible we have, whereas you might for an event, donate the premises, donate some food and donate the time of employees to come along and help us. So, the idea is to just make sure that so far as we can, everything that gets raised goes straight through us, never sits in a bank account that we own, never passes through any administration, and goes straight to the relevant charity. So, that kind of keeping lean, franchising out, and giving people a basic notion of how they might set about giving has proven to be very successful, and you'll have seen that we have people like Ishan who, you know, he cooks, so he's made a cookbook. And I was deeply sceptical, I said, who wants to buy a cookbook full of recipes made by lawyers? [Laughter] And the answer is, Nigella Lawson wants to buy a copy of this book and, you know, thousands of people!

It sold out! I couldn't get a copy at Christmas, which is why I started doing the sparkly, you know, wear something sparkly for December, and then eventually I managed to get a copy! Someone took pity on me!

I'm so pleased. I mean, there's some pretty dodgy recipes in there, some really fantastic ones, [Laughter] but it's just -I think what it showed me is what I've sort of always known, and what I hope has been your experience of the Bar and the profession generally as well, which is that for all of the reputation we have with being terrible ambulance-chasing heartless eejits, in fact, you know, it's - people are good people, they're people who want to help, and half the success of raising money seems to be to just give people the opportunity to do it, to put in front of them the opportunity to give, and they do, and that I can't - I can never begin to thank the people enough for what they've done. People like you who donated and publicised, just anyone who's participated is a hero as far as I'm concerned.

Well thank you and your co-founders with setting it up. I want to ask you about wellbeing, you know, you do quite a lot of jobs quite full on for all of us, and having a family, and I wondered really what you do for wellbeing, because you also write a column don't you with Professor Dominic Regan on wine?! I hope that wine is not the only thing you do for wellbeing!

I'm not in a position to advise anyone. I'm a disaster at wellbeing so I don't - I'm really bad at it! [Laughter] And I thought I was being very clever by doing a lot of work from home, but what happens is the home becomes a bit of a workplace.

Yes

And so the best bit of advice I ever got was from one of my Pupil Mistresses, as we then called them, Siobhan Ward, said, this job is really odd, there are ups and downs., there are quiet periods and there are busy periods, and you have to spend your quiet periods relaxing and not - as all barristers in fact do - worrying that you're quiet. So, she said, right, well, I've finished this bit of drafting, I'm going to the cinema. You go, what, on a Tuesday afternoon?! Yes, because I've finished this bit of drafting and now I'm going to cinema. So, I have, I've tried to take the relaxation where it comes, as it were, and not sweat about, you know, if there's a gap between two cases, or it's been a whole day without me having a telecon. I suppose if there's anything specific, it's probably running, although I treat that as work, so the only way to get myself out is to give myself a deadline and say, you have to do this much today, get out there. So, it has a certain work feel to it. But, if you ask my kids, they would confirm that I am disastrously bad at , you know, setting aside particular time. Sundays are probably the best day. So, I take the kids to Church and we tend to go out for lunch on Sunday, and I am - with a small 'r' - religious about making sure that that doesn't get disturbed, but otherwise this is just not a job that is ever going to take less than 100% of you. So, I think if you were thinking of coming to the Bar and you thought, well, what I'm going to do is make sure I never work Fridays, it's incredibly difficult to pull off. It's not impossible, but you have to be disciplined absolutely from the outset.

Yes, thank you, thank you. And now, the wine column, how did that come about?

That was a big surprise to me! I got a phone call at my desk from someone congratulating me on my wine column, [Laughter] and I thought, what wine column? And hung up, and I just thought that the person had had some kind of - just, mistaken me for someone else, and then I got an email from a prominent employment Silk saying, oh, I'm very impressed, I didn't know you knew anything like that about wine! So, this is getting very strange indeed. So, the third person, when they contacted me, I said, where is my wine column? And they said, it's in the back of Counsel magazine. So, of course, if I'm LexisNexis are listening, I religiously read Counsel magazine, but on that particular day it was still in its wrapping behind my desk. So, I tore the wrapping off and there it was, Dominic Regan and Sean Jones, and I'd had precisely zero input! [Laughter] I thought, this is odd! Then I call Dominic and find out what's going on and he said, ah yes, when I was approached by Counsel magazine to write their wine column, they said to me - apparently straight from the 18th century - no barrister will ever take wine advice from a solicitor, so you need a barrister's name to put on there, so I put yours on it! [Laughter] I said, what?! So, all of a sudden, I was Counsel's wine correspondent. So, we've, we've reached a working arrangement in which he and I drink heavily, and he then writes it up and I'm allowed to make suggestions. But I just don't have the gall to claim that it is my column. It really is, you know, 900% Dom.

[Laughter] I love it, I love it. Can I ask you about role models and perhaps any mentors? You've named a few already that you had in your career. How important have they been?

I would say, well, generally, I guess my grandfather, who was a good one, I didn't see him very much before he passed on. I started researching my family tree, you know, in the hope that I would find I was descended from William the Conqueror or, you know, there was some, there was some ancient estate I was ready to inherit, but in fact, simply, every line of my family, going back from about two generations back, just says "ag lab", agricultural labourer. Everyone was dirt poor, all of them, so, you know half of them appear to have died in workhouses of one sort or another. My grandfather was the son of an indigent, an occasional railway worker, and the story in the family is that he presented himself at the door of a school in Shrewsbury and said, I am clever, educate me – I can't believe it was that simple - but he was on, on a scholarship, and went on to be a headmaster in the reform school system. And he is, he was this enormous shift in the fortunes of the family through sheer determination and the faith in education. So that, that kind of kept me at the desk as it were when I was studying. In terms of law, the first person that really influenced me was a woman called Elizabeth Cope. She was a family solicitor who went on to be a Judge, and is now, I think, Lady Mayor of Colchester, which is where I grew up.

Yes

And she ran an incredibly busy family law practice. She was a family law solicitor. She was the most organised person I'd ever seen, and she had this phenomenal, practical empathy, so that people would come through her door - sometimes literally bloodied in a state of intense familial emergency, and she would - complete calm and wear a kind, of an implicit sympathy in everything, she said, calmed them down, take their instructions, identify what needed to be done and get it done. Now, that's not me, I really wish it were. She's my example. So, I daily fail to live up to the example that she set, but it was incredibly inspiring to see. Chris Jeans, my Pupil Master, dragged me by the ear into employment law, but also Dom, Dom Regan I think is a bit of an inspiration to me because, I mean, if you, if you know him, you know that he has this great gift for friendship, for connection. Once he knows you're trying to find someone else, he thinks you ought to know, you know, that some great thing might come out of you being connected with someone. And that's, I think, one of the keys to success in our profession is just - the evolution of a career is dependent on the evolution of friendships and the people that you get to know and the opportunities that present themselves and, if your him, the opportunity to just be kind and do good for other people. So, he's never thinking of himself, he's always thinking about how a bit of help here, a word there, a letter or an email, a clipping sent through the post that might make someone else's life a bit better. And that's extraordinary that he does that day in day out.

So, again, someone I'd love to be, but I fall well short of that standard. I don't say that necessarily to underscore, but he is definitely someone who makes the world better by just being himself.

Oh, well, I'm looking forward to inviting him on here, he is awesome. I've not seen him for a long time. We just talked about role models, I guess, and you name those. I wonder if there's a case that really may be a case that made you, or a case that has meant the most to you in your career?

The things I tend to remember are bad things, so I'm much more likely to remember the case where I accidentally locked myself in the toilet and couldn't get out, than I am some great victory! [Laughter] Because that first case will have me cringing until my, until I enter the grave, whereas I've been involved in all sorts of cases where I felt at the time I was making a big difference. Maybe I did, but I remember them less well. I suppose it would probably be my first one, which was a nothing case, objectively assessed. I had to go over to the Court of Appeal and ask for Legal Aid taxation of costs. I made an enormous mess of it. I tripped on my gown as I stood up, and then just [mumbled words] at the Master of the Rolls. He said, are you asking me for Legal Aid taxation of costs?. Yes. He said, well, you can have it. And that was it, you know, I was congratulated by my solicitor as if I'd won a case in the Supreme Court. But the reason why it was significant is because up until that point it's all a dream and an ambition, you know, what will I be when I grow up, and I'm working very hard in the university library in order that I will become a barrister. And then when you're in pupillage – it probably wasn't true of you – I was insufferable in pupillage. Once I'd been called, I told everyone I was a barrister all the time. I needed a dark suit because I'm a barrister. You know, I'm looking for a desk so I can do my barrister work on it – and that was before I'd done any cases! So, as soon as I stood up on that £50 case in the Court of Appeal, it all stopped being theoretical and all became practical. It's like a big slap on the face where you suddenly think, you know, literally people are trusting me with the most important moments of their lives. They're trusting ME with them, the fools! What do they think they're doing?! But you think one must now rise to this. This is all suddenly pellucidly clear. It's like, you know, it's a bath of cold water. This is reality. It's happening now. And that produced a sort of gear change where I stopped wandering about telling everyone I was a barrister and started trying to get it right. So, probably that very first one.

Wow! And do you have a favourite fictional lawyer and maybe a favourite book?

Yes, it's quite a disgraceful choice. If you ever watched Boston Legal.

Yes! It was after LA Law, I think.

It was, and it was genuinely terrible. [Laughter] But it had in it a character called Alan Shaw. Alan Shaw was revolting, and he's a vile man. He's, on the face of it, at the very, putting it as its lowest, he's a sexual harasser, and he has very little regard for ethics. But, if you could put all that aside, what the Church would call the glamour of evil, to one side, he has two characteristics. First is, an absolute inability to be anything other than entertainingly blunt in Court. So, there's a fantastic wish fulfilment element where, because we spend all day expressing the deepest and profound disrespects for whatever's being said to us - however, bizarre, however wrong - he just says that's wrong, or, you're an idiot, to Judges, so you think, aah, there's a kind of visceral thrill listening to someone say that. So, he's obviously much more entertaining than that, but that's fantastic. And also, he - there's a very odd thread through the series, which is that William Shatner, the man who was Captain Kirk, is head of the firm and has Alzheimer's and just becoming less effective as an advocate. And Shaw's friendship with him is redemptive. So, they share this extraordinary professional relationship, which is like a super-concentrated version of what's best about being in Chambers, that people - people don't stress this enough, I think, that the great crowning joy of being a barrister is your colleagues and relationships you form over decades working alongside, them sometimes against them, sometimes with them. The support that you give each other, the friendship which is inherent in all that, is absolutely the best thing about the Bar, and that that programme and that character somehow managed to, for all the other unpleasantness, epitomise that. Books, I'm, I think if you've got a favourite book, you're not reading enough. It's just, I don't have a specific book that I love. I mean, in different stages of my life, I've loved all sorts of books in the most cliché possible ways. As a teenager, I loved Catcher in the Rye, I loved I

Claudius … a book by Anne Tyler called Saint Maybe in my twenties, so, you know, for each decade there is some book which particularly sticks with me. There are books where I developed a great enthusiasm for and start - usually non-fiction books or something — start boring the pants off everyone, whether it's say - you are lucky not to be anywhere near me after I'd finished Thinking Fast and Slow, because I had about six months of overly talking about that in the most intense, possible way. But I think, it's like trying to choose a favourite book is like trying to choose a favourite leaf on a tree, or the favourite day in the year, there just too many and they're all wonderful, and my great regret is I'm going to die with only having read a tiny fraction of what I wish I'd read.

Sean Jones, it's been wonderful talking to you. I feel like we need like another two hours! [Laughter]

I don't think anyone could stand that! [Laughter]

But it's been really great. It's wonderful to talk to you. Thank you for talking to me. I wonder if you can just confirm the website in case people want to get involved with Billable Hours and donate.

So, it's www.billablehour.org. And thank you so much for having me, it's been a joy.

A huge thank you to Sean Jones QC for taking part in Talking Law. Do follow him on Twitter @seanjonesqc.

Joanna Hardy

On this episode, I'm pleased to bring you an interview from Joanna Hardy. Joanna is widely regarded as one of the UK's leading junior criminal barristers, practicing from Red Line Chambers in central London. She's ranked in both the 2019 and 2020 editions of the Legal 500, as well as the Evening Standard's Progress 1000, a list of the most influential people in London. As we recorded our interview during lockdown for COVID-19, there are times when you might hear technology glitch a little, so please do bear with me, thank you. I started by asking her how many years ago she was called to the Bar

Ten in July.

Wow!

Yes, very exciting.

Gosh, let's start from the beginning, shall we? Why law for you?

So, I was a bit of a geek at school. I was quite bright, I liked exams, I liked homework, I, I kind of excelled academically, and that led me to kind of travel through quite good GCSE results, quite good A Levels, which - I didn't go to a particularly academic school. I then ended up at Kings, and I read law at Kings, and I ended up in the postgraduate class with all the other geeks who were all going on to do these amazing academic positions and PhDs and teaching, and I just realised that actually, whilst I loved academic law, I also loved people and human beings, and I was quite nosey and quite interested in why human beings do the things they do, and so I realised that the combination of being obsessed with humans and being obsessed with academic law, that there is really only one job for that, and it is being a criminal barrister. So, I'm very fortunate that the stars aligned for me.

Wow! And did you know anybody in the law?

So, I had absolutely no links at all when it came to work experience, and my dad was a Police Officer. So, he was out all the time on the streets of Sussex, you know, coming home and telling us all the stories about criminal law. And it came to work experience week, and I didn't want to go and do what all the other kids were doing. I was quite interested in law and I wanted to go to work with my dad, and I can remember him laughing at the table now, imagining this teenager popping into, you know, the beat. [Laughter] And so he had given evidence in Court, obviously as a Police Officer, and through that way he knew one barrister, I think, who he felt able to approach and to say, you know, my daughter's quite bright, you know, we don't really work in these circles, we don't really know anybody in the profession, is there any way she could come with you? That barrister had actually become a Judge! So, I ended up doing my work experience in my school uniform. I'm sitting on the bench at Lewes Crown Court [Laughter] and it was just unbelievable! So, yes, and after that I still knew nobody. I knew him. So it was, it was a wonderful, wonderful piece of work experience. And even then, I didn't think I could necessarily make it at the Criminal Bar, but it certainly inspired me, and then when I did my degree and I realised actually this academic side isn't for me, that was what I wanted to go and do, and I was very fortunate to be able to do it.

Fantastic. Now I've been at the Bar 20 years in October, and you will have been at the Bar for 10 in July. I just wonder, when you came to the Bar what was it like, and what did you hope for it to be like?

I was terrified! I spent most of my pupillage and most of the early years of my practice thinking that everyone else was in on some secret that I wasn't in on, and I now know that's imposter syndrome, but I didn't have a word for it or a label for it then, and I just thought that everyone else was in this club where they felt very relaxed in this wig and gown, and I felt ludicrous. I was like, what am I doing, getting dressed up every day?! And I felt like all the people that refer to Judges by their first names in the robing room, like, John will do this, Fred will do that, I thought, how do you know the Judge?! How is this happening?! And it was only when I relaxed into my own skin and I started to make my own friends and find my own role models and, you know, really get to know Silks and Judges as decent people who would look out for juniors that I suddenly realised, oh, that's why they call them John, because they genuinely know them, and it's genuinely a pally and collegiate profession. But it took me a long time to be comfortable in my own skin, and I think more people should say that because I imagine there's a lot of junior barristers now, and I use the word junior not in age but in seniority, who are probably feeling that now, and I want them to know that I certainly felt out of place for years. I felt like someone was going to come and tap me on the shoulder and say, look, sorry, we've made a horrible mistake, if you could just leave.

Yes, we do. And actually, you know, you talked there about imposter syndrome. It's amazing, so many of us have it, even Lady Hale. Do you have any tips for perhaps those who are entering or have been in it on how to get over it?

I think the best tip that someone gave me was that there is no correct answer. Now, in law you have to be careful with that, cause there's a lot of wrong answers in law, but there's no real correct way of approaching certain ethical problems or certain legal problems. You'd get ten barristers who would do it in ten different ways, and they might all be correct. You know, your style and your approach to this job is a huge part of it. It's not a formulaic job, it's not like being a statistician or an economist. It's not mathematic, it's about human beings. And no matter what area of law you're practicing in, whether it's crime, tort, tax law, commercial law, at its heart will be a human being who wants an outcome. And as long as you're operating within the confines of the law and you're applying the law correctly and you're following the procedure, your individual nuances on how you approach your work and your work life balance, there isn't a right or wrong way of doing that. You need to find your way of doing it. And once I found my pace and how I wanted this job to work for me is when I started to relax into it and really enjoy it.

Well, can I ask you then, is there a case which means a lot to you really in your career? Do you have any?

I do, and I'm sure that what I'm supposed to do is show off about all the big cases I've done, and I have done some big cases and I'd love to show off now and say it was the murder or it was the, you know, high profile client, but do you know what, Sally, the case that ,honestly, I always go back to was about a parking space. And I won't say too much about it for reasons that you and your listeners would understand, but what I can say, which is what was said in open Court, so it's perfectly okay for me to describe it to you, was I represented a mother, who was a working mother, and she had a son who had some disabilities and they had a blue batch for their car. And he secured some part-time employment working in the same building as her, but he left before her, his hours were shorter. And for some reason, and reasons that never, I never quite understood, the Borough Council decided to investigate this use of her blue badge and the early return of the person who owns the blue badge, and they prosecuted her for fraud. And she took it to the Crown Court, she elected a jury trial for that, and it went in front of a Judge who encouraged the prosecuting agency to perhaps consider whether this was a trial they wanted to have. And they offered her a, a resolution that was very low and would have had a minimal impact on her life, but it would have been a criminal record for her, and she, she could see that the Judge wanted it to go away, the prosecutor wanted it to go away, the jury probably wouldn't be particularly impressed with everything that was going on about this parking space and all their taxpayers money, and I just remember that she stood her ground. She said, I haven't done anything wrong, and they've brought it this far and I'm going to have a trial and I'm going to be brave. And she was acquitted in such a quick time, and the jury were almost applauding her, you know, she was saying, I haven't done anything wrong, I'm just a mum and helping my child. And it was the type of brief that people sometimes would turn their nose up because they'd think, well, it's a load of work, it's a huge effort, the brief fee isn't particularly high, it's not particularly, you know, it doesn't look good on paper, it's not a murder, it's not this, it's not that, it was just about this woman and her family and the parking space and how a prosecuting agency can sometimes be dogmatic. And it sticks in my mind as somebody who stuck to her guns and showed her bravery in the face of the power of, of the State. And I came away thinking, well, good on you, and never again, would I let any, anyone, put administrative or any other suggestion that people shouldn't do what's right. And at its core, that is what the criminal law should be about, and sometimes we all need reminding of that. We all need to be reminded that it's within the power of every citizen to say, I'm standing my ground, and it's our job to stand their ground for them.

And be their voices. Can I just move on a little bit and ask you about diversity in the law? You know, what do you think we could do to improve diversity and social mobility in the legal profession?

So, the first thing we can do is to not stop. Sometimes I feel like there's so much noise around diversity and we have all these initiatives and we put them all into place and we have the articles in Counsel magazine, we have the initiatives on Twitter, everyone's talking about it, and then it's almost as if it goes quiet, and people think, oh, they're doing that diversity stuff in the background, and that's not how we change the demographic of this profession. We all need to be aware of it when we do little things. When we have a mini pupil with us who's from a background that might be underrepresented at the Bar, it should be incumbent on each of us to really encourage that person. And when we interview or do selection exercises, even for work experience for a couple of days, or for mini pupillages, that recruitment exercise needs to be fair, because those are the experiences that go on the CV of the candidates that get through for pupillage, and the candidates that get through for pupillage are the candidates that becomes tenants, and they become the Silks, and they become the Judges. So, nothing is too small in this profession. When we speak - I know you speak as well - when we speak at open days and when we take time out of our diaries to go and speak at schools, or we speak at pupillage fairs, or we just stand on the stall talking to kid after kid, after kid with their parents, every single one, I think that we should always seek to encourage them, no matter what, and to show them that, you know, this is not a profession anymore, that is closed to anyone. There's still a lot of work to do. So, my second step is we can't be complacent. I think sometimes we see encouraging statistics and we forget that it doesn't take much for those statistics to crumble. I mean, I'm slightly concerned about the coronavirus impacts on diversity because our most junior tenants, if they are very fortunate - and it's no criticism of them - if they're fortunate to have the cushion of private wealth, they're in a better position to weather the storm. And for those students that have scraped in with scholarships, with debt, with loans, now they're being asked to weather the storm and they may be not as well placed to weather the storm, and I'm concerned that all the work we have done in the last few years, and the work that you and I have done, Sally, with the Social Mobility Committee, that some of those people may now be vulnerable to leaving the profession. So, there's always work to do, we always need to respond to the circumstances at hand. And, you know, I'm, I'm always grateful and inspired that there are so many people willing to give up their time and their knowledge and their own experiences to speak at all levels of seniority and across all practice areas, and I think it's something that the Bar is rightly proud of, but something where we've all still got more work to do.

Absolutely, which is why we give up, as you say rightly, our free time. You were talking just about, you know, you're inspired by many. I wonder if you could just share some of that. Who are your role models and who are the people that inspire you?

So, my Joint Head of Chambers, Gillian Jones, QC, she, she is a great of the Bar. But she's somebody who I looked up to before she became my Head of Chambers actually, and I was doing a trial with Gilly when she took Silk, and it really stood out to me that she was one of the few practitioners who had a work life balance, which I thought meant that she was all the better for it in Court. She obviously has a wonderful family life, which is healthy and productive, she has interests outside of the Bar, she's interesting to talk to, which sometimes people you think all you do is this trial, this must be your life. And she's a person who shows you a warmth and depth of character, and that's why she's well suited to be our Head of Chambers. But also, she is somebody who breaks the mould. When people say that women in high-powered positions can't have it all, so they can't reach the upper echelons and have a healthy family life and have interests outside of the Bar and be nice, and I look at people like Gilly and I think, well actually you can, you can do that. And so, it's people like that, and there are many of them in my Chambers. We have a number of female Silks who I look at and I think, you balance so much and yet you maintain excellence in your work, and they're living, walking, talking proof that you can do it all and still have time and energy, I hope, to spare - they probably would disagree with me on that - but when I see them, they're still generous with their time and energy with me, and I imagine I'm not as high on their list as they are on mine.

Well, what do you do for wellbeing and really work life balance?

I always say this, and people always laugh as if I'm joking, but I'm not. If you can, if you have the capacity to buy a dog, every barrister should buy a dog, because honestly you come home from Court and you're really stressed, and the Judge's words are ringing in your ear that he wants the admissions by five o'clock or your opponent's going to send a Skeleton Argument overnight, and everyone's so het up, and I come in the door and his little face ... he just, all he wants is to go for a walk in the sunshine and have a cuddle. I have a cup of tea, and it forces me to spend an hour decompressing, it just forces me to do it, there's no excuse not to do it. And I just think that that hour is so precious to me. I have an hour in the morning where I walk him around the block, I have my coffee, I clear my head. I get ready for the day. I have an hour when I get home where I give him a big cuddle. You know, he goes off to doggy day care and runs around with his pals and we come home in our house and we have time where we really decompress together, and it's so good for anybody, I think. So, I thoroughly recommend any kind of pet. I do a lot of walking. I'm fortunate, I live in a lovely part of London and I often will just get up from my desk and just walk and just, you know, go around the park, with or without the dog, get some fresh air, clear your mind, rest your eyes, rest your neck ... I think we're a profession that will be all hunchback because we all are so scrunched over screens all the time, particularly at the moment because none of us are going to Court.

Yes

Sometimes I think we forget that the simple things can sometimes be the most effective. You know, we get emails about fancy yoga classes and all of this, and actually my downtime is quite simple. I just like to step away from the work, close the laptop, be with my friends, my family, my partner, and my very, very precious little dog.

Aah. Now I want to talk about some of your other activities if I may?

Yes

You gave evidence to the Select Committee. How did that come about and what were you giving evidence about?

So, the inquiry that the Justice Select Committee were looking into was the disclosure failings in criminal cases. So, there'd been a high-profile sexual case that collapsed because the police had not sufficiently or properly ..... disclosed material that was, that met the test. And so, there was a broader review, there was a lot of headlines, and the spotlight was really cast on the criminal justice system more broadly because the upshot of why disclosure failings were really happening was resources, and particularly the change with technology. So, whereas before the disclosure in a case, you know, 40 years ago may have comprised letters, but now they comprise 3,000 WhatsApp messages, you know, the landscape is so different, and a smartphone being considered by the police - and I make no criticism of them in the cases that I do because I know they're doing actually a very difficult job - is that it is very difficult to analyse all of the material with competing resources, time pressures, and a diminishing workforce, and it is hard. So, they were looking into that. So, the CBA, the Criminal Bar Association of which Angela Rafferty - now Judge Rafferty - was the Chair was asked to give evidence, and the solicitors associations were all represented, and they tagged me on the end, Sally. Who can believe it? Because I think they wanted a standard criminal - not too senior, not too junior - somebody that does this knockabout work every single day, and so I was asked if I would mind – when I say asked, I was very, very heavily persuaded. [Laughter] I had to go on what I then found out was being broadcast on live television. So, the only person in the world that found it enjoyable was my mother [Laughter] but it was an important activity. And it was actually interesting to meet the justice select committee because you see them on TV and you read their reports and you don't actually get a feel for how inquisitive they are, and they're really inquisitive, and they're really interested in the profession and in the problems and in the practical solutions. And that applies to disclosure, which I was talking about, but we also touched upon the wider funding issues and the wider issues for the Bar, and I left feeling a lot more impressed with the process and with the assessment, their assessment of problems and possible solutions than I did when I arrived. So, I was really glad I did it. And I think that, you know, the, the CPS now have new policies on disclosure of digital material, the police have new processes in place and hopefully those difficult days when we saw in the headlines the cases that collapsed, hopefully they're behind us.

Yes. Well, you talk there about, you know, participating in that, but I wonder, you participate in other things as well. One, how comfortable are you with using Twitter? Two, you've got lots of followers, but you also get a lot of aggro on there, and I wonder if we could go to the beginning and perhaps, you know, tell us about the Evening Standard article, or your comments that you made which led you to that. Can you just share a bit about that and then how you manage Twitter?

Yes, so I had what I would term to be quite a normal Twitter account to begin with where I was followed by my friends and a few of my colleagues and a few weirdos - and that seems to be the, you know, people that are probably bots ... or they seem to be just people that send you very strange private messages. But anyway, so that was my Twitter diet, it was very normal. And I used to tweet about the profession a little bit, and I remember there was a big campaign about retaining women at the Bar, at the juncture about when women have children really, and it was about how women will leave. And I got a bit fed up because I took the view that all we ever do is talk about this. We will say, isn't it awful, we wring our hands about women leaving, but actually keeping women at the Bar, the first steps are very practical, and I take the view they're very easy. So, I tweeted about them. I did a list where I said, you know, that the steps to retaining women at the Bar should be stop having listings so early in the morning that people can't drop their kids off at nursery. It strikes me that's a very easy step we can take. Secondly, abolish the warned list system, because women either juggling childcare or returning from maternity want to know what their diary looks like, so that they can say to any childcare arrangements that they have, I need you to be here on Monday, rather than I've got no idea when I'm going to need you to be here because I have a warned list and I'm going to find out at quarter past four. It struck me that's an odd system to retain women at the Bar, or any caregiver you know, men as well. And I tweeted all about these practical stats, about female mentoring, you know, upward mentoring, downward mentoring, and then one of my tweets was about people at the Bar who speak poorly to women during their cases. Now I must say, they're in the minority, but a male barrister had said to me during a debate about an attempted murder case, about the mens rea of attempted murder, at the end of the debate, which I was correct about, he said, you are worse than my wife. And I thought, do you know what, pal, I do not get up every morning for you to tell me that. So, I included that, and of course that attracted the headlines. People love having a little insight into a profession that they deem to be quite an established profession. They see it quite as a secretive profession, so just a young woman having a go I think they found quite refreshing, and it was the perfect storm because it was at the height of other prominent women, you know, sounding off about poor behaviour. And so, the Evening Standard ran it, they put it on the front page and then everyone else ran it and it all escalated. But what I've always said about it is this, and I honestly believe this, I think if I had been that girl a decade ago on the front pages saying, don't talk to me like that, I would have been ruined by it. I would always be, ah, that's the one that's the troublemaker, she spoke out about sexism.

Yes

The difference with how I was treated, I just couldn't believe it. The Chair of the Bar came out and supported me immediately, the chair of the CBA … it was referred to you by Judges in diversity speeches, and I believe it really made a difference, because almost immediately people, you know, I had young women emailing me saying, I just cannot believe that I've had to put up with X, Y, and Z - much worse than I'd tweeted about. And so, I don't regret it for a moment, but the upshot of it is, which is the second part of your question, is that people then seem to think that I had something interesting to say. [Laughter] I think I'd probably exhausted everything that was interesting about me in those tweets. So now there's 17,000 people!

And all I do is tweet about the dog! So, it's all become a big anti-climax. But no, I'm very fortunate. I still, I write both on Twitter and off Twitter, and I think that it's a really important medium, and that we need to accept it's an important medium, because it's not a fringe tech app anymore. It's how the Prime Minister communicates with people, it's how the President of the United States communicates with people, it's how the profession communicates with each other, and how we ought to think about how we're presented to people who might aspire to join us. And if someone sees me on Twitter - the other day I was saying that I'd been holding up hostage signs in my video link hearing because my microphone had broken, I had to hold up a little sign to the Judge saying 'help me'! If there's one applicant out there that sees that and thinks, well, she seems normal, you know, she seems completely normal and yet she's doing the job that I want to do, maybe I could, maybe I could do that job, I think that we're doing a great service.

I mean, what I love about you is that you're using that platform to actually give a voice and speak about some of the issues, but in a professional and candid way, actually, and if that includes tweeting about Billable Hours, or whatever it is, or whatever the event is, we're all very, very grateful to you. Just before I move on, I wanted to ask you about when you were correcting the thousands of members of the public who were adding QC to their name.

So, there was a, a huge thing going on about Brexit - and I know you've spoken to Gina Miller - and people on Twitter were a bit obsessed with Brexit. It was very much an obsession of many, many Twitter users, and some people decided that they didn't like the barristers who'd been involved in the Brexit litigation, and of course they were the QCs - and I had nothing to do with the Brexit litigation. I'm a criminal practitioner. So, what they'd all decided to do was to take the mickey really, or to try to diminish those that have QC after their name, by everybody on Twitter started putting QC after their name, everybody! You know, it's quite funny to begin with, but then you had people who didn't immediately seem to be joking. You had people who had, you know, a gentleman in a suit and tie who looked very much like a barrister with, you know, John Smith QC, and he's offering legal opinions on Brexit, which - you know, no-one is going to prosecute somebody larking about on the internet calling themselves a QC, and obviously no-one is going to prosecute that - but some of the people, it struck me were actually quite close to the line in giving legal advice with QC after their name, and you wouldn't do that if you were a doctor.

No

And so, I just pointed out the law, because there is a law, it turns out, that says you can't impersonate a barrister. It has to be wilful and you have to intend all sorts of things, so most people, with their comedy disclaimers, they were saying, it stands for quite cute or things like that. They would obviously all be fine, but then they took against that and raged against that. So, there's a lot of communal rage on Twitter, so it's a huge stress ball for people. But yes, it struck me that certain people were closer to the line than others, but we can't take ourselves too seriously, and sometimes the profession and the communicative nature of what we do, sometimes we're all guilty of taking ourselves a little bit too seriously. But it struck me that there were some people that were certainly closer to the line than others.

Yes, absolutely. Now, do you have a favourite fictional lawyer?

Sally don't ask me that, I get so cross! I cannot tell you how angry I get about all fictional legal dramas.

I know, I know, I know ...

I watched Quiz the other night and I was raging, I was absolutely pacing the floor correcting all the errors, pointing out the furniture that was wrong, outraged at the hair not being under the wig, so I'm not answering it. It's my bugbear, I cannot stand fictional lawyers. [Laughter] All I do is yell at the television. We can't watch them in our house, it's just, it's terrible, honestly, it's awful!

Well, I shall leave it, but just to let you know that Maxine Peake is going to be one of the few non-lawyers coming on this Podcast.

Tell her that I said, Martha Costello, just tell her! Do you know what? I met Maxine Peake and Rupert when they were recording Silk.

Did you?

Yes. They were sitting on a wall in Inner Temple Lane, and I was going in for Saturday Court. I'd been at Saturday Court and I was coming in to do my attendance notes, and I was miserable, and I met them both and they were charming. They were very, very nice.

Oh good. Well – and she, of course, is somebody who cares passionately about access to justice.

She came on the protest.

She did. I'll tell her that you said Martha Costello, which is about the only – I don't really watch them either, but my mother is very keen on them, so I end up watching them because she sends me messages to watch them. And do you have a favourite book that has really impacted on your life?

There's a book called *The Memory Police*, which is a translation, and so I'm not going to try and pronounce the name of the author. It's a Japanese book. I'm going to try and pronounce the surname now, cause I'm going to read it, so I don't get it wrong. Yoko Ogawa, which is honestly the most beautiful book, and I won't spoil it for anybody, but it's about everyday items and how they disappear and how the memory of those items is policed in a fictitious, kind of dystopian state. And what I loved about it is that the translation of it is so beautiful and the language is so crisp, and it's dealing with such simple items that everything about it is the opposite of my day job, which is noisy and cluttered and chaotic and often miserable, and it was just the most beautiful book. And I had the good fortune to, to read it in New Zealand. It's the most beautiful country, and quite a pure country as well with, you know, very low population, just hills and hills and hills and green and green and green for miles, and it's the most beautiful translation of this book. And honestly, it really, really moved me and I thoroughly recommend it to everybody.

Wow. Well, I should put that on my reading list and our book club. I've got two very short questions, really. What impact do you think COVID-19 is going to have on the way we work in our profession?

Yes, and I hope it will change the way that we work. I hope that we don't try and go back to - in inverted commas – normal, because I think that actually the digital hearings, once you get past all of the teething problems, I think that's brilliant for the small cases where you turn up to Court, all you're doing is working out if something's ready, asking for an order from the Judge, you're applying for bail in circumstances where your client isn't present anyway. Those kinds of hearings can sensibly and properly be conducted digitally, and what that means is we save time and money on travelling. You know, sometimes these Courts are four hours away and it's £100 in train fares. There's more time to do the rest of our job, which is not sitting on trains, it's working hard. So, I really hope that we transform some of the minor hearings. I take the view that any hearing where the liberty of the person is at stake, so any sentencing hearing, any plea hearing, anything like that should be done in person, once it's safe to do so, and I don't think that there's any realistic prospect of a jury trial with digital jurors being anywhere near fair, and I know that the Lord Chief Justice has sounded a word of caution about anyone approaching that reasoning. So, I really hope that everybody knows where we draw the line, and I think that the line has to be drawn with jury trials, even during the crisis, because - I tweeted about this, actually, the jury trial is often not so much about simply what is said but, you know, often in my trials and in your trials, you know, the most strange items take on real importance, you know, an eyewitness might have said the jacket was pink, and when the officer brings the jacket into Court and it's orange, but you look at it and you think I can see how someone thought that was pink at a flash or from a moving car, or if someone says, I didn't realize the drugs were in the bag, and you feel the weight of the bag, or you see how it rests on someone's back, you can't do that through a screen. You can't look at the jacket, you can't feel the backpack, you can't hold the weapons tube with a knife in it and think, you know, was that brandished? Would a member of the public have missed that? Or all those questions that we ask juries to fairly ask themselves. And I don't see a way, no matter how good the technology, that we can replicate what is a very good system, and so the answer to your question is, I hope it transforms the hearings where it can fairly and properly and quite inexpensively save us money and time and effort, but I hope that we draw the lines in the right places.

Yes. And so, my final question, really, if I can call it final - I'm sure I'll sneak one more in – is, what next?

At the moment I adore my practice, you know, I get up and - not at the moment in COVID, but normally - I get up every day and I am so fortunate to be briefed on the most interesting, challenging cases, working with amazing barristers all over the country, and I just love it. I just, I couldn't think of not doing it at the moment. So, for now I'm just consolidating the practice that I've worked so hard to get. You know, I've done an awful lot of slogging around to get to this stage. So, I'm really enjoying it, sitting back and enjoying the benefits of it. I would love to sit one day - and I wish more barristers would say that. Everyone gets very coy about it, no one wants to say I'd love to be a Judge because lots of us won't make it, and do you know what, if I say it publicly and I don't make it, that's absolutely fine by me. At least I've said it out loud and tried. So, one day I would love to sit, but not yet, I'm really, really enjoying learning my craft and I still have so much to learn. You know, it only takes you to do a case with a senior barrister who is of great gift and scale, and you think, I'm still at beginner, and I don't think any of us should run before we can walk, or sprint before we can run, and so I hope I'm taking my time and doing everything properly. In terms of a book, I spend most of my time denying that I've written a famous book, so I don't intend to start writing my own. But I'm so proud of the barristers that have put pen to paper. I think The Secret Barrister's book has changed the landscape in the mind of the public, and whoever they are, we owe them a debt of gratitude. And similarly, there have been some recent books and some books that I know are in the pipeline by practicing barristers, and it's wonderful to see the profession speaking to the public in that way, and really ending this closed shop idea that we don't tweet, we don't write, we're just this closed profession, it's very stuffy. I think it's lovely to see it opening up, and so rapidly. I think that, you know, I have senior members of the profession and sometimes people saying, I can't believe you go on that Twitter. I can't believe it. And I think, well, here we all are now, you know, you can't really stop the ball rolling, and I think that that ball is rolling. You know, I see more and more senior, and more and more established practitioners joining social media or writing articles, or really opening up the profession, and I think it can only be a good thing.

Absolutely, more accessible. Just before we finish, we are in COVID-19, people are dying and losing their lives. I wonder if you've got one thing that you're grateful for?

Yes. I'm just so, so grateful for my family actually, and I think that so often in this life we, particularly in our profession, we run around prioritising everyone else in need except ourselves, and it really has made me stop and realise how precious my mum and dad are to me. You know, everyone knows their mum and dads are precious to them, but, you know, all of a sudden I was on the phone just begging them, you know, don't go to Sainsbury's, I'm begging you. I'll get you an online slot, don't go to the petrol station, we'll put me on your insurance, I'll do the car. You know, and a real, to some extent, quite a role reversal I think for a lot of children my age - I say children, you know, I'm in my thirties - but a very sudden role reversal of us really trying to persuade our parents of various degrees of stubbornness of what is right - something which my dad spent most of his life trying to persuade me what was right when I was stubborn - persuading them to stay at home. Again, they used to try and persuade me not to go out all the time, to stay at home, and to keep themselves safe. And so, there's been a real role reversal, but in a, as you say, in a context that is terrible, and terrible in so many ways, and we mustn't become numb to it. But I think also that that's really put into sharp relief what matters to everybody, and that in all of the awfulness that's going on around us, that we might be able to scrape together, each of us in our own way, something that we've learned that actually is quite positive. And for me, in all the noise, you know, my parents are always usually the people that get the WhatsApp before I fall into bed ... absolutely fine today, trial's awful, or, you know, had to go to Bristol Crown Court today, knackered ... and now I think they won't be, they'll be the people that get the phone call. They're the people that will get the visit because, you know, we all need to learn where our priorities really lie. So, that's my takeaway from it. But I share your comments and the wider position that, you know, society, and the country, and the world as a whole has suffered an absolute sucker punch and a gut punch, and all of us are fortunate that we're literally one breath away from being one of the statistics, and behind each one is a family and, you know, any day now it could be any one of us, and so all we can all do is provide as much support and kindness as we can, and just take each day as it comes.

A very big thank you to Joanna Hardy for her time.

Chris Daw QC

On this episode, I'll be talking law to Chris Daw QC. After being called to the Bar in 1993, Chris built his reputation acting in high-profile trials, dealing with serious organised crime and commercial fraud. He was appointed Queens Counsel in 2013 and now acts in a broader range of matters whilst maintaining a substantial criminal practice at Lincon House chambers. As we recorded this interview during the lockdown for COVID-19, please forgive our audio quality, as we held all the interviews remotely. Chris started by telling me more about his work.

So, as you say, I've been a QC now for seven years, I've been practising for over 25 years at the Bar. I practice mostly in the fields of sort of serious complex crime, fraud, business crime, etc. I also act for a lot of sort of celebrity clients, footballers, and people in the entertainment business so, I spread myself all over the country. I'm in Chambers in London at Serjeants Inn on Fleet Street, and also at Lincoln House, which is one of the leading Chambers for sort of criminal and fraud work outside London based in Manchester. But I, you know, like most QCs, I go where the cases are, and also travel overseas a fair bit. I've had cases in the last year that took me to Ghana and all sorts of other places, so I'm very lucky. I have a very interesting and varied practice, and I really enjoy the job!

Phew! Why did you go into law?

It's a really good question that, because I grew up from a sort of working class background, my dad was a, was a builder and I didn't have anyone that had been to university, let alone anyone who'd qualified in one of the professions. So, growing up, I didn't sort of have that as part of my world. I went to a very ordinary comprehensive school in Milton Keynes, and there were low aspiration levels for most of the students and the pupils there, so really I, it was an entirely burst of luck that hit my life, because when I was 16, I decided to leave home, and my life's ambition was to leave school and go and sell doughnuts and cans of Coke on the beaches of the South of France. [Laughter] I hitchhiked there with a friend of mine, it took us a while, you know, to get there, and I don't know if you've ever wandered up and down a beach with a backpack on full of cans of Coke and ice and - it's pretty heavy and it's very hot! And, to be honest with you, at 16, I drank more of the stock than I sold and ate more of the doughnuts than I sold, and it was not destined to be my financial future. So, I ran out of money after about a month. I came back to England, managed to sort of somehow hitchhike and get my way back to England but, when I got back, my mum and dad had moved 200 miles away to another house! A much smaller house because I'd left home so, you know, there wasn't really the need for a bigger house, so they'd moved to a much smaller house. But anyway, they did have a little tiny back bedroom that they let me sleep in. But really, that was the best thing that they could have done because, as it happened, they moved about a mile away from a State sixth form college, which was at the time and still is one of the best in the country, and I managed to get in, even though I'd done really badly in my exams at 16 because I'd kind of had this ambition to go to the beach, I hadn't really done any work, but they let me into this college and I ended up just being inspired by the teachers. And, to answer your question, which was why did I become a barrister, I did the careers test at the sixth form college, which even then was computer-based, so you had to say, I like this, or I don't like that, and I filled it all in and it came back and said, there's only two jobs that you could possibly do, and one was actor and the other one was barrister. I wasn't really a very good actor. I did a bit of acting in the school like productions or the college production stuff, I wasn't very good at that. So, this is what happened, Sally. I went to the Crown Court in Liverpool, which was not far from where my parents had moved to, and I sat and watched a trial for about a week, which was to do with bringing drugs in via the docks in Liverpool, and I was 16 years old, no, 17 by then because it would have been the summer holidays of, halfway through my A Levels, and I just thought, wow, this is just like, can you really do this as a job? And there's these people dressed up and it's all dramatic, and there's all the family watching in the public gallery, and they're all going [gasps], you know, when someone says the wrong thing, and then eventually there was the verdict and I was just like, ah, you know, we've all watched verdicts on trials on TV, everybody has, but this was like, wow, is this guy is going to go down for 20 years, or is he going to go home? And I just thought that to be part of that is just, wow, you can do that as a job. And by that stage, because I was going somewhere that was, you know, focused more on qualifications and A Levels and encouraging you to kind of apply to university, I went to the careers teacher and I said, look, I've just fallen in love with this thing. I bought every law book I could find, magazines, I'd read all the – I'd read law reports in the garden about bloody housing case [Laughter] … just because it was law, you know, and I just got the absolute bug for it. So, so there you go. So, and then I applied to university, I took a year out and went to work for a year. I didn't have the money to go like to Thailand or whatever, like some people do, but I got a proper job and I worked for a year and I enjoyed that and I got a lot of experience working in a sort of commercial environment. And then I went to Manchester University and then from then continued right the way through until I, until I qualified and, obviously, the rest is history, so to speak.

Wow! That's an interesting route into the law, which is so important for people to know when I ask you later on about diversity in our profession. But why did you go into crime?

Well, specifically, I mean, that was the thing, I think like most people, most people who watch TV and see barristers in their wigs and gowns, it's always criminal cases. I mean, you don't really see, you know, complex Chancery cases, or your Civil trials, it's always a jury trial, and at 16/17 I, really, I'd watched Crown Court as a kid - probably bunking off school because I'm watching it in the daytime - but I'd watch Crown Court as a kid and I think, as I say, like most people, I didn't think to go to the County Court, I thought I'm going to go to the place where they, where they do jury trials. And, as I said, I watched a drugs trial, I watched a bit of a murder trial, and it just seemed like, just like, it was like being in telly, being inside a TV show, but it's real and much more dramatic and much more important. So, I just fell in love with the whole thing and, you know, as you probably gathered, because I've been rabbiting on, on your Podcast, but I do like to talk, and I thought that, you know, criminal law gives you the chance to cross-examine witnesses, to make speeches, to, you know, to be a bit dramatic, and maybe the acting side does come out a bit sometimes for all of us in crime. So, it just fitted my personality and it fitted the sort of the stuff that I was passionate and interested in, and from that moment of going into that very first Crown Court at the age of 17, I never looked back. There was nothing else that I could possibly have wanted to do with my life other than be a criminal advocate.

Yes. Now you have a breadth of cases, as you alluded to, from celebrity clients to, you know, vulnerable people, and you've become, you know, somewhat of a commentator on the law, you've been involved in a television program, you've got a book coming out, but I wonder, along your route, did you have any role models or mentors or sponsors?

Yes. So, two different issues there. So far as role models are concerned, I mean, when I was a teenager, you know, particularly when I got into sixth form and I was really kind of engaged with a politics A Level, I got interested in sort of politics and policy and so on, and I can remember that Michael Mansfield at the time was very sort of famous and, at the time, a fairly young lawyer, a radical lawyer representing sort of people who were on the margins and often the more unpopular characters like your IRA, terrorist suspects and the like, and he was always on Question Time. And, I remember thinking, you know, this is someone, you know, who's a real role model because he was standing up for people who had no-one else to speak for them, unpopular people, as I say, and that appealed to me. And, of course, there's other kind of even more famous people like Nelson Mandela, who was a lawyer, and a radical lawyer in his own right, and ended up of course serving a long time in prison for his beliefs. And it was these characters, I guess it was the sort of, counter-cultural kind of lawyers, those who stood up against the status quo, stood up against the system and perhaps advocated causes that were less popular with the public. And that, for some reason, appealed to me. I always kind of have a little bit of a sympathy for the underdog. I mean, even when I was at school I remember if someone was being bullied, you know, I'd be the one, I was quite big, I was quite tall, and I would say, look, kind of leave it out, and that kind of - so I guess anyone that stood up for people, the underdog, were the people that I would be most kind of admiring of, and Michael Mansfield certainly stood out in the UK, and people like Nelson Mandela in sort of world terms, and of course at the time he was still in prison. So, so those are two sort of big role models, heroes who were lawyers, and I know Nelson Mandela is nowadays not known as much for his legal career in the fifties and sixties as he is for his political sort of role later on in South Africa, but he was a massive hero and still is. And in fact, I've got Nelson Mandela's handprint signed by Nelson Mandela on the wall in my house, because he is such an important figure to me, and I just love his voice.

Wow! Oh, you must be one of the rare people. I think I only, my parents used to make us write letters for him to be free. I remember as a child.

Yes, I was part of the campaign at Manchester University. It was still free Nelson Mandela back in the late eighties before he was actually freed. Yes. I remember it well.

Amazing! Wow! Well, that actually takes me slightly nicely then to sort of the role of lawyers and barristers in society. And I really wanted to ask you really about, you know, you've got a huge Twitter following, you're quite comfortable on Twitter as some of my guests on this Podcast are, and you're not afraid to comment on legal topics, you're not afraid to go on Five Live to comment on things. How did all that happen? And then I want you to tell us a bit about the book and the TV show.

Well, so they're all, they're all connected. So, roundabout two or three years ago I met, through a friend of mine, I met Adrian Chiles, the broadcaster and BBC radio presenter. And we were out for a pint one night and we got talking about law and the state of the justice system, as lots of people know, particularly because The Secret Barrister book has obviously made people aware of a lot of the problems in the system. And Adrian and I got that chatting over a couple of pints and he said, look, this is fascinating, I don't think people understand this, people know that this is going on, how bad it was in the criminal justice system, and still is, and he said, will you come on my Five Live show and talk about this? So, I said, yes, of course I will. Because I'm very passionate, as you say Sally, about the system and about the fact that it lets so many people down, victims as well as defendants, as well as the witnesses, all sorts of people, and the rest of us, it lets down society as a whole. So, I went on Adrian's program and we did a 30-minute plus extended interview on the state of criminal justice, and it was picked up by - a lot of the media picked it up and they were interested. I then ended up meeting, through Adrian, a producer at BBC television called Paul Connolly, who heads up a lot of factual programmes at the BBC, and he was really fascinated and passionate about criminal justice. And he said, why don't we do a series? So, we ended up pitching the show to BBC One, and they picked it up very quickly. And we ended up making a five-part documentary series called 'Crime: Are we tough enough?' - which is still an iPlayer by the way if you want to have a watch. Then, so getting onto how the other stuff happened and the Twitter and so on, then I wrote a couple of articles about subjects that I was really passionate about, including drug legalisation, which I'm a big advocate of because of my sort of very strong view that drug prohibition is massively damaging to many communities and also causes untold costs and wasted time in the criminal justice system, so I wrote a piece about that for The Spectator, which they immediately agreed to publish and it went out - it was actually a cover piece maybe a year or so, or just over a year ago. Well, that article was then seen by an editor at Bloomsbury who famously published Harry Potter – hopefully, I can outsell her, we'll see! But I got an email from an editor, who's now my editor, saying, we're really interested in some of your ideas, they're quite radical, they're interesting, have you thought about a book? I hadn't at the time, I was just sort of playing around with the TV stuff and writing some, some media articles and so on, and then within about a month of that, they commissioned what is now Justice on Trial, which comes out in July and is already available on Amazon for pre-order and is already getting quite a number of pre-orders and moving up the Amazon rankings three months before it even comes out. So, all of that happened because of a chance meeting with Adrian Chiles and we had a pint.

Wow!

And, I didn't finish the answer about social media. So, basically as soon as you start doing TV and writing ... I now have a publicist and they kind of say, look, you need to have a social media presence, that's very important for books, it's very important for promoting TV shows and stuff like that, so, and also it's given me the opportunity, as you say, to make some of the points, particularly on Twitter you can make points very quickly and directly, you can react to events. And I also take - my approach to social media is, once again, a bit like I was talking about before about how I like the sort of counter narrative, you know, people who are standing up against the status quo, I just feel that the media often just takes a very simplistic party line to so many issues, and now that we've got Twitter, and now that we've got other social media, some of us who perhaps say, okay, let's just think about this more carefully than just assuming that, you know, the whole - the whole narrative, for example, around sentences are too short, they've been going down. They haven't! They've been going up and up and up for 20 years, they're longer than ever. We've got 80-odd thousand people in prison, higher than ever, and yet the media reports it as Judges are soft, everything's soft, so I'm using social media to try and put some of that truth back into the public domain. Whether it makes any difference, who knows, but hopefully the book will, because some of the points I've made in the book in much more detail, of course, with all the evidence to back it up.

Well, I'll invite you back on once the book's out because, as I say, I've not got a copy yet.

We'll get you one! It's very kind of you to pre-order one. I'll get you a press copy as well, so you can read it before July. How's that?

Oh wonderful!

But don't cancel your order though!

I just wanted to ask you, do you have a case that's really impacted on you on your life, or a really memorable case?

Yes, I mean, again, I do deal in - some of my sort of cases are fairly high-profile and made the news, and I do deal with some of them in the book and give sort of accounts in some detail. And there's one case in particular that I talk about in detail in the book, that was I represented a young man 20 years ago, called Olatunde Adetoro, who went on a shooting spree in Rochdale and shot five people. It was, you know, a very dramatic case, and it was a high security trial, it got a lot of publicity, and it was a case when I was only at maybe six years or so qualified call at the time. So, it was quite - you know, obviously I had a Leading Counsel, a Silk leading me in a case of that seriousness, but that was a case that was just so intrinsically fascinating. And, of course, the human interest of a case where people have just been shot at point blank range in the streets ... fortunately, none of them died, it was just a miracle, but that was a case that really impacted me quite heavily in terms of - and it advanced my career as well. I mean, one of the things I think that perhaps those who don't really understand how criminal law and criminal lawyers work is, you know, to most people, the idea of defending someone who's shot several people at point blank range, just members of the public, would find that whole idea quite awful, but to a criminal lawyer, someone who's got criminal law in their blood, you know, you actually have a passion for those really serious cases and the really kind of difficult cases where actually everyone's entitled to a defence, even someone who, in that case had been seen on video - I mean, there was a, the helicopter was filming the whole thing – been seen on video shooting people. So, it was a, it was a really, really important case in my career, it moved my career from sort of a reasonable level of success for my level of call. Suddenly I was up into a really high-profile case that was on the national news, and then after that my practice definitely increased in size, and also the nature of the cases I was doing was much more serious, much more complicated, and I went on then to spend the next almost 15 years doing almost exclusively complex, organised crime cases, large drugs conspiracies, murder cases, very large fraud, financial crime cases, and then ended up doing the largest ever trial for police corruption in the UK, which was another massive, massive sort of case for me in my career. The trial lasted over six months, there were ten defendants, it was all to do with a murder back in the late eighties and the conspiracy, alleged conspiracy, amongst police officers to fit up innocent men who ended up going to prison for murder and then were released on appeal. So, fascinating case, human interest case, and it was that case where I finished that case and realised now is the time to apply for Silk. I made an application within a month or so of finishing that case and was successful first-time round. So, that was a huge case for my career, a big, big impact, and I have no doubt was the bedrock of my Silk application.

Absolutely. Well, let me just ask you there then, you know, you are now very senior …

It makes me feel old when you say it like that. Can we say very experienced?

Very experienced, very experienced.

I haven't got my bus pass yet. [Laughter]

Well, the trouble is if you're not Silk, you're just referred to as a senior junior.

No, that's very true.

Now you're a Silk I'll just say you're a very experienced senior.

Very silky! [Laughter]

The question is about diversity in our profession. You know, I am a black woman, I'm 20 years call and, you know, I'm passionate about gender, social mobility, race … really, I'm passionate about just improving the makeup of the profession so that we're a bit more like the people we represent and society. And I wonder what views you've got about that? What ways can we improve, you know, the diversity in our profession?

Yes, well, that's something that I'm really passionate about because, as you say, we do still have under-representation in a number of groups, including State-educated people, whatever, regardless, you know, State education is still disproportionately underrepresented at the Bar, and there are many other kinds of diversity issues, and that's something I'm really passionate about. So, not only have I over the years tried to - as part of my role in Chambers I certainly remember encouraging, for example, mature applicants from non-traditional backgrounds as part of my kind of responsibilities when I became involved in pupillage decisions. But I also interviewed for scholarships for Gray's Inn, part of the interview panels for the scholarships, and I have always sought – I'm not going to giveaway sort of the internal stuff that goes on - but I've always sought to advocate for scholarships to be those who need the money and who are in groups that are most under-represented. So, you know, disabled applicants, ethnic minority applicants, and State school applicants, rather than giving scholarships to those who don't need the money. You know, I think that's an important part of it, but the truth of it, Sally, in my opinion, is that the Bar has still gone nowhere near far enough. We are still dramatically under-represented in terms of certain groups, and the only way I see through that is for the Bar as a whole to adopt a different approach to the assessment of candidates, particularly for pupillage, because for me the difficulty is this, most sets, particularly the more prestigious sets, place, an enormous emphasis on pure academic achievement. So, A Level grades, degree classification, and the institution at which the degree was taken. So, somebody who's got a first class degree from Oxford and a bunch of A's at A Level, and loads of A stars at GCSE, they are at the top of the pile and their chances are ten times higher than a non-traditional candidate from a State school background who maybe struggled with their GCCS and even their A Levels, and maybe got a 2:2 in their degree. They may be equally intellectually able, and in fact, the candidate with the perhaps lesser academics maybe a much more rounded candidate. They might have much more life experience. They may, as you say, you want sometimes, you want a number of lawyers, you want a good cohort lawyers who look and sound like the people they represent rather than talk down to them. And, of course, there are many very able criminal lawyers who went to public school and who had very wealthy backgrounds. Many of them very, very good at what they do. But the point is that the reason why a public school educated white male, who goes to one of the top public schools, the reason why they are so much more likely to get into Chambers as a pupil is because they, from day one, have been hot-housed, educationally, to achieve those specific milestones. GCSEs, A Levels, get into Oxbridge, get a First or a high 2:1. Whereas, those like you and me who perhaps come from more ordinary backgrounds and went to State schools, really the teachers just want to make sure you don't bunk off. So, the key thing to keep you at school, that's an achievement, if you can get a high attendance record. So, obviously, when I, as I said to you earlier, I didn't actually do that well in my O Levels because no-one was paying attention to what I was doing. It wasn't because I wasn't able. I could've got the same grades if I'd been to one of those other schools. But the fact is that Chambers do not make allowances for the difference in educational inputs that each of the applicants has received. So, my answer to that is a simple one, value added assessment of grades, which means you look at the school and the average grades for that school and you place the candidate against that average. So, someone from Eton where the average is everyone gets As anyway, they're no better off than somebody who gets Bs in a school where everyone gets Ds. In fact, they're worse off, because overachieving within your environment is much more impressive than simply achieving the average at a very high standard where you are given, injected with education from the moment you kind of almost come out of the womb, as many who go to the best private schools are. So, we at the Bar, there are brilliant algorithms, there are brilliant software programs, brilliant services around that can say you take Sally or you take Chris, you look at the average result from their school, where do they sit? Are they above or below the average? If they're above, how much above? And if you're 50% above the average for your school, you're pretty bright. If you're 20% below but you still got great grades, you've just been given lots and lots of help. And I would always want someone who's overachieved within their environment rather than someone who's underachieved in a much more elite environment where they're given so many opportunities. So, I think we have to absolutely look at - forget about the raw grades, forget about how many A's and if it's a first or if it's Oxbridge and look at the achievement relative to average in your environment and, if we start doing that, suddenly you'll find this huge pool of talent from the inner city communities that are underrepresented at the Bar, from many, many comprehensive schools that are dramatically under-represented at the Bar, suddenly that pool of talent - once people as well realise and have the aspiration they can do it, because we are going to actually give them a pupillage, then suddenly I think we'd see that that makeup, the social mobility and the ethnic makeup and the diversity of the, of the Bar actually start moving a bit further in the right direction.

Interesting. Well, I want to ask you about two controversial subjects, if I may. Number one is why you believe in legalisation of drugs and, secondly, really your view on - because we are in COVID-19 lockdown - what do you think about jury trials? Scotland's thinking of abandoning jury trials and for us to do trial virtually with juries. Do you think fairness can really be achieved?

Okay. So, so virtual jury trials, I mean, I think this is just one of those chip paper stories that's going to come and go, because during this period there's been lots of talk of different things, and if we're put in lockdown for years and that kind of thing. I suspect it won't be anything like as dramatic as perhaps some have predicted, and we're already starting to see the signs that maybe that will change. But the reality is you can't have remote jury trials, it's just ridiculous, because jury trials are - first of all, they are fundamental to our constitution, so the idea, and has been for almost a thousand years - there's a whole chapter in my book about jury trials and how important they are and how we've come to have the system that we have, and why it's been exported to the States and many other countries around the world, because it's, in my view, putting witnesses within the eyesight of the 12 jury members and allowing the 12 jury members to deliberate as we do in private, in a private room, is the most effective way of achieving a just and fair verdict that has been devised by the human species. I don't think there's any other system, and I've studied them being part of research for my book, but I don't think any other system that works as effectively as our English jury system, as practiced in other countries. And the reason for that is, as I always say in every closing speech to a jury, "members of the jury, the reason why that witness box is directly opposite you, the jury, is because you the jury then can make the best possible judgment of whether you're being told the truth or being told a pack of lies", and you can't do that by video, you just can't do it. Of course, we have video witnesses who gave their evidence on video link, but that's a very different thing, that's usually one witness out of an entire trial.

Absolutely. I wonder if I can ask you then about drugs?

Sure. Any criminal lawyer will have spent a considerable path of his or her career dealing with cases that have some connection to drugs. So, I would say my experience is that the majority of cases have some connection to drugs, partly because my practice over the years has involved serious drugs conspiracy cases and the like, but it's also because I've been involved in murder cases where people have been murdered because of drugs, either because people are on them or because there is a dispute about them and who's going to be allowed to sell them, and where. We know that the great majority of the murders of young people, we've seen so many shootings and stabbings on our streets over the last couple of years, almost all of those have some connection to gangs, and those gangs principally that deal in drugs. There are other forms of criminal activity, but it's the major form of criminal activity in this country. So, when I was, you know, looking into the book and, prior to that, writing other articles that I told you about, about the subject, I looked at the economic impact of drug prohibition, because of course they had prohibition of alcohol in the States, they tried it for ten years or so, and it was a total disaster and it led to the proliferation of organised crime gangs, it led to the untold misery that now is the prohibited drug trade, which was driven initially by the US. But the absolutely crystal-clear evidence is that the prohibition of drugs leads to more deaths because of drugs, leads to more crime because of drugs, you know, just think about the obvious. You know, if you have to pay the price, the black market price, for heroin, which is for most users between £200 and £300 a week, but it can be more, drug users do not have £200 or £300 a week, so they have to find it from somewhere. And how do they find it? They either sell drugs themselves, or they commit other crimes against members of the public, robberies of mobile phones, stealing from people's houses or exploiting women or others for sexual gain. So, basically, the long and short of it is that I have absolutely no doubt that the prohibition of drugs, not drugs themselves but the prohibition of drugs, is responsible for most crime in our society, most harm in our society, most deaths as a result of crime, and also, sadly, - I mean, one of the people I interviewed for my book was a woman called Anne-Marie Cockburn, whose daughter died of an ecstasy overdose at the age of, I think she was 15, I hope I'm right about that. But she had gone out and bought 93% pure MDMA powder from a dealer, not knowing that pure meant bad. She thought that pure meant good because pure means there's no additives. Her name is Martha. She took enough ecstasy to kill 10 grown men. Would that have happened if ecstasy was available as a licensed product, a known dosage with the exact strength written on the box at the points of sale in the way that alcohol is sold. I don't believe that and neither does her mother, and many, many of these overdose deaths, of which there are thousands up and down the country every year, come about purely because dealers do not have quality control. They will put anything by way of additives, but also they have no way of knowing - if you buy a £10 bag of heroin it might be 5% pure, or it might be 15, and you have no idea and you might well inject a particularly strong batch of heroin, and sadly, this happens all too often. It's not a suicide attempt, they just don't know what they're taking, they are putting a liquid made from powder into their veins with absolutely no clue how much heroin or other drug, amphetamine, or whatever it is that they're injecting into them. So, my take on it is that we should look at a welfare model for drugs, and I travelled to Switzerland as part of my book research and spent some time with their licensed heroin supply clinics out there, and the health of those who use heroin, their life chances, there's hardly any street crime associated with drug dealing there because they've kind of decriminalised it - unofficially as it happens - but I have no doubt that if you had a license to legalise model we would see a 50% reduction in crime and a 50% reduction in the prison population, and probably an 80% reduction in drug overdose deaths. And for me, that's much more important than ridiculous moralising about whether it's right or wrong to take drugs - but usually by people who were quite happy to sip whisky or vodka or some other legal and licensed product that already exists. So, I'm very passionate - and it's not because I want to be soft on drug dealers or criminals, it's because I want to get rid of them altogether, and they'll be gone.

Yes. I mean, it's an interesting viewpoint because there is a contrary view to that, which is actually we'll have more people as addicts and more deaths because they'll have more access.

Well, that's a contrary view that's disproven by all the evidence from all the countries that have decriminalised or freed up the supply of class A drugs as we would call them, like heroin and crack and other drugs like that, all of them - Portugal's the prime example, but there are others who have all seen a reduction in usage. But more importantly than the usage levels is the harm levels. So, the amount of associated crime, the amount of health damage and overdose all go down when you legalise and licence. And the more you legalise and license, the lower the rates of crime, the lower the rates of drug-related deaths. So, that's the evidence from every country that's experimented with the degree of liberalisation or decriminalisation is that they are - they don't, they don't change their minds after a year or two and so, 'Oh, do you know, we've made a mistake because it's … and look at all this terrible problem we've created'. Not one country that has decriminalised to some extent or licensed the supply of drugs to some extent, none of them have ever reverted course back to the original prohibition. Why is that? Because it worked and because it did have the desired impact. But none of them are perfect. The perfect model for me is complete licensing and complete regulatory and supply chain. So, I'm not talking about letting drug dealers off, they wouldn't be. You wouldn't be allowed to sell drugs any more than you are allowed to sell alcohol without a licence. You can't start selling booze without a licence. You wouldn't be able to sell drugs without a licence. You'd have to go to a licensed dispensary, you'd have to obviously make yourself aware of the whole impact, sign a form saying 'I understand all of this' to get a supply, but it would definitely improve the lifetime. I saw it, I saw it for myself in Geneva when - the people were coming in, into a licensed clinic, to get heroin twice a day and they were given a secure room, a safe - a hygienic room to take their heroin in - and they were given a measured and precise quantity of heroin, and they were given access to doctors, psychiatrists, therapists, rehab if they wanted to have rehab and come off the drugs, and 80% of them come off through that clinic. But 80% of street, heroin users don't come off it, almost none do in our current system.

Yes. Well, it'll be interesting to see, yes, what our listeners think about that because it is a controversial …

Absolutely, I get that.

Yes, but Chris you have so many passions. I wanted to ask you about wellbeing. You've got four children, two of them young …

Yes, 8 and 5.

Yes, and so I wonder, what do you do for your wellbeing, because burnout is high at the Bar, we know the retention rate, particularly for the publicly funded work that we do, and so what do you do to try and relax?

It's a good question, and it's something - I've done one of my videos on the YouTube channels about this subject, because I have been as bad as most lawyers over the years and, you know, certainly in my first ten years or so I gave no thought to wellbeing cause I was young! You know, you're 23/24, you're literally like any 23/24-year-old. You might be a barrister but you think you're kind of immune to kind of anything like stress or pressure and you think you can stay out drinking all night and still, you know, be fine the next day. But as I kind of matured and I, you know, I turned 50 in January, I guess that was a little bit of a milestone for me, as it is for many people, and I think I now, I do exercise a lot more than I ever did, probably since before I even came to the Bar! I mean, the last time I exercised the amount I do now I would have probably been a student, playing a lot of football and basketball and stuff. So, I think physical fitness is really important to me. I make sure that I try and get breaks in a way that I didn't in my younger – I would work seven days a week for months on end, that was deeply unhealthy, and actually deeply inefficient. I think it makes you less able to get stuff done in a sensible timeframe when you're overtired and overstrained. I did take a year out from practice. I'd been at the Bar for 12 years and I had worked in the way that I've just described, which was relentless, non-stop and, you know, yes, I'd take the odd week here and there but I didn't really take sort of proper holidays, and I do that now and I think that's really important,. But yes, after about 12 years I think I was in danger of getting to the point where I was kind of burned out by it, I was a bit kind of - a lot of the cases I was doing all seemed to blend into one. I'd do one case when another one had either not even just finished, or they were – you know, I'd finish on a Friday after a two/three month case, take no time off and immediately start another case, and that, I don't think is very healthy. I mean, sometimes now suddenly it's necessary because there have been such big cuts, as you know, in fees for the sorts of cases I did in those days, but I think I'd got to the point where if I hadn't taken a break from the law and I went off and started a business with a friend of mine and I spent a year working and running a business that had nothing to do with the law, if I hadn't done that – and I came back after that, absolutely refreshed and ready for action, and I actually started a big drugs conspiracy trial on the very first day back after that 13 months out of Court, and it was brilliant, I loved it. It was like, it was like being back on a bike but with new energy and a fresh approach, and I came back committed to taking Silk within five or six years, which I managed to do. So, I think breaks - I think having the odd sabbatical to do something different along the way, maybe every 10 years or so, if people can find a way to spend a month or two to do something else to get to clear your head a little bit. I think that's really helpful. I do think physical fitness and diet and stuff like that are absolutely critical. I mean, you can easily end up eating rubbish because you worked through to a silly time and eat a load of chocolate or whatever. You know, we've all done it and I've done it many, many times, just eat loads of takeaways because you, you know, and stuff like that, so I think looking after yourself that way. But also, massively important is to look after your mental health and wellbeing mentally. So, that for me meant I did take, you know, started doing things like the Headspace where you're trying to just sit and, you know, you could just put your headphones on and try and just take a bit of a timeout where you can take a breath and, and unusually whatever you do, anything you do as a break, whether it's physical exercise or just let's say some sort of Headspace, or to go for a walk or whatever and clear your head and stop work for half an hour/an hour in the course of a 12-hour working day that often, or more often we have to do, anything like that I think helps you to sustain yourself in the long-term, just as it does your body. You know, if you're relentless with your body, it's going to break down. If you're relentless with your mind, it's going to eventually kind of come into problems. So, take breaths, take breaks and look after yourself physically and mentally, and I just think that makes an enormous difference. And take time with your family, take time to see your friends. I know lots of people in our profession lose track completely with their friends, they don't seem them from one year to the next because they're always too busy. Friends text you, oh, I can't make it, I've got a trial the next day. Try not to get into that habit of constantly putting work before everything, I mean everything, as many of us have done. And I've done it, massive hypocrite, because over the 26 years I've probably done it for at least two thirds of the time. I've fallen into exactly the trap that I'm trying to kind of lecture people not to fall into, but it's because I've made those mistakes that I can kind of say confidently that you shouldn't do that, you need to - even at the beginning when you think you've got to prove yourself to everyone and you're chasing every brief, you know, because there's only so many briefs to go round if you're one or two or three years call, just still take - just go for a bike ride, just take an afternoon off. And also, pretty common sense, but try and limit the booze a little bit. I know lots of people in our job do drink a lot every night - and it's nothing to do with being a lawyer, it's just common sense. I mean, you know, we've all drifted into that – well, not all of us - but many of us have drifted into the habit of going to the pub every night or meeting people. You know, it's always worth trying to just have a bit of time off the booze and get yourself, you know, feeling good about yourself physically, and you will be a much better lawyer and hopefully much better sort of to your friends and family as well as a result.

Fantastic! Thank you so much for sharing that. So, Chris, I wondered, have you got a favourite fictional lawyer, and perhaps a favourite book?

Yes, definitely. So, I think, yes, I was thinking about this, my sort of favourite book, and the book that always comes into my head when I think about my favourite book is The Bonfire of the Vanities by Tom Wolfe, which of course was made into a film as well. And I remember reading that, but it's a brilliant book because it's, I mean, I love Tom Wolfe's writing anyway, but it's so real, but the book is about a guy who's from a very sort of wealthy investment banker-type earning a million dollars a year, etc. back in the eighties who has a hit and run and ends up in the justice system as a defendant, having come from this very privileged kind of Manhattan world. And it becomes a big kind of criminal case, and I just found the whole thing absolutely fascinating, this kind of two worlds collide idea that you have this guy who's very privileged who then ends up having to sort of defend himself in the criminal Courts amongst all of what he would see as lesser individuals and criminals there, I'm not one of them. But actually - it's a great read anyway, but it makes the point that all of us actually are only that far away. We're only one turn of our wheel on the car or one, you know, mistake away from potentially ending up in a criminal Court as a defendant. I love that book and I love that message because I think lots of people see the criminal justice system as about others, about some other kind of people that are not like us. And, of course, the main character in The Bonfire of the Vanities very much has that view until he realises, actually I need a good lawyer, I need to get some justice, I need some help here, and so I just think everybody – law students - should read that book. In terms of characters, I do have a favourite character but sadly, unlike my real life heroes like Nelson Mandela, he's not in that category of someone that you'd aspire to be, or maybe he is in some fantasy land, because probably my favourite fictional movie character is a character called Martin Vale, who was the lawyer played by Richard Gere in a film called Primal Fear, where he was the top defence lawyer, I think, in Chicago, and he was very wealthy and he defended wealthy people charged with murder and this and that, and he ends up defending a character, played by Ed Norton, for a murder. It's a psychological thriller, I won't give it away. But Martin Bell, he comes out with one of the great lines, which is - it sounds very cynical, but it's true - and he's asked in an interview by a journalist at the beginning of the film when he's describing how he uses all these clever legal trips to win cases, and the journalist turns round to him and asks the question that we often get asked as criminal defence lawyers, and the question that he's asked is, what about the truth? And Martine Vale's response, without hesitation, is the only truth that matters is the truth I create in the minds of the 12 men and women of the jury. And that's a very deeply cynical line but actually, when you think about it, it's not far off the truth about criminal cases, whether we like it or not. What matters is not the truth in reality, but what the jury believe. He's a great actor and it's just a great, great thriller with a really good twist at the end, which I won't give away if people have not watched it. But yes, he's my favourite character. Not because he's particularly likeable, but because I think he - a lot of his character is this sort of very high-profile, very kind of successful criminal defence lawyer in America, and a lot of what we look at in him and say, oh, we don't really like the look of that, is actually pretty fundamental to the system, which is being prepared to fight every case without fear or favour, and doing our absolute best for our client, whoever they are. And that message comes across in the film, even though he is often fighting for people who perhaps arguably don't deserve it as much because they're rich and maybe they have done wrong. But it makes the point, it doesn't matter who your client is, and I've acted for, you know, international footballers who are multimillionaires and I've acted for homeless people who've been charged with murder and, you know, literally every everyone in between, billionaires I've acted for. And every single client I approached identically, which is listen to what they have to say and do my absolute best to get the outcome that they are hoping for. And generally, in my case because I'm a defence lawyer, that's to be acquitted or to get them a lenient sentence. But yes, great film, everyone should watch it, particularly law students because, again, you learn a lot from fictional films.

Absolutely, absolutely! Gosh, I could talk, keep talking to you forever! But I can ask you this then, just on that point about being a defence lawyer, did you ever prosecute?

No.

When did you make the decision to then only be the voice for the other side, if I may say so? And would you ever go back?

Well, it's interesting. I didn't make a decision to be a defence lawyer as such. I was, you know, didn't come from the best of educational, etc. background, and therefore I wasn't really going to ever get pupillage at one of the sort of main prestigious sets, for many of the reasons I was talking about earlier when we were talking about recruitment to the Bar. So, I got pupillage in a very small set with only, I think, about eight or ten tenants, and my set only did criminal defence. You know, that was the place I got pupillage and, you know, I was incredibly lucky and grateful to get pupillage very soon after - I started pupillage within a few weeks of finishing the, what was then the Bar Vocational Course. And I was very lucky and felt very, very grateful and honoured to have got pupillage - and many then weren't getting pupillage - but now, of course, it's so many more. So, it just so happened that my initial exposure in practice, as everyone does, my first six following my Pupil Supervisor or Pupil Master as he was at the time, watching him do criminal defence, and I found it very interesting. And then in second six I did back to back trials, mostly magistrates, but one or two Crown Court trials, all defence, because that was all my Chambers did. And so, within a year or two, I'd begun to build a defence practice because that's what my Chambers did, they didn't do any prosecution. So, when it came to - I did eventually move sets because my Chambers kind of folded after a few years and I joined a much larger and much more prestigious set where they did do prosecution. But as you probably know, I don't know if it's still the case, I think it's still the case, but you have to start as a prosecutor at level one and move up the scale. So, by that stage I was doing level four work as a defence advocate. If I had elected to do prosecution I would have had to start doing committals for sentence and stuff like that, which I hadn't done for several years because my practice was jury trials exclusively, and usually quite serious jury trials. So, it was really a question of, I'm not going to go backwards in time and start doing really low-level work. As it happened, just as a sort of weird aside, I did actually go through the process of applying for the various grades of a prosecutor. I got to grade four, which is the top, having never prosecuted a case.! So, I don't know what that says about the system at the time, but I was at the top level of a junior prosecutor, as a grade four, having literally never prosecuted a single case. And I have presented cases in the misconduct arena effectively as the prosecutor, you know, on behalf of police forces and so on and if, you know, in the highly unlikely event now that the prosecution came to me and said, will you prosecute this case for us, Mr Daw? Well, if my diary was free, I would do it. So, I'm not actually, as it were, ethically or somehow politically attached to defending, it's just that's how my practice went from the beginning. And I was lucky enough - I mentioned that huge case I did it at six or seven years call, the mass shooting case - when you start getting cases like that and the alternative, so, two/three months complex conspiracy cases, and the prosecution are saying, will you go and do a shoplifting trial for us?, it makes no sense. So, that's the only reason. Anyway, any prosecutors out there who've got a nice juicy case for me, then you know where I am.

It's interesting what you say about the system, because of course I know many barristers who prosecute day in, day out, and they're rejected for reaching the category four. So, there is something about the system, and of course some barristers make that decision, there are many in my own Chambers - it's not the case for me, I prosecute and defend - but who ethically do not prosecute, and they've made that decision.

I don't really agree with that as a concept because ethically you should be prepared to advocate whatever cause you're asked to advocate. We're not there to make decisions about the morality of our client's actions, whether it be a prosecutor or a defence lawyer, we're there to advocate as best we can and, in fact, we're duty bound to do that. And I, I think there's a real conflict for me between our kind of cab rank rule and the obligation to take cases that are given to you, and making a personal, ethical, and moral judgment that you're only prepared to act for one side. I don't agree with that. I can see why people's practice, as mine, you know, end up being defence-based because that's the work you're exposed to, but I think if you're asked to do a case that's within your competence for the prosecution, then I think it's tricky to see how you can say, I'm not doing it on ethical grounds, because I don't see how you reconcile that with the Code of Conduct.

There are people who just say, well, I'm only defending, I prosecuted once, I didn't like it, I'm not going to, so, yes, it's a different argument. So, Chris, you do a lot - as I do really - outside our daily practice. You've got a much more glamorous and complicated practice than probably most of the Bar, you mentor for the Bar Council, you know, scholarship decisions at Gray's Inn – a great Inn, my Inn! I wonder, what's next for you? Might the Bench? I notice you don't sit yet as a Recorder, a baby Judge as we in the profession would know. Is there a plan for progressing?

I don't have any intention or desire to go on the Bench, for the simple reason that, if I did, then I couldn't do the campaigning work I do, I couldn't write the books that I write, I couldn't make the television programmes that I make about justice reform because, as a Judge, you have to be seen to be politically impartial. So, I couldn't become a Judge now because my kind of media and writing activities are inconsistent with being a Judge. And also, to be perfectly frank, I mean, I'm involved - not only do I make documentaries and I'm looking at making more documentaries about criminal justice - but I'm involved at the moment in a drama project for, you know, a potentially large kind of big budget TV drama as an executive producer, and you can't do this range of activity whilst sitting full-time as a Judge. There's just no way I'd have the time to do any of it, and I am really enjoying this stage of my career, you know. I settled into Silk after seven years and I've got a good established practice in Silk across a hugely interesting, and diverse range of areas, and I get these opportunities to do media stuff, to do TV, radio, to do, you know, books and journalism, and the judiciary just doesn't allow you that flexibility and that freedom in the way that the Bar does. So, it's for that reason I'm really happy with where I am, and I don't have any desire to go on the Bench. I'm not sure for me, after all these years, the idea of sitting in one Courtroom every day, all day, and being stuck with the timings of that and the lack of flexibility, I'm not sure I could cope with it, I'm afraid, so it's over to you, Sally, on that one. [Laughter]

Yes. Well, watch, watch this space! Well, finally, it's been so wonderful talking to you, Chris. I hope you will come back on. But one last question, really. If there were to be a film about your life and your career, who would you like to play you?

Oh, Tom Hardy, because, I mean, I know he's not quite as good looking or as muscular as me, [Laughter] but yes, he'd probably be all right as the second best. He's literally one of my favourite actors, I love him. In fact, I'm hoping to cast him - I shouldn't say this - but I'm hoping to cast him in my drama as and when we get it commissioned. Maybe he will play me, who knows?!

Yes!

Well, I'm hoping, you know, I'm not only to exec produce but co-write this project, and we've got to get it commissioned yet so, you know, I'm getting a bit ahead of myself, but I'm hoping to make it as realistic and interesting as I can and, as you say, people will find the book, which is Justice on Trial, and it's on Amazon. People will find that there's lots of juicy stuff in there. It's not, it's not a dry academic book, it's meant to be an airport read – if the airports ever open again anyway.

Yes, well that will be really great. Thank you so much for giving up your time.

You're welcome, Sally. It's great to speak to you.

Many thanks to Chris Daw, QC. You can find him on Twitter, @crimlawuk.

Brie Stevens-Hoare QC

On this episode, I'm thrilled to talk to Brie Stevens-Hoare QC. Brie is a highly experienced property Barrister, dealing with all aspects of property litigation, and she recently won Barrister of the Year at the Modern Law Awards, and Chambers Real Estate Silk of the Year award. I asked Brie when she first became interested in the law.

Aged 13 … a combination of watching Crown Court and Rumpole on the telly … having one of only two so far in my life personality clashes in that case with a biology teacher which meant I couldn't be the vet I thought I might be, and I hit on wanting to be a Barrister, so that was it! Little did I know that by pure luck I'd hit on the right thing for me, because I really knew nothing about the law, had no connection with it knew no one in it.

Wow! So, how did you then start and go about it? Obviously, you went to university - did people go to university in your family?

No, I was the first in my family to go to university, but somehow I always knew I was going to go to university. I was going to leave home, I was going to go to university. I think both my parents instilled in me a sense that life was out there, grab it by the throat, go get it, make what you want of it was very much an ethos. In terms of role models, I mean, different things. We all, if we're honest I think, have role models within our families. So, my grandfather who was a very straightforward man, Army, then postie, he taught me the most sort of positive approach to life. Whatever's going on, there's always something good, something you can take out of anything and forward you go. And then I was very involved in the women's movement as a teenager, so there were a lot of very strong women around me who were doing amazing things and making a difference.

My mum and some of her friends set up the first Women's Refuge in Reading, which was one of the very early ones. We got very involved in Reclaim the Night, all sorts of stuff. So, I saw a lot of strong women who wanted to change the world around me.

Would you classify yourself as a feminist?

Absolutely, absolutely. I have through the decades, it's been a dirty word.

Yes

I recall being asked in a pupillage interview in the eighties whether I was a feminist, because when at the LSE I'd done a course, Women in the Law. They looked at that on my CV and said, oh, you've done this, does that mean you're a feminist?' And my response, probably a bit too smart, but there we go, was 'you just tell me what you mean by that term, and I'll tell you if I fit that description.' [Laughter] Yes, I've always self-identified as a feminist.

Absolutely! I'll come back to the feminist and the dirty word later on if I may. But I wanted to ask you about your area of law and why you went, or why you practise in that area?

Well, when I set off aged 13, it was all about truth and justice. I thought I would be a criminal practitioner. In the early eighties, most sets, not all, but most sets were general common law sets, so I did, pupillage in a set that did everything, but thinking I wanted to do crime, and most of the advocacy I got to do was crime - and I did a third six and a fourth six, but that's another story. But there came a point, in fact, when I moved to a purely criminal set, that I realised it wasn't for me. I was loving it but loving the fact I was getting to do the advocacy. I realised that actually it wasn't for me long-term. At that point, there was very little paperwork in crime and if, you know, things were not effective when you got to Court, then you were kicking your heels all day until four o'clock when you went to the clerks room to see if there was something for the next day, and I wanted to have stuff to do all day, and I wanted a different balance of the sort of oral advocacy, the written work, the mental jigsaw puzzles of pleadings. So, because I'd done everything in pupillage, although most of the advocacy was crime, I sort of looked back and thought, what have you enjoyed the most? And bizarrely, it was property, which I'd hated at university, but I think it matters to people, it's people's homes, their heritage, their business, so it's not just money. I find the law in it really interesting because you've got culturally lots of different types of law that intersect with each other, and I thought, okay, fair enough, I'll try and be successful at this. [Laughter]

And you can obviously always remember all those millions of case law and cases. I seem to remember at university, you know, there there's cases, endlessly, you know, interesting, but just how do you remember them all? And for you, I guess it's a way, and it's a good area for you to kind of shape the law and the future of the law, you know, some of the senior cases you've been doing.

I did a leadership program which I found very, very useful in terms of looking back over my career and how I got to where I was and where I want to be, and thinking back to those women when I was a teenager and involved in the women's movement, and when I talked about becoming a Barrister, sort of half of them said, fantastic, brilliant, get on the inside and change it., and the other half were like, traitor, you can't do that, you'll become part of the establishment. And I think what I sort of realised on some levels was that actually what was important to me was … Come the day of the revolution I'm there, but in the meantime I will try and get into the inside and change things, staying authentic to myself but change things. But actually, what was important, therefore, was to be as successful as I could be, and there was something quite appealing when I realised (1) I was more drawn to property, (2) that it was one of those areas of law that, you know, you were getting all the signals – if you're going to be a woman at the Bar, which you shouldn't be anyway, you certainly shouldn't be doing this. It was very clear where if women were at the Bar what they were expected to do, and there was an awful lot they were expected not to do, funnily enough, the things that were money.

Yes, you know, and it's great to see. I wanted to digress for a moment if I may. Last year you were Barrister of the Year at the Modern Law Awards, with over, I think, 800 people, held in Manchester for the first time, usually in London.

There were Dodgem cars inside! [Laughter]

There were, which threw us all a bit! But everyone was sort of, you know, dressed up to the nines and so on and so forth, and then you won the award and went up and you were sort of, you were looking really nice, but you were kind of like, well, my intellectual ability speaks for itself. And I was like, I need to get to know that woman! I just wondered if, is that your persona? Is that how you've carried yourself across the Bar, really, just sort of get on with it and this is who you are?

When I, when I started out at the Bar I had a car and it was a pink beetle. [Laughter] I've spent a lot of time being told you shouldn't be that, or you should be like this, and I won't, I can't claim I've never bent and adjusted to it, but every time I've regretted it. So, yeah, it's a very powerful thing in me, the need to be authentically me and seen by the world for who I am. Either don't see me at all, or see me as I am.

Yes. Well, I wonder if I can ask you, you know, I'm obviously a black woman setting up an organisation focusing I guess on gender but also on race, and I wanted to ask you about diversity in our profession, in the legal profession and your views on it. Could we do better, and do we need to try and have more intersectionality?

Yes, absolutely. I mean, you know, it's not peculiar to the Bar, and I think there is managing inclusion so that you give the safe spaces to particular strands of diversity that need those safe spaces…

Yes

… but at the same time, recognise that we don't actually sit separately in those strands. You know, you and I are both women …

Yes

… that has certain impacts on our lives. You're a woman of colour, I'm a pansexual woman or living as a lesbian for the last, you know, few decades, so that means we have different experiences and different challenges, but we do share being a woman and perhaps share being other and outside. With that quite often comes, not necessarily, but quite often comes an ability to stand in other's shoes and to start to at least understand how impactful being a sort of other is, even if you don't understand exactly what being that particular other is. So, for me, the work in that space is about doing the two things, which in a sense are intention, but I think you just have to treat them as two different elements and two different ways of working …

Yes

… The safe space, strengthening any particular group that needs that and allowing them to flourish and grow and work out how they need the particular profession culture to actually change and open up for them, but also then to come together and work across all of those with allies, you know, with people who come from what I with affection call the WHAM group, white, heterosexual, able-bodied males. I think it's much friendlier than a lot of the names they often get called but, you know, they're invaluable as allies. So, actually once we all start to work in an intersectional way across the piece, bringing our understanding of what we don't understand about each other, then we start to make real change.

Absolutely. And, can I just ask you, you know, you were open about your own sexuality and how you identify, have you always been comfortable being like that, you know, you're very authentic. Did you make that decision? Because there are some studies that actually, you know, people entering the Bar and the profession open at university, but the moment they enter they go back into the closet, which concerns me. So, I just wondered what you thought about that, particularly being open and sharing it.

Yes. Well, for me, all my relationships up until I was about 30 were with men, and since they've all been with women - seen the light! No, wanting different things at different stages of my life, and wanting relationships that operated in different ways, and what I brought to them is what made the change. So, for me, that change happened at the Bar. I perceived myself and everyone perceived me as being straight, and then I was in a relationship with a woman - not only with a woman, but with a woman I was in Chambers with. So, actually that experience - and she has in the past said it's okay for me to talk about it - informed quite a lot of what goes to your question, or the answer to your question, which I think is two things. First of all, her family were homophobic. My parents had always had gay friends, so for me it was a voyage of discovery about myself. My blind assumption was and always is that on a human level, until there is some evidence to tell me otherwise, I assume people will be fine. So, it might be because of a particular culture or a particular religion that I think, oh, well they may not be find, I need to go a little cautious, but my starting point is people are fine, whereas her starting point was, it's the end, everyone will disown us, it's the end of our careers. So, I think your sort of base, your family, your parents' position, does inform what you expect from the rest of the world. The other thing is an intergenerational thing. I did some mentoring for a fabulous charity called Just Like Us, who were giving back to their ambassadors, who were students who go into schools.

Yes

And they wanted, as those students were leaving university and going into the professional corporate lives, whatever, to give them senior mentors, and that really opened my eyes to the fact that when you do that transition from university to a profession, for the first time in your life you leave being in institutions that are not controlled by your generation, but predominated and about your generation, and you go in organisations that have often a long-standing culture which has been created by different generations, possibly by generations that are no longer there, and large numbers of people who've come through and been assimilated to that, so you suddenly hit your head on a very different sort of institution or culture. And I think that is why a lot of people when they leave university go back into the closet, because suddenly they realise these are very, very different places and cultures that are determined by a very different perspective of the world, but they don't have power in it. And it's not for them and it's not about them. They're entering something that pre-exists, if that makes sense.

Yes, no, no, no it does. Can I ask you then, how do you think we could improve and do better? And how can our male colleagues and the WHAMs, you know, help?

Listening, to start with. I think we can all be allies for each other. So, you know, I should listen and understand people who have a strand of diversity, or multiple strands of diversity, that aren't my experience, and be led by them informing me what they need to have a culture open up to have it being inclusive of them, and valuing them, and not presenting more barriers to them. But also, being conscious of when you're the person in the room who can actually say, so if it was a white person, and I'm the person in the room who can say to another person, whoa, hang on, or male that can say to another male, because actually sometimes that gets through far more effectively than when the person on the wrong end of it says, hang on a minute.

Yes

So, listening and taking responsibility and care for each other across all of that. You know, I long for the time we don't even have to have the labels and don't have to think about it and we don't need the safe spaces. But we're a long way from that as yet.

Well, just talking of safe spaces then, how did you get involved with Jo Delahunty?

Jo's an amazing woman. She's a family practitioner and Silk. It turns out we were both called in 1986, although we didn't know each other at Bar School. Currently, Professor of Law at Gresham College and has used that platform in her last year as Professor to really sort of talk about the Bar, wellbeing and inclusion. And she did a callout on Twitter for people with experience of sexual harassment at the Bar to contact her with those stories, and promised confidentiality. So, I direct messaged her and said, happy to have a chat, and we spoke one Sunday afternoon and the similarity in our stories were gobsmacking. So, she asked me, I told her my story, you know, of being in pupillage, taken away out of London for a case, and there being a problem with hotel rooms. In my case, adjoining rooms with a door unlocked and a person presenting them – a male presenting themselves, a senior male who, you know, who was hugely influential as to my future.

Yes

Hers was arriving at a reception desk and discovering that a double room had been booked. Yes, so we sort of talked about, once I'd told her my story and some of the other not so glorious bits, we talked it through, she told me hers and we sort of decided, well, if we can't be open, if at our stage with our profiles and our status at the Bar, if we can't be open about what's going on, then that's a pretty poor show. We actually, I think it's fair to say, both felt that we'd sort of assumed, allowed ourselves to assume things had got a lot better. I do think things have improved a bit.

Yes

I think there is a recognition now, which there wasn't in the eighties, that actually it's completely out of order, whereas in the eighties you always felt, certainly with all the sort of comments and put-downs and patronising and outright sexual sort of banter – banter in inverted commas - that you really had to tough it out, and if you said anything, you would either be told you had no sense of humour, or you weren't tough enough to make it at the Bar. I think there's far fewer people who would say that now but, nevertheless, the behaviours still continue. So, I think we both felt a huge sense of responsibility for having taken our eye off the ball … It wasn't that it got that much better. And so, we came to the conclusion we actually had to be willing to use our names in stories. So, I told her that she could use me in her lecture, and she used me in subsequent press articles and stuff as, you know, along with her having some full-on abuse of power pupillage sexual harassment stories. And, you know, I think it's important that we acknowledge that is historically the case at the Bar, and it's still going on.

Yes, absolutely. Well, can I ask you with, you know, all that you do, and you do a lot for the profession, not just in Silk but outside of it. You've talked about mentoring before, you do lots of hard work. What do you do for wellbeing, because the burnout rate and stress and nervous breakdowns are high at the Bar? We're self-employed – and for solicitors and paralegals and so on - what do you do to kind of keep a work life balance, if you like?

Well, I'm not going to claim that I have a balance because my partner, Paula, would scream if she heard me ever claiming that I had that! But what I do do is a bit of being conscious about what nourishes me - seeing myself as a bank account was always running an overdraft in terms of what I put out, work and other stuff - and making sure I give myself some of the what nourishes me. So, I know I need in any seven days to have a 24-hour period where I don't work, even if that means the other days are longer. For me, that's a pattern that is sustainable, and when I don't do it, I notice a difference. A bit of adrenaline rush is always a good thing, roller coasters and stuff, and my guilty secret is soaps, soap operas.

What?! [Laughter] Have you got a favourite one?

No, I love them all. [Laughter]

There is something about downtime though, isn't there? I remember a very good friend of mine, Jenny, you know, when she did the kitchen but got a television in it. It was the first house, a flat, she ever bought, and the television would come down just above the cooker so that she could always watch Coronation Street. [Laughter]

Perfect!

Yes, and I think, you know, there is something about a long day in Court – and I don't get the chance now because of children – but a long day in Court, pre-kids or whatever, and then just switching off and watching the soap, the soap opera! I mean, The Archers is probably as good as I get.

I don't know how you do it with kids, I have to say. I absolutely, hats off, full-on respect for any barrister who has kids because, you know … It's an amazing, fabulous career, I love it, I absolutely love it, but I just don't know how you do it with kids. But amazing people do, like you, lots of amazing, successful women do, and guys, but more the women.

Yes, yes, quite. Thank you, thank you, keep going, keep going, despite having all these Skeleton Arguments to draft, and home-schooling in COVID, that's a new challenge isn't it.

Yes, that is, that is. I've spoken to some of my colleagues in Chambers and, yes, so, we're now all Chambers meetings and all the rest of it, kids, pets, all welcome, don't worry about it!

Yes, well, interesting, just thinking about that, do you think it will affect the way that we work and the way that we think about things, our approach?

Yes. On the Criminal Bar side, you guys, as I understand, it have been working with technology in a way that on the civil side, we really haven't been.

Yes

Yes, a few telephone hearings, yes, but that was pretty well it, and I have to say my experience of videos in Civil Courts has been, oh there is one in a cupboard somewhere, and it somehow never works when it gets brought out. I think this will - we, as a profession, will be far more, if I can use the word, articulate, with the technology ...

Yes

... to actually advocate with it and through it. And so, we won't, you know, undoubtedly the professions have been resistant to that change, oh it can't quite work, and suddenly, you know, it will, and we'll make it work. Juries obviously is a completely different aspect ...

Yes, yes

So, I think the profession will be more skilled, and is already, remarkably, skilling up, and by the time we emerge from this properly, because I do think it's going to go on quite a bit longer, the Court system will have had to, you know, they clearly, really are determined to keep the justice show on the road, which is the right thing, and so it's going to have to deal with technology, remote use of hearings, etc.

Yes. Now, do you have a favourite fictional lawyer? I know you mentioned Rumple, so it may be that it's Rumpole. And then books, you know, do you have a favourite book or books that have really impacted your life? Whilst you're thinking about it! [Laughter]

Favourite lawyer ... well, I'm going to say Miranda from Sex in the City.

Oh gosh, yes! I've not had that before, yes! Miranda!

... red head, the voice of reason, good mates she goes out and has a proper good laugh with and, you know, restore her, nourish her.

Yes!

So, yes, I think probably her. Who knows if she was good as a lawyer, but she seemed to be successful.

Yeah, she did. Now, did she, she ended up - did she marry the guy with the glasses and he was a restauranteur? So, very different to sort of her corporate ...

... me with Paula, the artist, so ...

Yes, yes.

Mostly, I don't like legal dramas. I mean, I watched them a lot before I became a lawyer, but they drive us mad. But the one that should have driven me mad, but didn't, was Silk. You know, anything Maxine is in, I think is amazing. I would sit there and say, that's completely unethical and all the rest of it, but I was a bit nostalgic with that as well, actually. People would say to me, is that real? And I would say, oh it's about 20-25 years out of date, but yes [Laughter] Book, I think the book that probably changed my life most, it's very dated now, is The Women's Room, which was Marilyn French's first book in, I think it was about 1977. So, I was about 13/14 when I read it.

That's the year I was born!

Well, thank you for that! [Laughter]

I was making a note to read it, and I thought, oh!

Do you know, I think it was a key part, my sort of sense of how important personal authenticity was. There's a section in the book where she, the main character, Mira, is pregnant, and she sits in a toilet cubicle – we've all done that, haven't we? - weeping, because she feels that she's been invaded by this pregnancy. And a lot of her feelings around - she didn't want to be pregnant, it was an accident - but also that everyone is treating her as a pregnancy rather than even a woman, and certainly not as Maya. You know, people think they can come up and tap her belly and, you know, and I think it was the first time - and it's a very well written section in the book – the first time I sort of really understood that pain and agony of the world treating you as something you're not, not respecting you for the person you are, not seeing, being seen, you know, that whole sort of piece, which for me also, for instance, if you look at trans issues, it's the thing that comes up there, and I feel very strongly about that sort of - you determine who you are, not for the world to decide that and impose it on you. And I think that runs quite sort of deep as a theme for me and a lot of my inclusion-type work and interest. Yes, I think that's the earliest time I can think of really starting to understand that.

Yes, interesting. And so, Brie, can I ask you then, just from that, you know, what sort of three tips or advice and guidance would you have perhaps for those entering into the legal profession at present, whether from the LGBT community or not, and perhaps those who are in the job now, you know, we've got issues with retention, we've got other issues … you know, we know we love the job we do, you know, I love being an advocate, as do you, but are there any kind of, I don't if motivational, I hate that term, motivational speaker, you know, but are there any kind of inspirational tips maybe for future lawyers or future entrants, and those who are in it?

You and anyone listening will be absolutely gobsmacked to hear me say, be yourself. But the sort of add-on to that, be yourself and don't leave your personality at the door. I particularly say that to people who are looking for pupillage. Yourself is the person you're best at being. Trying to be something that you are not, because that's what you think the group of people you're trying to impress want – (1) you may be wrong about what they want, (2) being someone other than yourself is not sustainable, (3) you're not going to be as good at it as you are at being yourself. And I'm sure you, like me, have sat in lots of pupillage interviews where people have left their personality at the door, and it's the interviews where people engage and you see their personality that you actually really think, yes, there's something about this person, I can see how lay and professional clients will be happy to work with this person.

Yes

That's number one. I think know yourself and be kind to yourself, understand what, for you, you need to keep your show on the road. And for some people that's holidays, and for other people it's music, you know, it can be anything, but the things that nourish you that actually enable you to keep going, because it is a hard profession. I think we all have to try and run, not at 100% percent because we know we'll be forced up to 110 and 120% periodically …

Yes

… not to be 100% plus all the time. But it's really important to understand how your body and your mind work, when they've had enough and what you need to give them, whatever that is for you personally, and I'm going to nick from - I don't know if you know, Nicola Davies, amazing woman, she's the ombudsman of all things military, as far as I can work out - she says, you need a board, not one person, so you need a sponsor, a mentor, a connector, and a friend. A sponsor, someone who's in the important places, who's a senior person who knows you and will sort of reference you and sort of give you those tips. A mentor who mentors you, we all know that. A connector, someone who has a network and will take you with them and introduce you to their network. And then a friend, the person you can go to when it's all gone wrong, or you think it's all gone wrong, or it's plateaued, or you don't understand what's happening, or just, it's all too much. An excellent summary, but it's not mine.

Well, it's yours now because we'll quote you on it. It's amazing advice. I feel so privileged to be able to interview you and for you to take out your time. But just before we finish, I wanted to ask you really, what's next? You know, could the Bench be the next stop? Might we see you either there or in the Court of Appeal or in the High Court?

Certainly not in the near future, because one of my roles at the moment is I'm the Barrister Commissioner on the JAC, which feels to me like somewhere where I can be actually having more impact and trying, working in terms of inclusion and improving the balance of our judiciary and trying to drive it towards a stage where it properly represents the society that it Judges, because to me that's really important. So, at the moment, that's the position that I have, that I'm really enjoying working with, and I think is really an important thing. I can have more use and more impact.

A huge thank you to Brie Stevens-Hoare QC for taking part in Talking Law.

Jodie Hill

This month you will hear from the very inspiring Jodie Hill on how law needs to take an active responsibility for its employees' wellbeing, and why she felt compelled to start her own firm. Jodie is Managing Director and Solicitor at Thrive Law in Leeds. She has also been shortlisted by the Law Society of England and Wales for Personality of the Year 2018. Jodie, thank you so much for talking to us today, welcome. Tell me what inspired you to get into law.

A few things really. I grew up without anyone in the law, so I didn't have any experience, so I looked more at the ideal situation of, well I suppose what people see on television, and helping people and that kind of inspirational person that they're perceived to be in the media. So that was my initial reason to want to go into the law, to help people really.

Interesting. So, did you have any female role models? Who were your role models? I'm just interested in your background and maybe education.

Yes, so I'm from a working-class family but I did get a scholarship to go to a private school, so I had a bit of a mixed upbringing. In terms of role models, more later in life than earlier was Michelle Mone because I know that she had quite a working-class upbringing and then she's obviously, well she's a billionaire, which is slightly different to me(!), but she has been really, really successful and I think it's really admirable a lot of the work that she does. Also, Lady Hale, she's obviously from Yorkshire like me. She's so fantastic and obviously she has the most senior role in the legal profession.

Yes, because she's President of the Supreme Court.

Exactly. So, I think both of those are inspirational for very different reasons.

Yes. Amazing. Now, can I ask you a little about challenges. So, what were the biggest challenges that faced you at the start of your career, and how did you overcome them?

A lot of my challenges were in relation to the network that I had because it was very, very small. I didn't have any network from family or friends, so a lot of that was quite difficult to get work experience and to get into some of the firms, so those things I found particularly difficult, but threw myself in, continually attacked people online – well, not attacked them, but you know constantly messaging them – because otherwise if you don't put yourself out there then people are just simply going to ignore you because they're so busy. So, I actually used LinkedIn and contacted Managing Partners and they reluctantly said, 'yes, come in', and actually that's how I've got every single one of my jobs. It's from just being really proactive online. So, whilst I didn't have a network, I was able to use modern technology and embrace it.

Fantastic, and not be fearful of it.

Yes, of course. So, I think that's a lot of the issues now is that people are so scared to approach, and it seems quite a daunting prospect to approach somebody in that position, but actually we've all been there and we know how difficult it can be, so Yes, I think that's it, just embrace it.

That is so awesome. Yes, and don't let it - don't be scared!

Yes, don't be scared.

That's great advice actually. I'm thrown off now! Can I ask you a few other things then? What surprised you most about working in the law?

I suppose the way that the law is perceived perhaps, especially when you're younger. There's not a lot of admin work on the telly! So, there's lots of admin, but I think a lot of it is people skills and it's people management as well. It's simply being able to communicate effectively. That's a lot of what being a lawyer is about, and it's time management and it's admin, there's so much more to it than the law, and I think a lot of the time people assume that you just charge a really high fee and just sit there and kick back like you're on an episode of Suits where they're just drinking Bourbon all the time. When actually you're doing a lot of hours! We put a lot of hours in and a lot goes into being a lawyer behind the scenes. I was also taken aback by how much marketing and business development is required from the legal profession, because a lot of firms don't have their own department for that, and you're required to bring in all of your own work. So, it's very different to how it's perceived in the media, I think.

You're absolutely right. Across the profession really for solicitors and barristers. Let's talk a bit about diversity in the profession, the "D" word. What do you think about the diversity in our profession?

I think that, well my understanding that there are more women entering the profession than men. However, in the senior roles there appear to be very little women, and I might be wrong in my statistic but last time I checked it was only at 16% of equity partners are female, which is outstanding. I mean, how is that even possible? So, my view is that I don't think it's diverse and I think my own experience was that it was really difficult. I actually trained at the Bar before I became a solicitor.

Fantastic, good choice!

One thing I did find was that that was even more difficult for me, having come from a working-class background, because the Bar is notoriously difficult to succeed at, and whilst I was offered pupillage and I didn't take it, it was still for me, I was still thinking well where am I going to get my work from, you know, there was so much pressure and the amount of money that they pay for pupillage, when I had no financial backing, it didn't even cover my rent. So, if you don't come from a higher-class background or have funds surplus to just fund yourself for a year, then it can be really difficult unless you get into one of the big Chambers, which is really, really difficult obviously again to do. So, I think from a diversity perspective, obviously that covers gender and class, but it's similar you know for race as well. I think the profession is very under-represented.

What do you think about how we could tackle this problem? I mean, it's a big issue and you know some of the stuff Women in the Law UK is doing is tackling it, but how do you think we could tackle the problem?

It's about empowering those people who it effects and showing them that actually they can succeed in any career in the law regardless of their background, regardless of their ethnicity or their gender, and putting initiatives in place within the workplace, within the profession, from the Law Society, from the SRA. So, I think there's lots of different things that we can do as a society, but I think individual firms can look to empower individuals so that they actually apply to those types of firms as well, or Chambers, vice versa. I know there are things ongoing at the moment but I'm not sure that it's quite enough to reach out to some of the harder to reach areas, for sure.

Interesting. So, do you think retention is one of the biggest issues when it comes to diversity, and how do you think we could deal with that?

Certainly so with women, because I think the issue we have with women and retention is that they'll go on maternity leave and then that year or so, it might be shorter or might be longer, is crucial for them because they're out of the loop, they often aren't put on any return to work scheme that's sufficient enough to put them back in the position they would have been, they might have missed promotion, career progression, overlooked for other opportunities, and so I think that we have issues around retention when it comes to returning to work from maternity leave for sure.

Yes. And how do you feel that the profession would change if it was more diverse?

Well, I think it would be more approachable for people. At the moment the profession still, regardless of what most people's opinions are, I think it's still quite inaccessible to a lot of people. There's a perception that we're very expensive, everyone's middle-class, and actually those perceptions don't truly reflect it, but I think there are still changes that could be made, and if there was a more diverse profession then it would potentially be more accessible to more people for sure.

So, if we had more working-class lawyers, or more disabled lawyers, or …

More relatable to society.

Exactly, there'd be more entrants from those backgrounds.

For sure, exactly. And the whole point of the legal system is access to justice for all, not just for a particular race or class.

Fantastic! Can I ask you then about you, more about you? It's all about you! About setting up Thrive Law. Why did you set up Thrive?

Well, two reasons. So, mainly because I felt that there was a bit of a gap in the market in terms of having a law firm where you could really just be your true self, so you can talk about your disability, talk about your religion, your beliefs, so we employ, every one that we employ here either has a mental health condition or their very close family are suffering with something and they're very open about it in the office, so we wanted to create an environment where people could just be themselves, basically. And I think there's a lot of issues entrenched in traditional firms because of what's seen to be successful, what's seen to be the right way to be, you've got to bill a certain amount of hours, and we don't adopt that structure so we've created a really flexible working environment whereby people can be themselves, they can work from home, which obviously gives access to return to work mothers as well, so Yes, I think I just, for me, I wanted to create an environment that I could work in because I have mental health problems as well, and where I felt that I could really be myself and get out the message that I wanted to get out, so I created the brand Thrive because I wanted to thrive at work, and it really encompasses what we're all about. It's not just about disability and race and religion, it's about all protected characteristics and about everyone just being able to thrive as themselves.

So, I think that nicely sums up nicely the next question I was going to ask you about the ethos of the firm, really. Is that generally the ethos, allowing people to thrive in the firm?

Exactly, and it's about just being really open and honest. For example, if I've had therapy, I'm quite open about that in the office and I'll say, 'oh I had therapy this morning', you know, so making it a conversation that's just normal. Like, if you had a bad back or your neck was hurting, you'd be like 'oh my God, my neck's hurting today'. Not saying we should all come in and just complain, that's probably the wrong way to look at it! But it's just about normalising those conversations and making it a bit more real, because most of us suffer or have suffered, and even if we've only suffered with minor stress, we all know what it feels like to have a really, really bad day, and how actually that could be made better if we could perhaps talk about it or feel as though we're not going to be punished for appearing weak.

Absolutely. I know that you're a Mental Health First Aider ...

I am!

What is it, and why are they important?

Okay. So, Mental Health First Aid is an accredited course. It's created by Mental Health First Aid England and it's actually accredited by the Royal Society for Public Health, of which I'm a Fellow by the way, I thought I'd just drop that in! The reason why that's important is that you've got the consistency of an accredited programme that's rolled out across the UK. There are three different types of courses – there's the two-day course which means you become a Mental Health First Aider, there's a one-day course and a half-day course which is about being Mental Health First Aid aware. So, what is a First Aider? They are similar to a physical First Aider in that they help with a crisis situation in respect of mental health rather than the physical, so if someone is having a panic attack at work, or if somebody is appearing suicidal, there's a very high rate of suicides at work at the moment, so they are equipped with skills to intervene and basically to signpost individuals to the correct support. So, they're not a counsellor, they're not a therapist, they're not a doctor, but they're there in a way to signpost and support them in that crisis moment. But they're also there to assist people whilst in the workplace, so it might be they're struggling with their employer and they don't really know how to communicate, so they might go through the Mental Health First Aider as a third person to communicate about reasonable adjustments, or to communicate about sickness. The other thing they can do is they can help spot signs of mental ill health. So, they can show, well they can talk to that individual and try to signpost them to the correct manager or a doctor or a therapist, or it might be that they assist HR in determining what might help that individual to stay in work. So, it can help with job retention as well as absenteeism.

That is fantastic.

It's just a proactive approach I suppose.

Yes it is, rather than people shying away and then dropping out of the workplace and the work environment. It's great.

Exactly.

And do you think the law has an issue with wellbeing?

What, as in the law as in the legal profession?

Yes

Yes, I think so. I think we're very targeted on money and hours, and that doesn't account for mental ill-health I'm afraid, because when you're mentally ill you struggle to concentrate, you struggle to sleep, and if you're struggling to sleep and concentrate and that cycle is constant, you are going to really struggle with achieving the same amount of work in the same amount of hours as someone who doesn't suffer. So, it's about looking at adjustments and I think there are firms doing fantastic things, but there are also lots of firms that lag behind, and I appreciate there are targets that people have to meet and they have to cover their costs, but the cost to someone's long-term mental health is, in my view, more important.

Absolutely, absolutely. And you talked about the way that you are tackling that in your firm, and perhaps more firms can adopt that in the flexibility of work. What do you think about newly qualifieds? Are they bringing a different attitude to the profession?

Yes, I think so. I teach on the LPC and I see a lot of the students coming through, obviously studying on the LPC, and from that they tend to want firms to support them with other things not just simply offering a training contract. I've noticed that the ones, I mean we have six students coming between January and May all doing work experience with us and they've all said they were attracted to us because we were doing something slightly different, we were looking at wellbeing and I think that's what firms need to be looking at. What is their wellbeing strategy? Do they consider mental health as something that they would support people with, like they would with other ethnicity and sexual orientation? These things need to be taken into consideration when looking at initiatives within the firm for sure.

That is fantastic. What about you? What do you do to relax and switch off? You know, you've got to take care of your own mental health really. I know we're not great at it, but I was wondering if you could share some of your own.

Well, I do have to practice what I preach. I actually do meditate, so I find that meditation is really helpful and not just kind of sitting there and being all zen. You can meditate at any point, so I do three minute meditations if I'm feeling really stressed, I'll actually go and sit in the toilet and just meditate, because I think just breathing and stopping for a moment, it's so powerful, and I have a dog and I walk my dog and I spend time with animals and I think that's also really, really helpful because it makes you think, well it stops you from thinking about work and about all the problems and you're actually like, 'aww, look at his face'...

I know you haven't brought your dog here, but we'll need to post a picture.

I will post a picture, definitely, but he's all over my Twitter, bless him. But, also, he comes into the office, so the girls love that. And I know that for law firms that's a huge no-no for most firms, but we love it. He's just like, he came in for Christmas jumper day, he dressed up as a reindeer, it was great. And, do you know what, you don't have to be boring about it, there are ways, just find your niche, find what chills you. Exercise is a huge thing for me. I play netball and I do a lot of training in the gym, and that's my therapy really. I just, if I know I'm feeling stressed I'm like, right, I need to go to the gym, and if I haven't been for three days I kind of notice it – and you're nodding, I like it!

Yes, I know, I know, you're like, 'I really need to get down there', if you're getting maybe aggro at work. So, how do you see the future of the profession shaping out?

I think the roles of solicitors and barristers are going to change significantly in the next ten years with the introduction of technology. I think it's a huge, wow, I mean it's going to change the way we use paralegals, it's going to change the way we train our future professionals, so I think there's that side of it. There's also the wellbeing side and the needs of individuals. The people coming up now have different needs, they have different wants. They don't necessarily want to just all become partners and take on the world. A lot of people are looking more for a lifestyle choice, and whether or not that is going to be encompassed as part of the legal profession remains to be seen, because right now I couldn't imagine, you know, just doing three days a week just for fun. That's not an option. It's hard to do that even as a working mum.

Yes, it is.

So, I think the roles will change significantly. I mean we're looking to develop our own app next year and working with some AI as well, so that's on our agenda and we're in the design phases of that at the moment. So, we're already thinking about it and we're only eight months old. So, I think it's something that you know the big firms, if they're not already doing it, they need to be to keep up-to-date, and I think a lot of the students that are coming up will have to think of things like psychology and technology and coding as part of their learning, because they're going to have to understand how that works in practice. It's not as simple as just learning the law anymore.

No, it's not, it's not. Now, Jodie, we are in the headquarters of the radical city and home of Emmeline Pankhurst here in Manchester, and we now have a statue here of Emmeline in St Peter's Square. What do you think she would think about the profession now; her husband of course famously was a barrister. What do you think she would, you know, this famous suffragette, make of our profession?

Well, I think we've made significant progress. I mean look at where we've come over the past 100, it's been 100 years now hasn't it, pretty much.

Well, next year it is, yes, 100 years.

Exactly, so you know we've come such a long way from being not even able to practice and now being, as I said before, we've got more women entering the profession than men. So, the fact is that, you know, we've come a really long way but it's about retaining those women in those roles and getting more women into leadership roles.

Fantastic, fantastic. Now, I'm going to ask a slightly different thing now. What's the best book that you've read this year?

Ooh, it's a difficult one.

Just because I'm nosey.

I'm trying to think of how – it's got a swear word in it! It's called "The art of not giving a ...."

I'm reading that presently!

Are you actually?

Yes, as well as "Becoming" by Michelle Obama, but I have to flick through the two and it's really funny ...

I think I read a lot, I like to read autobiographies and I like to read a lot about personal and self-development really and trying to kind of work out where your headspace is at, and I think we can always learn from other people. Most people have done something already, so read the autobiographies, read the self-help books and the professional books as well.

Fantastic. And who's your favourite fictional lawyer?

Oh, I have a few!

What?!

Well I think I may have already answered this question online, so I'm going to have to stick with it, and it was Elle Woods from Legally Blonde, which is really cheesy! But the reason is, everybody says …

But we all love it!

But, do you know what, I'm just being real. So, the reason is, is because everyone thought 'what the hell, she can't do this', and actually, whilst it was a complete extreme and it is obviously not what being a lawyer's really like, it just showed that actually you can do anything if you put your mind to it.

That's so fantastic. And is there a quote that you live your life by that you'd like to share, or maybe a saying that you've adopted?

I have two – I have "create your own destiny", which I actually have tattooed on my body! I don't know whether I should announce that, but I've just announced it. And also, "everything happens for a reason", and I know that's really cheesy but some things in life have really set me back and I had a mental breakdown last year and I was off for four months and I thought about quitting the profession, and that drove me to set up Thrive, so had that not have happened, I wouldn't be here, so everything really does happen for a reason. When you're feeling that low, or you're having those weeks where you're thinking I'm literally not going to get through this, there's another day and every day will get better, and I just think everything does happen for a reason, it does make you stronger, and I couldn't have done Thrive had I not have been through that, because I had nothing to compare it to.

Exactly, exactly. Well, I totally agree with you. Jodie, thank you so much for taking the time to come and talk to me today. You're an inspiration and it's been wonderful having you on.

Thank you so much.

Cherie Blair

In just a moment this month's guest, Cherie Blair Queen's Counsel CBE, will be discussing the personal memories of her extensive career and the biggest challenges she feels the profession has ahead of it. Cherie is a leading Queen's Counsel and committed campaigner for women's rights, as well as a lecturer, writer and founder of the Cherie Blair Foundation for Women. I asked Cherie what attracted her to the law in the first place.

Well I think it was probably down to the influence of my grandmother, who was always very interested in affairs of the world and what was going on, and in particular she was fascinated by a woman QC called Rose Heilbron, who was the first woman QC, and happened to come from Liverpool like obviously my grandmother and I did. Rose was very famous in Liverpool, and in the early days my grandma used to come and watch her in Court during the, what we called then, the Sessions, and she was very famous because she was the first woman to defend someone on a murder charge, I mean she was the first woman to become Recorder. She did so many amazing things, of course the first woman QC, so my grandma was very fascinated by her and I think it must have rubbed off on me. Otherwise, I remember when I was thinking what I should study at University, my then boyfriend's mother at the time said to me, 'oh Cherie you like an argument, you're good at debating, why don't you try the law?' So, I thought, why not?

That's wonderful. And so, would you say that she was your role model, your grandmother, or Rose? I just wondered who are your role models?

Well, Rose was obviously one of my first legal role models, if you like, but yes, of course, my mother and my grandmother were very influential to me, not least because both of them were very strong women who left school at the age of 14 and who were the bedrock of their family, for sure. My own mother of course, after my father abandoned us when I was eight, she had to pick herself up and find herself a job, you know, in order to support her children, and that in turn made me understand the importance of a woman being able to earn her own money and be able to stand on her own two feet, because you never know what the world may throw at you, and that in the end led to me setting up, years later in 2008, my Foundation for Women, which is about helping women entrepreneurs in the lower middle income countries to develop their businesses, so the whole thing sort of comes full circle.

Well, I'm going to ask you a bit more about that a bit later on actually. Can I just ask, just before we get to there, when you became a barrister there was a tiny minority of women in similar roles. I just wondered what challenges did that offer, and did you ever feel your voice wasn't heard?

I think that I was very young when I became a barrister. I was only 21 when I was called to the Bar, which was ridiculously young and probably wouldn't happen these days, so for a long time I was often mistaken for the secretary from the office rather than the actual barrister.

Crikey!

But you're right, there were very few women called to the Bar. In fact, when I was called to the Bar in 1976 it was the first time that the number of women called to the Bar went into double figures, so that was a sort of milestone, but I was not aware of at the time but became aware of later on. I think the main thing was that, though there were women in my pupillage Chambers, two to be precise, I didn't for the entirety of my pupillage, my training, my on-the-job training if you like, ever see a woman speak in Court.

Really?

And, well there weren't that many women and the cases I was doing with my Pupil Master, Derry Irvine, he was always against men not women, so that meant it was quite difficult for me to work out how a woman's voice should sound in Court, if you like.

Wow! So, did you just sort of, you know, be just yourself?

Well, I think also I realised Derry is a very large, larger than life figure, and his approach to cross-examination was often very much like a bull in a china shop, and I remember a case when he was against Lord Bingham, well Tom Bingham then, and in those days I think neither of them were QCs, or maybe they were both just QCs, and so I saw Derry cross-examine this witness like a rhinoceros, and then Tom Bingham came and he, I thought, was much more subtle and much more like a snake and I decided that, given my age and size, a snake was probably a better role model for me than try to be a bull.

Well, can I ask you then a bit about wellbeing and wellness at the Bar. There's a big movement at the moment to advocate wellbeing and wellness at the Bar, and so I was just wondering, how did you deal with the pressures that being a barrister presents? You've got a family, like I have, and certainly for that era I just wondered how you got through it and if you had, maybe, I don't know, any tips?

Well, I very much support the recent efforts to advocate mindfulness and wellbeing at the Bar, because it is a very pressurised profession. I think in some ways I was quite lucky, because when I started in the 70s, mid to late 70s, there was a boom in the Bar in relation to Legal Aid work, there was money available for the new kind of work that I was able to get into, the public law work, the employment law work, and, you know, one was paid reasonably well. I mean, today I think a lot of the pressures, particularly on those who do Legal Aid work in the Bar, are due to the fact that there is real financial pressure, particularly for those just starting off, and that in itself of course is very, very stressful.

Yes, absolutely, and of course entail access to justice.

Yes, and makes a problem, I think, for people like me coming, as I did, from a family that had no connections. I was the first person in my family to go to University, you know, we had no private money to support me, so I supported myself and I was able to do so thanks to scholarships from Lincoln's Inn, a loan, the fact that I could work part-time at the Polytechnic of Central London, and the fact that actually, you know, that it took some time for the money to come in, at least there was money coming in, and all those things are not so easily available to today's young Bar and I think it creates a real problem. Not so much for diversity, not so much between men and women, but between those with extra resources and those who don't have them.

Absolutely. I couldn't agree more, and certainly social mobility. And can I ask then, in the early days and now, how you coped with professional disappointment, if you like. If a case didn't go your way, can you remember how you coped with it, or anything of that sort?

I think, to be honest, that in those days the Judges were often a lot more unkind than they are today. I know that there's recently been studies showing that there still are some bullying Judges, and my daughter is a junior barrister and I know that that does happen, but certainly in the Higher Courts, I think in the High Court and the Court of Appeal, many of the Judges were often very severe, particularly on young barristers, and you know sometimes it was difficult to remember you aren't supposed to cry in Court.

No, I know

I never did though, but I think that generally, and certainly in the Higher Courts, the Judges are much better behaved than they ever were. It was great training in those days doing, as I did, general common law so I could do crime, I would do family, I do personal injury, and you would just, have wig would travel around the country and you would just plead your case and you would make mistakes and you'd learn from them.

Yes, absolutely.

But it was also, I can remember going over to one circuit, going off from London and going into the robing room very early on in my career, and them all falling silent because they thought 'what is this woman doing in this robing room?', you know, 'she must be a secretary'. Then, when I brought out my robes and they realised I was actually going to robe in there, there was, sort of, consternation!

Wow!

Nowadays you don't get that. I think that the one thing is that you are often, you know there's plenty of women at the Bar now, which is a good thing.

Yes, absolutely. Can I ask you then about, you answered this earlier, but does the law in the UK still have an issue with diversity, gender, racial, and social mobility? And really I was interested in maybe your views about how we remedy that, and the work that Women In The Law UK are trying to do is great in encouraging those specific areas aside of gender, but do we still have that big issue with not just gender but racial and social mobility?

I think the statistics speak for themselves, don't they? Both in relation to gender, where we see a real improvement, and you know 40% in the Bar, 50% in the solicitor's profession entrants, but then when you look at the senior levels, you know down into the 20% which says to me, and I'm sure to you, that we're still not doing enough about work life balance and how to support women through maternity. And I feel very strongly that this should not just be about women, this is about parental leave and it's about how we support both men and women being parents, because it's not good for the men either if all they do is work 24 hours a day and never see their families and children. So, I think work life balance still remains an issue and we need to talk about that, and some of the recent proposals about late sittings for Court, weekend sittings, are good in one way in enabling Courts to be accessible, but they do have a knock-on effect in relation to the work life balance of those who work in the Courts, which needs to be seriously considered.

Absolutely.

As for race diversity, I think again that is very much tied up with resources, because if you're from a wealthy family, whatever your race or colour, I think you know that we see many examples of how people can progress in the law, but the problem is that we still don't have enough support for those from less fortunate backgrounds who want to go into the law. It starts very early on when you go to, as I sometimes do, I go and address schools about being a lawyer, and the absence of knowledge of just simple things, like what's the difference between a barrister and solicitor, or what our Courts do, particularly in our State sector, means that people don't even think that the law is something for them. Now, we've seen a growth in apprenticeships in the law, which I think is an interesting approach, particularly for those who want to become solicitors. I say that not because I think we couldn't use apprenticeships for the Bar, it's just that we haven't got a system to do it and I think we should think about, you know, is there a way that we could also do that, but it's much more difficult at the Bar because of course we're a profession of self-employed.

Yes, absolutely.

And that's one of the problems I think in relation to how do we support. The Inns can do so much, as they do with their scholarships, as they're doing with the move to make the professional training more accessible and less expensive, but there is a difficulty in a profession of self-employed people, many of whom went into the profession because they didn't want to be part of the larger organisation, to deal with these problems.

Yes, absolutely. And when we mentioned remedy and you talked about you speaking in schools, which is fantastic, do you think that's one of the remedies? You know, providing information in those areas, particularly in social mobility, just about what the law is and the difference indeed in the law?

Yes, I think so, and I think that certainly, when my husband was Prime Minister and David Blunkett was in education, they introduced citizenship training and I was on the Board of something called the Citizenship Foundation that had programmes making sure that school children understood about human rights, understood about how our justice system works. I think unfortunately these days, both with the cuts to education and also the emphasis on core curriculum, that sort of information is less available, and that I think is a shame.

Absolutely. What's the biggest challenge do you think facing the profession presently?

What is the biggest challenge for the profession generally? Well, I think the biggest challenge actually is what I've said before about making sure that we get diversity and that we get sufficient income so that people who have a passion for justice and the rule of law, from every area of life, can still come into the Bar. Because if the legal profession does not reflect the diversity of the population at large, we're not properly serving the principles of accessible justice.

Can I ask you about your Foundation and your work to support more women entrepreneurs in developing countries?

Well, I can simply say that as I mentioned before, because of the lessons I'd learned both through my mother and through my own life of having been able to make my own choices, I realised that women who have their own money can make their choices. They can walk away from abusive relationships, they can say no to pressures that society might put onto them to conform, and they can become leaders in their community. And I felt that across the world, particularly in low and middle income countries where the societal pressures perhaps ae stronger, that if we could help women entrepreneurs set up and grow and expand their businesses so that they employed other people, so that they got respect in their community and that they could be a voice for change, and so for the last ten years the Cherie Blair Foundation for Women has supported women in over 104 different countries, and we use technology to reach those women. So, we have a global mentoring platform, which is an online mentoring relationship which enables us to put women in the UK and all over the world, and men as well, in touch with women entrepreneurs all over the world, and they give a year of two hours a month supporting those women and helping them achieve their business goals. And then we also have programmes where we use mobile phone and the internet to provide business training and skills to women, plus the ability to network with other women in similar situations. And so, because of that, we reach 140,000 women, as I say, in over 100 countries across the world, and we have big ambitious plans for the next ten years, including extending our work into helping young girls from 15 onwards who, a recent report by Plan International shows of the 628 million young people between 16 and 25 who are neither in education nor in jobs, the vast majority of them are young girls. And one way, it's not the only way, but one way of helping them start off and stand on their own two feet of course is to help them set up their own businesses, and that's one of the things that we hope to do with our programmes in the future, and we've been very lucky just recently having a partnership with Avon.

Fantastic!

We have reached one hundred million women a year, not only through their sellers but also through their supply chains and the women who are their customers, and we're going to help provide business training and advice to women through that network, which will be fantastic.

That is awesome. Well, I'm sure our listeners will be keen to go on the website and donate or support in any way that we can.

Oh yes, www.cherieblairfoundation.org.

Fantastic, fantastic. Can I ask you then, Cherie, two more questions really. If a young person was considering a career in the law today, what advice would you give them?

My advice would definitely still be, go for it! And the advice I give when I go to schools is, if you think you want to be a lawyer, I always advise them, and the schools always encourage this, to take a law degree. Why? Because at least with a law degree there are loans available and therefore you avoid the extra cost of doing the law conversion course, which you don't get the same sort of support and help, and if you've got limited resources that's an important consideration.

And, we always ask everybody this. What's your favourite, who's your favourite fictional lawyer, and why?

Well, I'm a bit of a groupie for reading crime novels, and at the moment I'm reading some novels by a Swedish author called Asa Larsson, and she actually was a lawyer herself. In fact, she was a tax lawyer by profession, and she's invented this lawyer called Rebecca

Martinson. She's got four books, I think, about that, and I've been enjoying reading those stories, set as they are in Sweden and so a bit Scandi Noir about them, and also about this woman with her struggle first as a commercial lawyer in the capital and feeling disillusioned with the pressures of work there, and then going up to the North of the country and ending up as a Prosecutor.

Wow! Well, you know we've got a Women In Law Book Club, so we've got to read all of those.

Yes, you should look them up.

What a joy to listen to a true trailblazer and inspiring woman in the legal profession and beyond. That was absolutely brilliant. We really enjoyed having Cherie on. A huge thanks from us.

Nigel Poole QC

This month, Head of Chambers of Kings Chambers in Manchester, Nigel Poole QC, tells us about the cases that changed his life, and the challenges that face the future of the profession. Nigel is Head of Kings Chambers in Manchester and is ranked as a Leading QC by Chambers UK and the Legal 500. He sits as a Recorder and a Chair of the Bar Tribunal and Adjudication Service and has appeared in the Supreme Court and the Court of Appeal. He also writes a successful blog called "Learned Friend". We began by talking about his path to becoming a barrister.

I came to it halfway through my university course. My dad was a solicitor, but he did, he was a solicitor in a small High Street firm, and he did Wills and conveyancing, and I thought that was deadly boring, and it's not litigation at all, it's not Courtroom work. I liked reading 'Rumpole of the Bailey' ..

Yes, hear hear, I agree!

Watching 'Crown Court' on the telly, but it was through my dad. He had a contact at the Bar, and I did a mini-pupillage when I was, I think, in my second year of University, and I loved it.

Which is what's now the training period, yes?

Well, no, because I did a non-law degree first, so it was during my first degree.

Oh, I see.

And it was coming to the end of that and thinking 'what am I going to do', so it was the end of the second year. There was a Careers Service, and there was a sort of computer program, or what passed for it in those days, and I put in information about the sort of career

I might like, you know, self-employed, not tied to a desk etc., and out popped the answer 'barrister'!

Oh, wow! I think we need that program now!

Yes! And so I did a mini-pupillage in Leeds. They had a common room in the Chambers I went to, in those days, in Park Square, and they'd come back and tell tales of their cases at Court, criminal cases mostly, and it was just brilliant. I just loved it. The whole atmosphere and, you know, all the eccentricities of the Bar.

Yes, yes, all coming back.

And I just thought, this is what I want to do.

That's amazing. Well, Leeds is a great city, but we're glad you didn't stay there. Apart from your dad I suppose, who you'd have to say was one of your role models, I wondered if you have any role models, and why they're role models, that you can share with me.

Well, I was really lucky, my pupil supervisor, Alistair Forrest, and he specialised in medical negligence, which is what I – we call it clinical negligence these days – but I sort of followed him ultimately into that. But he was a real role model for me. So, I like to think I was a pupil really for 16 years because I stayed in those Chambers for that long, and he was always there to answer questions and give advice, and he was very clever, really good with clients. And I think what I got from him, and others that I've admired at the Bar was actually a sort of modesty. He wasn't a bombastic barrister at all, quiet, you know that doesn't mean he was good at cross-examining someone, he just did it in that penetrating, quiet way, and when I've seen other barristers do that, David Allen QC and so on, that's what I've tried to adopt a little bit myself.

Yes, rather than that sort of aggressive – I think Cherie Blair was talking about that sort of aggressive style …

It doesn't work.

... which didn't appeal, yes, and it doesn't at all. So, Nigel, your work is in human rights, personal injury, clinical negligence or medical negligence as you started, why did you pick that area? We know you followed your pupil master, but what impact, for example, did the Human Rights Act have on the law in this country, in your view?

The reason I enjoyed and ended up in clinical negligence, to be honest, is it's a way into another world which I enjoy finding out about. There's times where you think, 'actually I could do a laparoscopic cholecystectomy because I've done six cases on it.

I hope not!

A dangerous belief I know, but you'd learn a lot about different areas that I just think are inherently interesting to do with our health and so on.

Yes

Also, at the risk of sounding a bit sort of epic about it, it is life and death in medical negligence, so you're dealing with cases from birth you know through to geriatric care, and so the whole of human life is there. And the privilege of representing clients who have been through, you know, some life-changing experiences is great. Human rights hasn't made a huge difference to clinical negligence work but it has, to a certain extent at the peripheries, so with inquest work that often follows from healthcare negligence, and a case that sort of really helped me in my career, called Rabone, had a big human rights aspect.

Yes, I was coming to that, actually. A case that's changed your career I would say.

Yes, it was that, I would say of all of them.

Can you tell us a bit about it?

Yes. So, the tragic case of a woman who was 24 and committed suicide. I represented her parents.

Oh, I'm sorry.

She'd been having in-patient treatment, she was allowed home when she shouldn't have been, and she took her own life. And under the existing law, and certainly before the Human Rights Act, there was really no recourse for justice for them.

No.

They had no claim because she was over 18. There was a claim for the Estate, but it was relatively minor for funeral expenses and so on. And the solicitor who was representing them, who I knew well, Emma Holt, came to me and said, 'Isn't there something we can do here? How about the Human Rights Act?' We looked into it and it was quite a novel claim. We brought a claim for them under the Human Rights Act to say that their daughter's life had not been protected and that the State, through the Hospital Trust, a public authority, owed her a duty, an obligation under the Convention, Article 2 of the Convention, to protect her life and had failed to do so. There are certain hurdles you have to overcome to get to that point. We lost in the High Court, we lost in the Court of Appeal, and we won – I was led at this stage, I wasn't a Silk, but was led by Robert Francis in the Court of Appeal, ...

Oh yes ...

... Jenny Richards QC in the Supreme Court. They were both brilliant, and we won, 5-0 in the Supreme Court.

Was that one of the proudest moments in your career?

Certainly, professionally that was -in terms of conducting a case - it was the proudest. I mean, if you win a case, particularly if it feels as if it's been a fight and it's been against the odds, you always get that sense. It's one of the reasons we do the job is that sense of righting a wrong, you know, that's what brought you into the profession.

Absolutely, absolutely.

So, to actually achieve that, and on such a stage was a great, you know, it did feel like a great achievement, or to play a part in it.

Can I ask you then about the Medical Innovation Bill? Is that one of your proudest moments?

Well, it was a curious sort of episode in my career. I'd started a blog …

Yes, it's called Learned Friend

That's right. And I'd become aware of Lord Saatchi, Maurice Saatchi, who lost his wife to cancer, and he seemed to blame the legal profession really for it. But he felt that the fear that doctors have of being sued had prevented there being a cure for cancer. He put it no lower than that. And his solution therefore was effectively to introduce a law that would render doctors immune from being sued if they gave innovative treatment to their patients and it failed or harmed or killed them. And I thought, at first sight, this is entirely wrong, and I thought so when I looked at it again, and again. So, I wrote about it and it snowballed into something of a campaign and ended up sort of meeting an MP in Parliament and, you know, doing public debates about it, and letters to The Times and all of this. We lobbied, and a group of disparate people got together, and we campaigned against it, and pretty effectively. Ultimately, for various reasons, it ran into the ground, so the Bill was passed but with all of that part of it removed.

Yes, excellent! Excellent in the sense of, you know, what one person can do, and through your blog as well. I just wanted to pause for a moment and just think about, you're a barrister, you're Queen's Counsel, Head of your Chambers, a father, you've been at the Bar for a number of years, but you're doing all this extra stuff, or perhaps new, innovative stuff. Do you think the law gives an opportunity to write blogs, to campaign and be effective in more than just litigation preparation and the Court? What's your view on that?

I was saying to you earlier that we are attracted to the Bar, to the legal profession, ultimately because we have a sense of injustice and justice, you know, fair play. And you do have and you encounter through being a lawyer certain issues that may be directly concerned with the law, or indirectly, where you feel that's not just, and we do have a platform to do something about it and to speak out about it. And you know, like it or not, if you're a QC people will sometimes listen when they wouldn't otherwise.

I totally agree, yes.

So, it's not necessarily that you have an obligation to use that, but if you wished to and you do feel there's something you want to speak out about, then you do have a platform.

Yes, absolutely. Well, can I ask you about some interesting developments coming up? The Ministry of Justice is consulting on extending fixed costs in some civil cases, and I wondered how significant this is and what the results are, and hopes are for you. Can you just share a bit about that?

Well, you don't want people to not listen anymore to this Podcast …

No, stay tuned, stay tuned!

… if I went into detail about it!

Just very quickly, now move on! [Laughter]

Funnily enough, I'll answer it this way. I've long thought that on the civil side of the Bar we charge at an hourly rate. I've long thought it's an incredibly inefficient way of charging for the work we do.

Absolutely.

And the reason I say that is of slightly self-interest because I'm quite quick! So, I'll do a set of work and I'll do it in four hours …

Crikey, I'm quite slow then! [Laughter]

So, my colleague might take ten hours. Why should he be paid for ten hours for doing a piece of work that takes me four hours and I only get paid for four hours? So, I'm actually quite attracted to the idea of a fixed fee for a fixed piece of work. Because I think the hourly rate can reward inefficiency.

Ah, interesting.

But anyway, that's a personal view about it. That said, of course, the devil is in the detail and it depends how the rates are set.

Yes

And they have to be set at a level where people, there are people who are willing to do the work for that rate, otherwise they'll give up and do something else.

Well, that's been a problem in the criminal sphere. We haven't got long enough for me to start talking about access to justice, but yes, okay, I see the logic.

Well, Sally, I think that you're a criminal lawyer, I'm a civil lawyer. When I started at the Bar we were much closer, the different areas of the profession, than we are now.

Absolutely.

Because it's financial. The profession has gone in two different directions and basically, this is a simplification, but civil lawyers are doing alright but criminal and family lawyers are not, particularly at the Bar, so you've been really squeezed because you depend entirely on public funding really for your rates.

Absolutely, which in turn means that those who are the weakest in society are not getting the best that they could, it's a denial.

Very arguably crime and family are the most important areas of law, but they're the most underfunded so far as the profession is concerned, so it's gone, if anything, in the wrong way. But that is how it's gone.

No, it has, and we must work hard to protect access to justice. Could I ask you some other questions now about diversity? Do you think the law has an issue with diversity?

I think that structurally the Bar doesn't have a problem with diversity in this sense, but the structure of the Bar – it's a very free, competitive market actually at the Bar. So, if someone had a clinical negligence case and went to a solicitor, that solicitor could choose from one of, you know, 200 barristers alongside me for that case. It's very competitive and there's a lot of free choice there. And structurally, women, ethnic minority barristers and so on can fit easily within that. It's competitive. If they're good enough they'll be chosen. I firmly believe that in terms of the structure. The problem that there's been is the age-old 'we'll select people who are like us'. So, when the Bar is recruiting, that's been a tendency over the years, and I've heard things that I won't repeat, you know, and embarrass anyone, you know, 'can you believe this person applied to be a barrister because …' and then an unacceptable comment. And it's just a tendency to say we want people like us because we know what it takes to be a good barrister because we've seen it, and it's people like us. So, you tend to sort of go to the same mould. That is changing and it will continue to change. But within the structure itself, it allows diversity. The structure itself can work. The other problem I see – in our Chambers we just do civil law. If you take an area like planning, is there a tendency amongst clients to look for a certain kind of barrister that they're familiar with, someone they can go out for a drink with after the case or whatever? This is something you just have to be aware of. There's a limit to what you can do at the Bar because we are serving clients, but it's something we need to be aware of, but it is a problem.

It is a problem, you're right, but this is an opportunity, particularly for those who are in leading positions, to develop the sort of environments we want to work in, and those who we're training and bringing behind us by way of pupils and trainees isn't it? So, you're absolutely right, the fact that you know you're aware that in certain areas people want certain types of people, but if we make it an effort not to have drinks after work, or golf days or football, whatever it is, that is rather more inclusive because, you know, the man who doesn't want to drink may not necessarily want to go cycling either. So, in terms of the way that we attract, and we have to be careful about the Bar because we are self-employed barristers working, so it's much easier for solicitors' firms to deal with some of those issues I suppose. Can we move on to deal with some of the other questions I've got? Is there one misconception that the public has about barristers?

[Laughter]

Or are there too many for you to comment on? Fat-cat lawyers, that sort of thing. And the reason I'm asking is, you know, what piece of advice would you give a young lawyer today, for example, who may have heard some of those misconceptions?

Yes, well, I think it is open to everyone, and anyone can succeed at the Bar, and a diverse range of people do succeed at the Bar. But there's still a perception that, you know, you say fat-cats, but, you know, the lawyer who sort of washes his hands after he's shaken hands with his client is a somewhat Dickensian approach, and we don't help ourselves in many ways. I mean, personally I voted to dispense with wigs for civil cases …

What?! What?!

I just don't understand why we wear those.

Fancy dress! [Laughter]

I can see an argument in crime to a little small extent, but, you know, there's that, dining in the Inns etc. It does create – Geoffrey Cox QC standing up with his booming voice in Parliament talking about his codpiece and so on, it does rather, you know it fits this image. It is unfortunate, because actually the Bar is quite diverse, there's all sorts of people on all sorts of levels of income working at the Bar, and of course the Bar should reflect the people that it serves as well.

Absolutely. And a piece of advice you would give a young lawyer today?

Resilience. I don't know if that's advice, it's just – trust yourself and trust your own judgment. You spend your life at the Bar surrounded by people telling you you're wrong. So, certainly in civil cases, if I bring a claim and I have a negotiation with, you know, a barrister on the other side, they're there to tell me I've got it wrong, and you do need to be resilient. You do need to have - I suppose it's a certain amount of self-confidence. You finish that case, you start the next one and you retain your confidence. You have to. So, I don't know how, you know, you can give advice to be resilient, I mean you have to learn resilience, especially when you start off. There'll be lots of confident people around and you'll think, you know, gosh, they're really good at this, and do I really belong here? I suppose that's another thing, is, I mean I'm, I've told you, the son of a solicitor, independent grammar school, Oxbridge, white male … Pale

[Laughter]

But you're not stale, no, no, no

All sorts of other things … [Laughter] … but I still feel an imposter. So, everyone feels that. Don't feel that you are unusual thinking, on occasion, 'I'm out of my depth', 'What right have I got to be here' – everyone feels that. So, you've got to learn resilience to get over that and just carry on. You're there for a reason and, you know, over time you will gain confidence and more resilience and then you learn to trust your own judgment, which is after all why you're doing the job, because people are asking you to exercise judgment.

Absolutely. I think you touched on imposter syndrome there actually in what you said, which is quite a common theme now, but getting over that imposter syndrome. What's your biggest concern about the future of your specific area of law?

So far as clinical negligence is concerned, the biggest threat really is the occasional perception, which is fostered I think from certain politicians in particular, that it's all a bit of a scam, that there's a compensation culture, that patients win cases and pay-outs, that it's like a lottery win for them. In fact, it is a means of compensating people for terrible things that have happened to them, which were not their fault but in fact were the fault of either individuals or, more often, a sort of systemic failing. So, the threat is just an undercutting of all of that for financial or political reasons or public perception, and I think that can cause great injustice to people. I'm not saying the system's perfect, but these claims are justified. In terms of the Bar generally, I think we have to think about how we organise ourselves in Chambers and so on. So, when I started out back in the day, we would be in Chambers more, we would talk to each other more, we would learn from each other a lot more. I mean you say going out for a drink or whatever, but we would …

Yes, we would.

… sitting round for a coffee, there was a chance to learn from each other just by sharing experiences …

Exactly, and discuss cases.

Yes. And that was invaluable. It was an informal kind of training programme.

Yes, it was.

But now, people tend to work from home more, we don't see each other as much, we don't talk about our cases as much in that way, so I think we've got to find ways of replacing what happened naturally. And I do think the Chambers model I hope will survive, that people won't just work from home by themselves, but we need to think very hard about how Chambers works and how it can serve barristers well, and ultimately therefore serve our clients well. So, I think that's the real challenge is how a modern Chambers should operate.

Yes, well that brings me nicely to wellbeing and how the profession needs to adapt. I mean, Women in the Law UK, as you know, we have several events and seminars and masterclasses which are designed partly for that. So, you know, for people who are working those long hours, briefs electronically, not seeing people, it's an opportunity. But I wondered if I can ask you this – the Northern Circuit where your Chambers and my Chambers are is in Manchester, the home of the Pankhursts. Do you think Manchester is still a radical city?

Yes, I think it does have a character. I'm a Yorkshireman actually.

Oh, are you? Oh, crikey, I wouldn't have let you through the door!

[Laughter]

Yes, I've been on the wrong side of the Pennines for 30 years! …

I'm joking, I'm joking!

… And I still get a tear in my eye when I go back to Yorkshire ..

Do you?

… and see the beautiful stone houses rather than the red brick and so on. Anyway, it is God's own county! But Manchester has a slight sort of, I'm trying to think of a polite expression, you know, sod you, radical …

Yes, radical!

Oh, radical [Laughter], thank you, attitude to it. It's a fantastic city and it's a great place to work and live, and it does have a slight edge to it, Manchester, which I hope it doesn't lose as it develops. More generally, the North as a whole I think has a different culture to London, and one that we really need, particularly in our profession, well, I say particularly across the board but it's something we can do something about in our profession, is to, you know, encourage people to realise that the North has a specific and distinct offering.

Absolutely.

Internationally as well as nationally. So, my Chambers joined the Northern Powerhouse Project. I mean, you know, all we had to do was sign up to that, but I hope at some point we'll really make something of that and work with business partners and professional partners who are also in that to try and do something about it.

Yes, well can we talk a bit more about that, because the Northern Powerhouse Partnership is huge, and I wondered if you could just tell us what is it and why did your set join, because there aren't any barristers Chambers in the Northern Powerhouse?

Well, we decided to join because I think there are sort of three goals that I would have out of it, or at least that we can harness, you know, the resources perhaps of the Northern Powerhouse. I just mean the other partners and so on, work together with them, I don't mean financially necessarily, but to try and achieve three goals. One is to encourage graduates to come North. So, you can have a fantastic career at the Bar and not be in London.

Yes, hear, hear!

I don't have a London address, professionally.

Don't you?!

No, I don't need it. There's good work in the North, and if we all go to London, or half go to London, why is that ever going to change? How are we going to encourage more work to come North?

Yes, good point.

So, we need the best and the brightest to come to the North and join the profession. We need to attract work internationally to North, that's the second thing. And the third thing we need, and probably the most ambitious – I'm not going to achieve this I'm sure – is devolution within the legal sector, because all the main institutions, nearly all in the law, are in London.

Yes, they are.

All the Inns of Court, Court of Appeal, Supreme Court, the Royal Courts of Justice, and this creates, I'm afraid, some injustices.

Yes, it does.

So, you know, I looked recently at QC appointments ...

Yes, so did I.

... and was troubled by the success rate for London barristers at that time compared with barristers outside London.

Absolutely, yes, and of course for women and minorities.

Yes, yes, but specifically in relation to the North, you see, a successful commercial barrister here will go to the local Court in Manchester, and we tend not to have High Court Judges doing the same value cases as his or her colleague in London who's in the Royal Courts of Justice in front of High Court Judges, fill their QC application form with High Court Judge Referees, it looks different, but they're doing the same sort of work. So, these are the sorts of things that do happen because we don't have a properly devolved legal system. Actually, most people live outside London, so they should be served by a Bar that is more balanced than it is at the moment. So, you know, this is another reason to join the Northern Powerhouse to see whether – it's not just about railway lines ...

No, which would help!

Well I don't think it would!

Don't you?! Have you tried to go to Leeds?!

Well that would, so HS3 would, but it seems a strange concept to generate the North to produce a faster trainline to go to London, to me.

Oh, I know, I totally agree. Without a significant reduction in the time, it seems absurd.

But, in the professions we should also be part of this, you know, generation of the North, or regeneration of the North, because the professions matter as well. It isn't just about infrastructure, it's about the people and serving the people, and the professions and business community as well.

Absolutely. I was thinking, Nigel, that Richard Pankhurst, we are in the home of the Pankhursts, which I know I say all the time, Emmeline Pankhurst and the city of the suffragettes. Richard Pankhurst was a barrister. Did he practice from your set, what is now Kings Chambers? I seem to remember a Judge who's now passed away, Mr Justice Gilbart Queen's Counsel, telling me this, that that was one of his early homes.

If Andrew Gilbart told you that, it'll be true.

Well, I'll check my emails, but I used to write to him when he was having his treatment for cancer and he had very little else to do, so he would write his long emails.

Great man, Andrew, and very sadly so, as you just mentioned, he died recently after being Head of my Chambers and then a High Court Judge. We also lost Frances Patterson, who was a great female barrister …

And a supporter of Women in the Law.

… and also Head of Chambers and then a High Court Judge. I was looking it up recently. She was the 92nd QC – have you seen this list of female QCs?

Yes, I have.

So, she was the 92nd in 1998.

Can you believe that? 1998 is not that long ago.

No, the most remarkable I thought was, so Rose Heilbron's number 2 on the list, although at the same time as Helena Normanton. So, that was 1949. Her daughter, 38 years later, Hilary Heilbron, was only the 29th QC. Isn't that remarkable?

I know. We think we're progressing but let's not forget it's taken some time and those who came before us.

Yes, well since your involvement in Women in the Law – when I joined, I joined another set, 18 St John Street not Kings at that time, it was a really big criminal set at the time, and Helen Grindrod was one of the QCs, but she was the 21st on the list of QCs to be appointed. She was a formidable, brilliant Silk.

In fact, she's mentioned in an interview by Lady Hale for Counsel magazine. I think she was a bit before my time, so that's good to know actually. You see, the Northern Circuit produces some of the best advocates aside from present company. [Laughter] History tells a story, you know, she said the same.

I know, and a lot of the first female High Court Judges as well came from the Northern Circuit.

Absolutely. Well, we are a true powerhouse and the Northern power women and the awards showcase those as well. Nigel, just a couple of final questions, if I may and if you can indulge me. Your favourite fictional lawyer, and a book that has changed you?

Horace Rumpole.

Yes, I wholly agree.

No hesitation, sorry, you probably hear that all the time.

No, no, it's one of the reasons I became a barrister.

Well, I was talking about when I had my first taste of life at the Bar in a mini pupillage in Leeds, and all the eccentric characters and the stories back from the criminal Courts, and it was just like Rumpole really. John Mortimer, obviously a barrister himself, but he just had that whole culture and atmosphere down to a T, and I loved that. The book – Dance to the Music of Time by Anthony Powell, which is – when I was about 19-20 I read back-to-back the 12 novels in that sequence, and I still sort of dip into it occasionally.

Do you?

One day I'll read them all again from beginning to end.

We might read them for our book club. That's why we ask that question.

Well, it's a long read because there are 12 of them. But, funnily enough, I mean there the narrator is a sort of calm, reasonable, sane person surrounded by - and married to a reasonable sane woman - but they're surrounded by all these eccentric, slightly insane and colourful characters, and I sometimes think I like to identify with the narrator a little bit. And I saw life at the Bar as a bit like that, that you are surrounded by these sometimes extraordinary individuals.

Yes, I suppose we are. And, have you got a quote or a motto that you live your life by that you can share? No swearing please, we've got peculiar associates and pupils. [Laughter]

Yes, well you're asking the wrong person because I sort of hate motivational quotes, I'm sorry.

What?!

Yes, I'll tell you one …

I'll share mine then, fine! [Laughter]

This'll play into the image of the Bar being elitist because it's in Latin! [Laughter] My school motto was "hoc age", right. What does that mean, Sally?

I don't know. My Latin 's very poor.

It's effectively, I suppose it's like the Nike, it's just do it! Do it – hoc age! And honestly, there's certainly times in my life where I've sort of thought, actually that was a good thing to learn, because my school was a bit like that and it's just don't worry about it, don't fret about it, don't over-reflect, don't, you know, just get on with the next thing and do it.

Absolutely.

So, actually, I suppose having said I don't believe in motivational quotes, there you are, that's one!

Yes, see, you do! Good job I asked. Well, I think it's a good, that's actually quite a good quote for Women in the Law actually. Whenever those moments come and we're all hesitant, should we apply for – whether it's Silk, should we apply for this, should we do that, should we, you know, progress, just do it!

Absolutely, and I really believe in that. I don't mind saying most of the things that have happened to me, in terms of appointments, have been second time. And people mustn't be afraid to put themselves forward. People are sometimes afraid because they think they will get rejected. It's not a rejection.

Well, it is.

But it's not rejecting you. You just didn't meet the criteria that time, or the person who is deciding it didn't think you did. Have another go. Why would you take your bat home and not have another go? So, yes, put yourself forward, you are good enough – you're good enough to have a go anyway – but this is where your organisation, Women in the Law and so on, really helps, because I think it encourages people to think, 'well, I've got support and encouragement to do it', and everyone at some point needs that, don't they?

Absolutely. Thank you so much Nigel Poole QC. Do visit his blog. Just search online for 'Learned Friend'.

Paulette Mastin

For this special episode of Talking Law, you'll hear from Paulette Mastin, Counsel in the capital markets practice at Linklaters in London, a Magic Circle firm, where she advises corporate trustees, other service providers and companies on a wide variety of capital market transactions, including Islamic finance. She is also the Chair of the Black Solicitors Network. I asked Paulette about her route into the law.

My journey or route into the law was somewhat unconventional.

Oh good, I like it already!

I actually started out in the field of investment banking, working the swaps and derivatives team of a foreign investment bank. I actually thought that financial markets was where I would establish and grow my career, and that was until an opportunity arose for me to assist with a House of Lords case involving a derivative contract that the bank had entered into with local authorities, and that experience really piqued my interest in terms of, you know, how to apply the law to transactions, and the implications when things go wrong. And, you know, with the law as I then discovered it, and in particular commercial law, I thought I'd found my vocation and calling, if you will, so I left the bank. This is sort of high stakes because it's not as though I had a training contract or a job to go to, or even knew very much about training contracts and the whole process, but I left the bank to pursue post graduate legal studies, eventually setting my sights on joining a commercial law firm. And, with a great deal of perseverance and determination and applications – there were many! – and a few interviews, I was fortunate enough to secure a training contract with leading global law firm, Linklaters, and I haven't looked back since!

Wow! And could I ask you, as a black woman, I can't imagine there were many lawyers who looked like you when you were starting out?

Yes, you're right, Sally. When I started out, some 20-plus years ago, there were very, very few, if any, in particular senior female role models in corporate law who looked like me, you know. And, for that reason, I really can't overstate the value of role models and, indeed, internal and external network support in navigating a legal career in a sort of demanding and dynamic environment like the City.

Absolutely. And did you have a mentor at all?

Not in my junior years, no. I would say that I've had some support and guidance in my career, but I would definitely have benefited early on from having senior mentorship. Not least because of, you know, the opportunity to share and learn from others, you know, those who have navigated the same path, and it's for that reason that I have to commend the work that you do, Sally, with founding and leading Women in the Law, providing career support to countless women in the profession, and this is a really useful resource, particularly for those who are starting out.

Thank you. I was wondering actually, just on that point, you were attracted to the financial world, but again a very male-dominated environment. Were there times that you felt like your voice wasn't being heard?

Well, yes, I mean, you know, why was I attracted to the financial world? I would say from a young age I've always been fascinated by how the City works, you know, the financial systems, the nuts and bolts that drive the economy, and indeed the global economy, and that was the initial attraction then. Then I got the bug for practising law and now I enjoy both worlds as a finance lawyer and, you know, I do hear what you say, it is a male-dominated environment but that doesn't make it any —

Yes, the perception -

Yes, absolutely, you know, but that doesn't make it any less interesting or attractive, and the financial markets and the practice area into which I qualified, which is capital markets, has become more diverse over the years but, dare I say it, it still has some way to go in terms of female representation in senior roles. And, you know, in terms of having my voice heard or feeling as though my voice isn't heard, I mean, as you know Sally, I've been championing and advocating for greater diversity in the profession for some ten years or more, and in that, you know, with a particular focus on ethnic diversity, and as Chair and now Co-Sponsor of Linklaters BAME network we had achieved a number of successes with the network, certainly in terms of recruitment, but we really struggled with, you know, internal traction and engagement with senior management on issues of race and ethnicity. It seems that the ethnicity strand was not really a priority and the focus was more on social mobility, as somehow, you know, there was a conflation of the two strands, ethnicity and social mobility. No-one really wanted to talk about race, and at that time I felt that my voice on this issue wasn't being heard and, you know, perseverance of course is the key, which is sort of like my second name, and helped by some really heavyweight reports on race in the workplace, including, you know, the Race Disparity Audit which was a Government research piece, and the McGregor Smith Review, and thankfully, as I'm sure you've observed, race is now firmly on the diversity agenda, certainly at our firm, and we're now seeing positive change, slowly, and most recently with the launch at Linklaters of a BAME Talent Development Programme.

Which is absolutely fantastic. Just before we move on to find out more about the Black Solicitors Network and diversity league tables, I understand that many years ago you were specially advised that you would never make the grade, that you are a black woman. I mean, how did you react to that? I know how I would react, but maybe our reactions may be slightly different. I mean, do you think you had to work differently or think differently to your male-wide colleagues when that comment and observation advice came, which is appalling.

Yes, Sally, I think that certainly sums it up really. It was appalling, but I was disappointed really to hear that this was said of my dream and my ambition to pursue a legal career, and in particular in the City. The individual in question had made this remark to a colleague of mine, not thinking that the colleague would tell me ...

They never do.

Yes - and he'd said, he was a lawyer himself as well, that there were two reasons why I, Paulette, wouldn't make it or would seriously struggle to do so. One, she's female, and, two, she's black, but you know I don't know about you, Sally, but I'm negatively motivated. [Laughter] You know, if you say I can't do something, then it becomes my determination to prove that statement, and in this case this individual, wrong.

Absolutely.

To really work hard and just strive to be the best that I could be against even those odds.

Yes.

And, you know, thankfully a year later I was offered and accepted a training contract with Linklaters, and the rest is history.

Absolutely. So, tell us now then about Black Solicitors Network. Tell us a bit more about the work of the Black Solicitors Network and your involvement because you are Chair.

Yes, that's right. So, the Black Solicitors Network, which I've Chaired just for the past two years, was founded over 20 years ago and is committed to the recruitment, retention and progression of black lawyers right across England and Wales, and I became a member in 2005 and, you know, it took me a while, I qualified in 1997!

I did want to comment, but, yes. [Laughter]

I didn't have a mentor as such and was just feeling my way around the system actually, but I discovered BSN in 2005, and then in 2008 I led an initiative to create the City branch of the Black Solicitors Network. This initiative was conceived in the midst of a challenging economic environment. As you can remember, the financial crisis, there were widespread redundancies and we were acutely aware of the challenges facing City lawyers, in particular BAME lawyers, so there was no question that a support network of this nature was needed. BSN City group's core mission is to focus on the needs of and issues affecting black corporate and commercial lawyers practising in and around the City and Canary Wharf. And the group has grown exponentially since it started, from about 40 people, including myself, a few mates and others that we reached out to, to around 400.

And you're in Manchester as well, aren't you?

Yes, we are, but that's the BSN on a sort of national level. The BSN membership is in the region of about 4,000 at the moment and, you know, we have region-specific groups. As you know, Manchester has been established for some years now and it was re-launched in 2016. Carl Blackburn is the Chair there, and I know, Sally, you've been extremely supportive and we really do appreciate your help and support in that region, and also we have BSN Midlands which is fairly active, and we're looking to re-energise the efforts there in Birmingham. And of course, you know, we have BSN South. So, you know, it's a national network with an extensive platform of initiatives and events supporting those looking to enter the profession and those looking to progress within it.

And so, do you think that, well two questions really, do you think things have improved since its formation, and do you think that BSN is still needed in the same way as, you know, one asks all the time. Are gender-specific organisations like Women in the Law UK and others still needed?

So, in response to your question ' have things improved in the 20-plus years since BSN started?' – yes, I think things have improved. The proportion of BAME, black, Asian and minority ethnic individuals entering the legal profession has almost doubled in ten years. In 2006 around 10% of the trainee cohort were BAME individuals, and in 2016, some ten years later, BAME individuals accounted for 20% of trainee solicitors. I think this is commendable and it can actually be described as representative of the proportion of BAME comprised within the UK population. Of course, you know, when you look at the City it's more diverse, but certainly the wider UK I think BAME individuals make up some 14% or so of the population, so that is commendable progress. To your point or question as to whether networks such as the Black Solicitors Network is needed, I would say yes, several times over. Retention and progression for BAME lawyers remains a critical issue, and it's the same for gender I'm sure, and so in stark contrast to the number of BAME candidates entering the profession is the representation at the top, at the partner level, and what BSN's diversity league table has revealed in its survey is that the levels of attrition for BAME as we move up the professional ladder are worryingly high. I actually mean that only 8% of partners are BAME and, you know, in the ten-year period of our study, the diversity league table, progress at the top has been painstakingly low, from 3% in 2006 to just 8%, and those of African and African-Caribbean origin comprise just 1% of partners in large law firms, and that's the current state of play with senior BAME representation. And the challenge here is that we have a massively leaky pipeline which leads to a dearth of BAME senior leaders.

Yes, which is worrying. So, yes, we are still needed. Now, I want to ask you about what advice you would give a young lawyer today perhaps, and then specifically advice on longevity and progression in the law. Have you got any very quick tips?

This is probably more in the vein of advice I would give to my younger self.

Yes, fantastic. We all need that, God I do! [Laughter]

I would stress the importance of taking responsibility for your own development. You know, I thought I had worked hard at securing a training contract, and that provided I applied myself and worked hard, you know, head down, I would climb the greasy career pole. Progression would just happen naturally. Well, that's what I thought, and indeed that was the work ethic that my parents drummed into me, but I have come to realise that progression is driven by several factors. Some individuals are fortunate to be in the right place at the right time, they have been prepared and highly favoured and so they're promoted. And then there's the rest of us.

Yes.

The hard truth for me was the need to recognise and understand what it takes to drive your career forwards, and I've learned that you need hard technical skills to land the job, but you need soft skills to progress your career, seeking out those stretch assignments, you know client and business development business opportunities, networking internally and externally. That is how you build career capital, and that's a message to my younger self and to the junior lawyers coming through. And, in terms of advice for longevity, one might say 'well, you know, I put one foot in front of the other and hoped for the best' but, seriously, in addition to the advice to my younger self, I mean I have three maxims that have driven me in my career thus far, you know in terms of my craft, getting your profile out there and professional relationships. It's be committed, be consistent and be courageous.

Excellent! I'm going to remember that. That's fantastic advice. And, for you, have you maintained a work life balance? You work hard, you're in the City, you're in a sector that is very busy and complicated. Because, as all we women, you know, we struggle to try and find that. I just wondered if you could share with us some of your sort of wellbeing.

Yes, well it's not easy, as you rightly point out, Sally, as the working environment is quite demanding. I have worked flexibly by working from home one day a week for a number of years, which helps me to connect with my family and helps me maintain some form of equilibrium in my life. I also play tennis – badly – at the weekend, as a means of escapism from the pressure of work.

Which is really, really good. Now, I love these questions I always ask. I want to find out a bit more about your favourite fictional lawyer, and then I want to find out about your favourite book, and then maybe a quote that you live by. So, in that order.

Okay.

Who's your favourite fictional lawyer? Mine's Rumpole. I have several now actually.

Really?

Yes, I've got several. The more I do these Podcasts I'm like 'oh, why didn't I think about that!' Some people say Elle Woods from Legally Blonde …

Oh, wow, okay.

But I wondered if you could share.

Yes, so this is funny. So, favourite fictional character. Jessica Pearson?

Ah, I like it!

Managing Partner in the law firm featured in Suits. I don't know if you've ever watched that?

I have, mainly because my husband's a huge fan. [Laughter] But I've grown to love it.

So, it's the series with Meghan Markle. So, Jessica Pearson is formidable. She's strong, she's talented and she's gorgeous. So, yes, she's one of my favourites. My second favourite is a bit cookie. It's Ally McBeal. Am I allowed to have two?

We'll let you off. So long as you answer the last two questions. [Laughter]

Ally McBeal, she's one of my favourites. It's a comedy-drama TV series and she's quite crazy and she has these random hallucinations at work. Like the time where she just visualised a funny dancing baby on a meeting room table. In a meeting, you know, you close your eyes for a few seconds and imagine the sort of dancing baby on the table, it just helps you to mellow. So, yes.

Fantastic. Gosh, we're all laughing in the studio here, including my wonderful producer, Sam Walker. She's trying to contain her laughter. And have you got a book that's changed you?

So, there was a book that I read some time ago called 'Who Moved My Cheese?' I don't know if you've heard of it.

I haven't. Sam's nodding. I'm writing it down to read because it just sounds great.

Yes, so it's called 'Who Moved My Cheese?' and it's by Spencer Johnson. And cheese is a metaphor for what you want to have in your life. What will make you happy and, of course, when circumstances take it away – you imagine that you're a little mouse and that cheese, you know, these things that you want in your life, have been taken away. Different people deal with that change in different ways. And this book actually, a fairly short book and quite funny in places, it's actually enabled me to be a bit more open-minded and adaptable in dealing with changing times, so yes, I'd recommend it as a read.

Fantastic. I love that. I'm going to be straight on there. There'll be a Women in the Law Book Club soon. So, finally, have you got a quote that you live your life by, or a meaningful one that perhaps you could share with us?

Well, one that I have sort of stuck on my desk, and I can't remember who the quote is by, but it says something like 'Real joy comes from a grateful heart'. So, it just prompts you to, when things are not going according to plan or you're beset with challenges, just take a moment to just assess what you have and realise, you know, that that actually is something that can bring you real joy. You know, what you've achieved, what you've overcome, family, and that can bring you joy just, you know, having that sense of gratitude about what you have and where you are.

Absolutely. Thank you so much to Paulette Mastin. You can find out more about her work at www.linklaters.com, and more about the Black Solicitors Network (BSN) at www.blacksolicitorsnetwork.co.uk.

Helen Pankhurst

This month, activist and author, Helen Pankhurst, talks about the legacy of her surname and how the law still needs to work harder for women. Helen is an activist, an author, granddaughter of Sylvia, and great-granddaughter of Emmeline. She is currently a senior advisor of relief agency, Care International, working across the UK and Ethiopia where she was brought up. I asked Helen how much the legacy of her surname led her to her career.

The legacy was really important, but I would say it was only half the story. The other half was being brought up in Ethiopia and seeing the reality across two different cultures of how women are treated and the difference between their lives and the drudgery and the difficulties, and yet the way women are often considered to be less important, less powerful, less strong. So, it was the contradictions within society and the comparison across societies that was as important to me as the surname in terms of my own journey.

Yes, absolutely. So, Helen, you moved to the UK at 12 years of age. Did you expect things to be different in the UK?

From what they were like in Ethiopia?

Yes.

I think I was always aware of the differences. We used to come every summer, so I'd seen the UK and I'd lived in Ethiopia. But, right throughout I think my sense has been continuity and change, differences and similarities, you know. So, for every time you think something is different in a particular country, you see echoes of similarity, and I think I've felt that right throughout and linked to that ideas of progress and then retrenchment. So, sometimes you think a particular problem is resolved and then, guess what, it comes back, and you realise that the problem is still there!

Yes, and what do you say to people who argue that women have parity now? We're in 2019. Do you think that women have parity?

I think you have to be blind to think that women have parity, and I'm talking about not just numeric parity but a sense of how you're valued and your sense of self, and the epitome of this has been the research that I've done looking at how far we've got over the last 100 years and the book that I've written called "Deeds Not Words – A story of women's rights then and now".

A fantastic book.

Thank you! And when you divide it up and you look at what do we feel about the political context and you say, okay, how can we score that? Do we score that as parity? Have we got there? Are we equal? And you say, no, of course not. Then you look at issues of economic equality and you say, well, have we got that in terms of women's jobs, in terms of wealth? Of course not. What about in terms of society and social attitudes? What about women's own sense of self? What about issues like surnames? What surnames do we take? What about issues of violence against women? As soon as you break it down it's very, very difficult to say, no problem.

Tell us about the Pankhurst Fawcett Scorecard which you've just launched here, in Manchester especially.

So, one of the things I'm particularly excited about at the moment is the sense that actually you can be involved in activism at different levels. You can be involved in it internationally; you can be involved in it locally. And Manchester, and in particular Greater Manchester with its strong links to the suffragettes, it's the home, it's the starting point of where Emmeline formed what became known as the suffragette movement. There is the sense here of radicalism. There is a sense of wanting to do something for women, being aware of the need to continue to address women's issues. So, a bunch of us formed something called GM4Women2018 – Greater Manchester For Women 2028 - with the idea that between now and 2028 we really want to see change in terms of gender equality. And one of the initiatives, a starting point, is to say, well, what is the situation like in

Greater Manchester? How can we score it? What do we think the data is telling us? And, as a group of us across different backgrounds, lawyers, politicians, civil society, people in finance, people in many different backgrounds, education, we came together and looked at the data and ended up with ten indicators, five key issues – so, education, work, safety, culture, employment. And we have found we've got, not ideal indicators but some indicators, and the Fawcett Pankhurst Scorecard is bringing together those two iconic names around feminism. What we're saying is, this is the data at the moment, and it's showing incredible gaps still, and once a year we will continue to look at whether we're reducing the difficulties, whether we're getting there, or whether in fact some areas of these aspects are getting worse. And meanwhile, part of the initiative is not just to have these scorecards at the Greater Manchester level, but to also encourage people and companies to pledge with their own data. So, companies saying well, this is the situation we have now, for example in terms of gender pay gap reporting, or it might be some other indicator, and we commit to actually trying to make things better and to reporting once a year on the data. So, the Fawcett Pankhurst Scorecard is at the overall level but we're also encouraging individuals and companies in particular to say we can engage in this, we can have our own data as well.

Fantastic. And, as you know, we're part of the Scorecard so we support it, Women in the Law, wholeheartedly. Tell us about the Care International's Women's March, the march for women which carried out the theme of Women in the Law UK. I was there, so I don't want to just tell people, I want you to tell us really about why Care International has been encouraging that march, because it was awesome. What is it and why was the theme Women in the Law?

So, March for Women has been going on now for about seven years and we've picked up different themes each time. Last year it was the centenary of women getting the right to vote, some women, and also women being able to stand as MPs. This year it's the centenary of women in the law, the Sexual Discrimination (Removal) Act, so it felt like a critical moment to celebrate, to look at how far we'd got, to look at how far we still need to go. And right now, beyond that issue of the centenary, there is a sense, I think a global sense, that workplace harassment is the issue - Time's Up, Me Too - so many countries now realising that that isn't just a problem that happens in Hollywood or in the film industry, that it is something happening in every single industry around the world. And a number of different organisations, including the ILO, the International Labour Organisation, is looking at whether right now we can seize the moment and actually do something about it.

And, the Head of the Supreme Court, Lady Hale, spoke at the march this year. Is that right, Helen?

Yes, that's right, and it was lovely having her there, you know, we have a woman at the Head of the Supreme Court which is absolutely wonderful. We also had women who challenge the law, so people like Nicola Thorp who had challenged the issue about having to wear high-heeled shoes as an employee, Leyla Hussain talking about FGM, Muslim Women's Network, a representative talking about the fact that women who were escaping from having been taken abroad without their will in order to be forced into marriage had to pay for the flight back, so a number of women who are challenging the law. So, it was lovely to have both lawyers and people who are outside the law actually challenging the law.

And it showed the power of individuals, because of course we had the lady - is it Gina Martin? - the up-skirting legislation which is now in. So, that was very good, but do you think the law supports women enough or there's a need to be new legislation, or does perhaps existing legislation need to be implemented better? What are your views on that?

So, I think the law does need to continue to be more sensitive to women's interests. It is still man-made, the whole structure of it. If you look at the numbers, so in the North West, so in this area, only 29% of Court Judge appointments are of women. So, we still have a way to go in terms of ensuring equal representation and therefore a legal system that's more likely to take women's interests into account. It doesn't mean to say that men will not do so, but surely a more diverse – not just in terms of gender – but a more diverse and representative legal system is more likely to reflect the interests of people in the round. So, I still think we have a lot to do. There's then the question of laws that are not implemented, and both in the

UK and globally you here often that there are laws, it's in the application of them that we have again many, many problems.

Absolutely. Do you think that women are currently treated equally to men in the eyes of the law?

I think the law still expects lawyers to be men and is biased in terms of not understanding women's concerns, women's interests. That's not to say that it's always the case, but I think then there have been a number of studies looking at how again, globally, whether the law treats men and women equally, and the UK is not one of the six countries which were identified as doing just that.

No. In your view, what does the profession need to do to ensure it reflects the whole of society, not just gender – race, social mobility, those from different socio-economic backgrounds and diversity of thought. Have you got any thought on what the profession, what my profession, our profession, need to do?

So, I think the first thing is being reflective and understanding the privileges and the vulnerabilities that individuals have who are represented in the law, and those who are being represented by the law. And the more reflection and sensitivity to difference we have, I think the truer the justice will be, the more equal, the more relevant, the more appropriate the decisions made.

As we've discussed, it's 100 years since women were given the right to practice law. What advice would you give young women in the law who want to go about implementing change?

So, there are many ways I could answer that, but the first point would be that as individuals, as women, we can affect change three ways. Firstly, in our own sense, in our own spaces, as women, as individuals, the way we parent, the way we live our lives, the choices that we make, the day-to-day minutiae of how we live and whether we resist the dominant story of our roles as secondary, or whether we are just too tired and we just accept, or we accept the pinkification of the toys and the clothes that we buy our kids, our girls, and the blueification, etc. There are so many examples, you know, the cultural spaces that we occupy, the books that we buy, the music that we listen to. To what extent do we enforce, reinforce traditions and norms, or to what extent do we say actually let's challenge women being subordinate in all of this. As a very small example, Netflix has a whole category of films directed by women, so I just watch those at the moment, and they're brilliant! Otherwise, you're just perpetuating what gets the most visibility.

Absolutely, absolutely. Be careful, we'll end up in a Women in The Law Film Club next. [Laughter] We've got a book club, theatre club, now we're heading towards film club!

And the second one is, it's by lots of people, lots of women standing up, demanding change, that you change social norms, and that's important. And the third one is through work, through structural or institutional change, and, as lawyers, you have incredible power. I mean, Emmeline used to talk about wanting women to be law makers not law breakers so, as lawyers, women have that chance, and the question is, do they use that power with a feminist perspective, or not? And, hopefully, they use it with a feminist perspective and also for broader social change.

Absolutely. What role do you think men have?

So, men have a critical role in all of this. We can't change the whole of the world with just half the population, we have to ensure that the other half is totally engaged, and it's a really tricky one, because as soon as you bring men into a space where you're talking primarily about feminism, men feel very uncomfortable. And that's right. And they have to feel uncomfortable because quite frankly women know that sense of discomfort so well, and it's important that men, for once, feel that. Having felt uncomfortable, I think it's then really, really important that they feel included and we, as women feminists, find ways to include men, as I've said, because nothing is going to change unless they are involved. After all, they are father figures, they are husbands, they are partners at home let alone in the workspace. So, men, as feminists, is critical going forward. Quite how we do that I think is a really difficult process, but it is happening, and we need to encourage it.

I wholly agree. That's why we allow men in our network. 2028 marks the centenary of equal franchise. I just wondered what change within wider society do you still think we can inspire in the next nine years?

So, I'm really hanging on to this idea that we can do it. So, we can do it, we've got until 2028, that's a large amount of time, and if individually and if collectively and if society as a whole says 'come on', it's going to be on us. You know, in 2028 people will be saying 'what did you do?', and if we all hold onto that and if we all make as much noise, as much change as we can, I'm hoping that right across the board, you know, in terms of the political structure, in terms of the legal structure, in terms of workplaces, in terms of society's cultural values, in terms of violence against women, right across the board, that we will have a more diverse and more equal society. A richer society for all of that. It'll only happen if we all take responsibility.

Absolutely. You're so right, you're so right. I have to avoid saying that. Now, I want to ask you a couple of other things if I may? You're really a very good author, you've written several books, especially Deeds Not Words, which I love, and I wondered what was one of your favourite books?

So, right now I'm reading a whole set of books because I am one of the judges for the Orwell Prize of political writing, and I can't tell you which books I'm reading because that's not out there yet! But the reason I'm mentioning it is that I might not have picked up a number of books that are in that list because instinctively I go for certain types of books. I go for feminist books, I go for international books, you know, I've got a default mechanism, a default line, as we all have. And the fascinating thing about this has been it's encouraged me to read a whole set of books that I wouldn't have normally read, well beyond my comfort zone, and I think what I would encourage people to do is to do just that. You know, pick up books that you wouldn't normally read because you can learn so much by doing it.

So, you've basically just got tons of books that are your favourites! [Laughter] And, do you have an inspiring quote that you live your life by, or one that you tell your daughter? I met your wonderful daughter. Do you have a quote that you can share with us?

I do. I've got a favourite quote and I'm not even sure who initiated it, but I live by it, and it's 'fun and purpose'. It's the idea that you combine doing something that's meaningful, but you do it with fun and verve, and that's what life should be about.

A huge thank you to Helen Pankhurst for her time. As I mentioned, Helen spoke at the Women in the Law UK annual dinner in March this year, where guests also heard a song which was specially commissioned to celebrate the 100 year anniversary since women were allowed to practice law, and I wanted to give you the chance to hear it. Here's singer-songwriter, Claire Mooney.

Song plays (Lyrics below)

A hundred years ago just after some women got the vote
There was another change in legislation
At last the time had come when sisters of note
Could practice law all around the nation.

It takes a fearless spirit to cross new frontiers
To make a place for women to excel
Where would we be without these bold pioneers
Who within the law were ready to rebel?

To each and every one
Who laid the foundations for all the years to come
Lawyers then Judges too
From the bottom of our hearts, we thank you.

Bebbs versus The Law Society found women were not persons
Carrie Morrison, Mary Pickup, Maud Crofts, Mary Sykes
Took great strides against the prejudice that cursed them
To work in the law and promote equal rights.

Ivy Williams, the first woman called to the English Bar
Helena Normanton took the first High Court case
Be proud to know that since those days your sisters have come far
As we practice law with brilliance and with grace.

To each and every one
Who laid the foundations for all the years to come
Lawyers then Judges too
From the bottom of our hearts, we thank you.

All QCs and Judges who pushed each boundary
For the benefit of all who share your gender
First Justice as the Supreme Court and President a plea
Let's give our heartfelt thanks to Brenda

So, raise a glass, remember, all the things we've done
Don't forget, each and every day
All our brave sisters and all the battles won
Women in the Law UK.

To each and every one
Who laid the foundations for all the years to come
Lawyers and Judges too
Clerks of the Court, thanks are overdue
Reporters, admin staff for all you do

Sally Penni and all speakers for your overview
From the bottom of our hearts, we thank you.

(Claire Mooney, March 2019)

Thank you so much, the brilliant singer-songwriter Claire Mooney, for that specially commissioned track.

Gary McIndoe

For this special episode of Talking Law, you'll hear from Gary McIndoe, an immigration solicitor and founder of Latitude Law, a firm which specialises in business immigration and refugee human rights. Gary is also Chair of the Electronic Immigration Network, and also a trustee of human rights charity, RAPAR. I asked Gary what specifically attracted him to this area of the law.

So, I got really rubbish A levels and I started a degree in linguistics that eventually I realised I didn't want to do, so I dropped out and I got a job and I moved away from Manchester down to Croydon to work for the Home Office in fact.

Oh, I didn't know that!

And that is how it started really. So, I worked there for three years, did a bit of travelling after that, and then went back to study law. I graduated and I looked to immigration law because it's kind of what I'd been working in and I had some experience, so I was more likely to get a job in that area, and to be honest, it's not been a bad area to specialise in. It's interesting, you know, to do stuff like judicial review. I think a lot of lawyers don't get the opportunity to do that kind of litigation, and obviously there's a big human rights element, so I was kind of lucky really.

Yes. Now, you came back to the North then after London. Were you ever worried that your career might not flourish in the North?

I didn't really think about it to be honest. I was in the same situation that a lot of law students are in. I didn't have contacts, you didn't know lawyers, and I had to really work hard to get a training contract. I ended up getting one in Newcastle-upon-Tyne …

Oh, did you?

… and I was up there for a while.

I was going to say, how was that?

It was pretty cold, [Laughter] but it was really good training. I worked at David Gray & Co, which is a good multi-discipline practice, again, a good human rights background, and I qualified back in Manchester then and I – it didn't really occur to me to go back to London, event though I'd kind of lived, you know, lived and studied there for about eight years.

Wow! And can I ask you about this sort of North/South divide in law when it comes to career opportunities and financial success. Do you think there is one?

I mean I'm sure there is in terms of financial reward, but I don't see that, you know, there's a big difference in the substance of the work we do. I think, I suppose I notice it when we're instructing Counsel, because we work in quite a specialist area, it can be a bit tricky, you know, to get people locally. There are Chambers that do, including yours Sally, that do immigration work, but you know you want someone at short notice, you've got the big sets like Garden Court in London who, you know, they've got a good range, so we do tend to instruct out down there quite a bit, but I don't think, I mean I think Manchester's a great city to practice in.

Absolutely, absolutely. Interestingly, you mentioned travelling before when you've been all over the world, Brazil, New Zealand, Indonesia, Israel, Burma, India, do you think that has actually impacted your view on immigration law here in the UK, and your interests in human rights?

I think so. I think what it's going to help me with primarily is, kind of, improving my geography. [Laughter] I think what it also teaches you is to be a bit more resilient, sort of self-sufficient. So, definitely helpful from that point of view. I would definitely encourage, well, not just lawyers and you know prospective lawyers, I would encourage anybody to do it really. I think it, it kind of helped me to get into a job, because I did that before I got my training contract. It gives you something to talk about and some, you know, rather than just going straight from University, Law School, straight into a training contract.

Absolutely. Now, so, talking about the job, can you remember a case that's changed your career?

I was thinking about this. I would probably pick a case that I've been involved in on and off for probably about 12 years now on behalf of various family members. The case involves a Rwandan family, and the mum and dad they're accused of involvement in the genocide in the 1990s, and it's been a mixture of asylum and extradition. I mean I'm not an extradition specialist, but at my previous firm we worked closely with a criminal team there who were handling the extradition matter. And I think what it really taught me was the value of solid research and case preparation. I think, you know, we put a hell of a lot of resource into that case and ended up with a good result. It didn't stop the Rwandan Government coming back and having another go at extradition, but again that was successfully challenged. It's reached the point now I'm acting for the children. You know, there are some children who are now adults, you know, and they require separate representation. So, it's kind of the case that keeps on giving really.

Wow! Yes, really, absolutely. Well, and actually impacting people's lives in a positive way. So, I really wanted to ask you about whether you think the legal sector has an issue with diversity, and if there are any specific areas worse than others, if you like. You know. We're, I suppose our concern is gender, because we're called Women in the Law, but actually we have lots of male members and male champions, but do you think there are other areas? You know, there are very few BAME practitioners, social mobility is still an issue. How can we rectify some of these?

Yes, I think that what you've got is quite a significant divide in the legal profession between those with contacts and, as I said earlier, I'm not, I wasn't one of those people you know, from a white, relatively working class background, and you know I didn't have any kind of the leg-ups available to certain people who might then end up in larger firms. And I think how it impacts, or how I see it impacting on black and minority ethnic practitioners, or potential practitioners is they are often pushed towards working for smaller firms, and I think they're pushed towards starting on their own earlier, you know, because they're being denied kind of career opportunities, and I think that kind of stores up problems for some people, and I think those smaller practices they suffer from lack of supervision, lack of systems perhaps, lack of resource, they are far more likely to get in bother with the regulators than larger businesses. And I think that comes back to the, you know the kind of denial of opportunities early on in people's careers really.

Yes, in the same way as, you know, women who have suffered some form of discrimination on grounds of pregnancy or so on, then set up on their own, and then trying to build, rather than the large organisations supporting and nurturing those talents.

And it's hard, I think, I mean I set up my own practice, you know, 11 years ago. I, along with the rest of the immigration department at Robert Lizar's in Manchester, we were made redundant basically. The firm decided they didn't want to be involved in immigration work anymore, and I had a big decision to make then. I could have applied around, you know, looked at working for another firm, but you know we decided, as a group, so there's me, one other solicitor and a couple of admin people, you know we decided to kind of go it on our own, and that was a, it was a daunting time for, well for me because I kind of borrowed the money to start things off, you know, to rent an office and buy a computer and stuff like that, but I mean I'm really glad I did it but I see the pitfalls, I can see the dangers, you know. I mean, I was probably lucky really, we had an SRA inspection, within probably 18 months of setting up …

Wow - I'm not sure if that's wow in a positive way! [Laughter]

… and I think it was, it was quite helpful. [Laughter]

Yes, now you reflect on it.

Yes, reflecting on it, exactly right, yes.

So, I suppose that probably set the grounds as to how you wanted your workplace to be really, because I know you're very keen on wellbeing, which is something I'm going to ask you about. You know, what you do for wellbeing and how you are trying to monitor the wellbeing of the staff, the solicitors in your firm because, you know, you have yoga and stuff like that. What do you do for your wellbeing, and what do you do for theirs really?

Yes, we do try to create a good office environment. We've just moved to St James's on Oxford Street in Manchester. It's much larger, we've basically tripled our floor space.

Wow!

We've got everybody on the same floor, which is a really positive move. We've got much better meeting space and what we've done over the years as well is kind of promote a collegiate atmosphere in the firm really. We have staff a conference every year, and the last few years we've been lucky enough to be able to take everyone abroad, so we've been to Spain a couple of times, we were in Morocco a few weeks ago, and we take everybody. You know, we take from the senior solicitors down to the admin team and the reception team. Everybody comes with us, and I think it's really helpful ...

Brilliant!

... and we also take, we have a former employee who decided she doesn't want to be a lawyer and she's now a mindfulness practitioner, and we took her along as well and she did sessions with us while we were all in Marrakesh.

Fantastic!

Now, I think yes, it's a relatively small thing, it's for a few days in a year isn't it? But, it's kind of a nice focus for the practice and it kind of informs how we, you know, how we run the place for the rest of the year.

Yes, and building the team. Yes, interesting, interesting. So, what do you think is one of the biggest misconceptions that the public has about lawyers?

One of the biggest misconceptions I think would be that the legal profession is a homogenous bunch of people. The differences are not between barristers and solicitors, they're between the corporate world and the kind of personal/private client Legal Aid aspect of law. Working in a law centre, you know, you've got such a gulf between people who work in those two you know very different sectors, and I think the whole idea that lawyers make a load of money is – it still exists in the public eye I think, and you know clearly it's completely, completely wrong, you know, when Counsel's doing work on graduated fees on …

£46.50

… you know, hearings, it's worse than driving a taxi isn't it?

Yes, yes, absolutely. So, what piece of advice would you give a young lawyer today?

I think the advice I give would be as well as being a lawyer you need to be a business person as well, you need a commercial mind. And that applies, I think, even if you're starting out in a law centre, you know, that law centre still has to survive economically, you know, it has to think about fundraising and it has to be viable, because you don't get the same kind of local authority grants that I had when I was running a law centre in North Manchester.

Absolutely, absolutely, and that's very good advice actually, whether for solicitors or barristers, to have a commercial view. So, what's your concern? What's your biggest concern about the future of your specific area of the law?

I think that the challenges that are presented by the UK leaving the EU, or potentially doing so, are a big issue for us.

So, Brexit.

Yes, I meet lots of people who say, "oh this is going to be great for you, isn't it?". And I say, "Well, you might think that, but what we've noticed over the last couple of years is that the flow of people, you know, moving into the UK has gone down, you know, there are not so many people interested in coming to live and work here, whether they're from the EU or from elsewhere to be honest.

Yes, yes.

There's no, there's been no evidence that the Government's going to make life easier for non-EU migrants as well. I think that was probably a bit of a misconception at the beginning, you know, a lot of people who are pro-Brexit were talking about it creating a more benign environment for, you know, the Indian sub-continent or African visa applicants, but I don't see that that's going to happen. And I think, you know, for the corporate clients we represent, while the, you know, the challenges are there, and you might think that would increase the amount of work we get from them, what's actually happening is – especially with the Brexit uncertainty – people just aren't making decisions, people are just putting things on hold, and we've definitely seen a slowdown in the last, well I suppose in the last quarter of last year, first quarter of 2019.

Interesting, because the Bank of England says the same thing about economic growth, so it is all linked. Now, Gary, you're dealing with some of the most vulnerable people in society and sometimes going through very difficult times, how do you ensure your wellbeing?

Cycling's a big thing for me, yes. I was in Wales a couple of weeks ago and I got out early in the morning. I did 70 kilometres around the reservoir and up some hills and down some hills, and it was, it's just amazing, you know, you can just lose yourself. You're struggling up inclines and there's no room in your head for anything else really, you know, it's a good way to get away, I run a bit - and I've to parent teenage kids [Laughter] – that takes your mind off things! It's not exactly a stressbuster but it kind of puts work stresses into perspective.

Yes, absolutely. Now, one of your roles is that you're a trustee of the human rights charity, RAPAR. Why is that role important to you?

I came across RAPAR through Dr Rhetta Moran who was an academic, she was working at Salford University at the time – this was quite a few years ago. RAPAR's about what the academics call action research. So, it's about involving the individuals in active work on their own behalf, so you're not just treating them as subjects – the academics are not just treating them as subjects – they are assisting them and empowering them to do work on their own cases and to think about the contacts they have, you know, and to use those contacts rather than just be the subject like a lab rat or something.

Yes, quite. Interesting.

And it's kind of an interesting approach because especially with cuts to Legal Aid. I actually was at the Emmanuel Church in Didsbury yesterday, I was doing a talk to – they've got quite a large Iranian congregation – and I did a talk after Sunday Service and we were talking there about the need to do work on your own behalf and to think about what corroborative evidence you might get, you know, to support your asylum claim, because your lawyer working on a fixed free or a graduated fee really doesn't have the resources. Not that that lawyer's a bad lawyer, it's that they've got a lot of cases and they've got a couple of hundred pounds per case that the Legal Aid Agency allows. It's extremely difficult to do everything that needs to be done in an ideal world.

Yes. So, how does that you know affect your day job, if you like, the RAPAR work?

I suppose it kind of keeps me in touch with that field of work. The asylum work's something that we still do at Latitude, but it's less of an emphasis now, you know, we're much more kind of commercial immigration orientated. So, it's good to maintain those links. RAPAR's a good grass roots community organisation. It's very good at getting volunteers in. We've had crossover between RAPAR and Latitude, you know, people who've shown themselves to have promise within RAPAR, and they're quite often from refugee or immigrant backgrounds themselves, and it is really nice to, you know, to see people make that transition and once they've got their status, you know, to kind of transfer into the work and perhaps getting some work experience with us.

Yes, and sort of be paying back.

Yes.

Yes, interesting. Gary, just finally, you've got quite a lot of women who work for you, specifically one of your staff who started really – is it Gemma, or have I got this wrong?

Gemma.

Yes. I just wondered if you could share really her journey.

So, I worked with Gemma when I was at Robert Lizar Solicitors in South Manchester, and Gemma had joined from school. She was 16 or possibly 17, and she worked on reception, and when the firm closed the immigration team, Gemma was one of the four people, including me, that came to Latitude. She's a real kind of paradigm of how, you know, or a really great example of how you can do things a different way. You know, she didn't do A levels, she never went to University, but she's, through a lot of hard work, she's put herself through the ILEX process, she's done exams and she's qualified. She's become FILEX and then she's cross-qualified as a solicitor in the last couple of years.

Amazing!

She's an amazing fee earner and she's, you know, a really great personality to have around in the office as well, and she, even though she's – I don't know how old she is exactly, you know –

Let's not skirt around there [Laughter] But she's a great role model for people coming from non-conventional roots.

She is, and she's got that kind of authority to talk to law school graduates who are joining the firm who know nothing, and you'll do well if you're in that situation to listen to Gemma because, you know, she will guide you, she's a great mentor within the firm, you know, to new starters. Yes, she's an amazing example of how things can be done. You don't have to do it one way.

No, no, and I think it's great to see Latitude Law supporting that sort of, you know, route and journey. Now, I want to ask you about your favourite fictional lawyer. Have you got one?

I had a think about this. I think my favourite would be Kim Wexler who's the kind of foil to Jimmy McGill's less than straightforward lawyer character in Better Call Saul. She's really tenacious but she needs to learn some delegation skills, I think but you'd want her on your side. She puts together a good argument.

And have you got a book that's changed you?

I don't look for books about lawyers, but this is another book about a lawyer.

This is great for the Women in the Law Book Club, I tell you! We've got such a big list now.

This is a big book. It's nearly 1,000 pages.

Crikey!

By a New York public defender called Sergio De La Pava. It's called A Naked Singularity, and the lead is another public defender called Casi. He demonstrates I think that there's more to life beyond your work. You can be – and your work can be kind of informed and you can become a better lawyer if you've got outside interests. I mean, the kind of stuff Casi gets involved in you probably wouldn't want –

Oh right, oh right, so she's not making Podcasts or giving speeches or speaking at schools like I am? [Laughter]

She's not making Podcasts, it's a little bit more challenging than that [Laughter] – a little bit closer to the edges of legality, but he's an amazing character and I would definitely recommend that to your Book Club.

And who's that by?

Sergio De La Pava.

Sergio De La Pava, right, fantastic. That scribbling is me writing it down for the Book Club. I think it's going to be on the WhatsApp group. Fantastic. And Gary, I wanted to ask you then about any quotes that you live by, or any sort of sayings that are meaningful to you.

I'm not very good aphorisms, I can never remember stuff, but what I did for this - because you reminded me of the character of Casi - I went back and had a look through –

Who's not making Podcasts in addition to the day job!

So, here's Casi's take on life. Intellectual discourse and investigation is admittedly great fun but only truly meaningful when conducted in the service of others. There you go!

Wow! I didn't think the book was profound, I thought it was fun, but that sounds quite profound.

It's got the lot! It's a great American novel.

Thank you so much to Gary McIndoe. You can find out more about his work at www.latitudelaw.com, and more about the charity, RAPAR, at www.rapar.org.uk.

Dame Laura Cox

Dame Laura Cox, one of my heroes, titled The Honourable Mrs Justice Cox, which was in practice, took to the Bench in 2002 and was an English High Court Judge of the Queen's Bench Division. She was formerly a barrister who specialised in employment law, discrimination and human rights. She recently carried out the enquiry into the bullying and harassment of House of Commons staff. I asked Dame Laura what sparked her passion to become a lawyer.

I think probably spending a lot of time arguing with my mum and dad. [Laughter] But to be fair, I mean when I say arguing I don't mean always having a row, but discussing and questioning things and asking why, so my father used to joke and say, 'you'd be a really good lawyer'. He was very interested in the law, and one of the things that happened when I was a bit older was that he used to take me around the old Quarter Sessions and I used to sit in Court and just watch some of the advocates, and I became really interested in the whole notion of using your arguments to help somebody and to achieve a result. So, I think that's probably where the passion started, because by the time I left school I had decided I wanted to read law and, if I could, practice it.

Wonderful. Now, despite representing just 10% of the practising Bar in the 1970s when you first started your career, you said Cloisters Chambers in London was an enlightened place to work, and that helped. Can you explain what you mean? How did it help you?

Because it was a set which was full of progressive people with progressive ideas. It was progressive politically. There is a joke that Cloisters in the 1970s was called The Kremlin of the Temple, because it had quite a lot of really left-wing – it's a laugh now to record that – but there were a lot of left-wing lawyers. The Head of Chambers was then John Platts-Mills, who had been severely criticised for having Communist sympathies during and after the war …

Really?

… Yes, and it was full of lawyers with progressive political ideas and ideals, and part of that very much was dealing with sexism and racism at the Bar, which was then really institutionally sexist and racist.

Yes

And so I think I was just very, very lucky to arrive at that time in the mid-70s when there was a sort of really interesting political time in the country generally, in a very enlightened, progressive set.

Which is brilliant! Now Laura, Cherie Blair when she was interviewed on this Podcast, said one challenge she faced is that she never heard another woman speak in Court and so didn't know how a woman's voice should sound in Court. Can you empathise with that?

I can, I can, and that's because there were so few women at the Bar when I first started. So, when you were in Court it was mostly men. That did gradually change and you know I began to notice because women at the Bar in Court became very noticeable because there were so few of them, and so that the ones that there were you became quickly very aware of and able to assess their skills and watch them and admire them.

Yes. And how much did the availability of Legal Aid have on your early career, and those of juniors around you?

Yes, a great deal, because when I was taken on in Cloisters in the late 70s, Legal Aid was freely available, you know, so we were very lucky because we were able to be instructed in cases for which there was Legal Aid, and so I could gain my forensic experience going around Courts and tribunals up and down the land and be paid for it …

Yes, which makes a difference.

... which makes a huge difference really, so I'm very aware of how fortunate I was to be practising law at that time when Legal Aid was readily available.

Yes, unlike now. Can I ask you then, re your career, you took Silk in 1994, I think I was still reading law then, but from when you started your career at the Bar until 1994, how had the landscape of law changed in that early 20 years since you started?

Are you referring to equality law really?

Yes.

For women particularly? Yes? Well, at the time that I became a pupil in Cloisters in 1976 we had just passed the Sex Discrimination Act and in 1976 the Race Relations Act was passed, so I spent the first couple of years working with Stephen Sedley who was my Pupil Master in Cloisters ...

Wow!

... on some of those early cases, and I became very aware of the legislation and how it worked, and the Equal Pay Act had been brought into effect at the same time as the Sex Discrimination Act, so there were early equal pay cases as well. But over the next 20 years what happened was the European Union law, which made a huge impact on our own law, and so there was a whole plethora of European legislation which came into effect which we then had to ensure that our own laws gave effect to that European law, and that was hugely important in terms of advancing women's equality. We're talking about workplace rights because the European Union laws were all about equality in the workplace, but a lot of the jurisprudence about equality, the principles of sex equality law, were established in the workplace setting, that is undoubtedly true, so by the time I took Silk, you know, the landscape of that law had changed dramatically.

That year you won a very big case in the ECJ, the European Court of Justice, which many said was an unwinnable case. Can you explain that? Because I love this.

Yes, this was, and I do really describe it as my big break, I think it was, because it was an important case. We, in our law, had been struggling up until then with the whole concept of pregnancy discrimination, and because the way the Sex Discrimination Act worked was a woman had to compare herself with a man, there's no comparator that you can think of, and so the largely male Judges in the Courts were trying to have this weird construct of a comparator. So, for example, during some of the early stage arguments in this case that I went on to win, one of the Law Justices thought that it was, the problem with pregnant women is they had to have time off work. So, a pregnant woman who had to have time off work should be compared with a man who had been selected to play cricket for England, for example! You know, that was the kind of ludicrous argument, but this case, Webb v EMO Air Cargo, was a pregnant woman who'd been dismissed because she was pregnant, and the European Court decided you didn't need a male comparator because a woman who's dismissed because she's pregnant is sex discrimination – end of – and so that's when I say people had been saying 'ooh, you know, that won't happen, you won't win that argument, and I do describe it as my big break because I did win it and …

Thank goodness!

… these sorts of victories can shape your career and it's, you know, it's a very fortunate event because it was just as I took Silk and I got a win, and I really feel it helped me then with my future career.

Amazing! Now a lot of your work was in the field of sex discrimination, including pregnancy as you've just said, maternity discrimination, sexual harassment and equal pay. Why did you choose those fields of work, or specialised in those areas in particular?

What was remarkable about the school I went to back in my hometown of Wolverhampton was that it was a girls only school and it was a grammar school, and I can vividly remember by the time I hit the sixth form a number of our teachers would talk to us about women's rights.

Really?

Yes, yes, even in the late 60s I'm talking about, and there was a lot happening in the US at that time in terms of women's equality. The 60s, as you know, was a very heady time …

I wish I was there! [Laughter]

Well I was! It wasn't always heady, but anyway … The thing was, I began to get really interested even when I was at school, and then at Uni that continued and progressed, and so part of the reason of asking to do a pupillage in Cloisters and with Stephen Sedley was because I was very interested in those issues and knew that that sort of work was happening in those Chambers. So, I went out to find it, and then it sort of found me, because of course even though you may be interested in that sort of work, it isn't guaranteed that you're going to get it, but through working with Stephen on a number of these cases I got known about by solicitors who would then instruct me, and it all started from there really.

That's fantastic. And just looking back, has this area of law moved on for women since then, do you think? Because on the surface it seems that it has, but in reality, I wondered if you could comment on that?

I think the law has moved on, not least because we now have our own Equality Act, which was radical, is radical, and has moved things on a great deal for women, and I think we're now at a stage where the law is in a very good settled state, but it's what happens in practice that really counts in terms of what's happening to women out there in all the different forms of, you know, access to services in the workplace, on the streets, you know, and the question you need to ask is how is the law working in terms of its practical impact, I think, which is a different issue.

Yes, given we've got MeToo and sexual harassment on the increase.

Exactly.

Now, you became a High Court Judge in 2002. I just wondered how many of you were there, particularly in the Queen's Bench Division?

Very few, very few, I think there were three of us in the Queen's Bench Division at that time. There were more in the Family Division. But the numbers were very, very low.

And did you notice or feel it? Because I think sometimes, you know, one has a 'just get on with it' attitude. You used to see it, I suppose?

You certainly did notice it, yes. There would be termly meetings. There are still termly meetings of the divisions in the Lord Chief's Court and sometime, you know, I was the only woman sitting in there, or there were just a couple of us, you know, out of 108 or however many – the whole thing was ludicrous.

Quite. Now, you were involved with the Association of Women Barristers, but also you were the Vice-President of the UK Association of Women Judges. How close are we to gender parity on the Bench?

We're not at all close.

Why is that?

There are some who think that we're doing quite well, and when you look at the numbers now there has been progress and I don't say there hasn't been any progress at all but that progress has been at a glacial pace and part of the problem is that initiatives that were being advocated 10/15 years ago as needing to be implemented to bring about gender parity have not been. So, the reality is that we don't yet have gender parity on the Bench, and I'm afraid to say if you wanted any more detailed answer you'd have to have an entire Podcast devoted to why there isn't gender parity on the Bench and what we need to do. But the best thing to read is the Justice Report on increasing diversity, which came out a couple of years ago, and which sets out in great detail what the problems are and what needs to be done to rectify the position.

I think we'll all do that and maybe we can have a whole Podcast on that. Over the years you've been involved in many of the issues affecting women at the Bar. You were the Honorary President of the Association of Women Barristers, as I said, but what issues do women in particular face, do you think?

At the Bar?

At the Bar.

Yes, I mean I think as long as I can remember there have always been issues about access to work, i.e. women having access to the sort of work they want to do, as opposed to the work they're given to do that they're thought to be capable of dealing with, so I think access to work, I think access to career development, and the recent publicity that's been given to the possibility of unequal pay is extremely worrying.

Can you tell us a bit about that?

Well, I don't know. I only know what I've read myself about what some senior women are saying about it, and I know that anecdotally over the years women have been saying similar things to me, and if this is just, you know, the beginning of something that is a very serious problem, then the Bar has a major problem there because that is completely scandalous.

Yes, it is.

The other major problem forming at the Bar is sexual harassment, because I thought this had all been dealt with years ago and yet the recent studies reveal that it is happening at a level and on a scale which is truly horrific, so I'm very, very upset about that. Because I spent a lot of time in the 90s working with the Bar Council to try and deal with that problem, so the fact that it's now come back, you know, in 2019, it's just awful.

Yes, particularly the year when there's 100 years since the Sex Disqualification Act.

Absolutely.

Whilst in practice you worked on implementation of the first equality code for the Bar and was trained to mediate in sexual harassment cases in Chambers. I just wondered how prevalent were they?

It's difficult to know. I mean what we knew at the time was that there was a confidential hotline established at the Bar Council so women could call one of the two equal opportunities officers who were excellent who were in post at that time, and they would talk through with them what the options were for them, and often they didn't want to make a fuss about their careers but they wanted it to stop. And so a number of us were trained as mediators to go in to Chambers, and I did go in to a few sets of Chambers and mediate, and in some cases it was just thoughtlessness and blokes not understanding what they were doing and the effects of their behaviour. In other cases, it was more serious and then you had to deal with it. But, you know, what had led to the Bar Council setting up a Sex Discrimination Committee in the early 90s was some independent research that the Bar Council had commissioned which just revealed that there was a huge problem of sexual harassment of either young women pupils or young women tenants by senior male members of Chambers. We seem to have come full circle. You know, we went through a stage in the 80s and 90s when this was really big, a big issue, sexual harassment for example, you know, and this had to be dealt with and, you know, we thought we'd dealt with it and now it seems to have come back again. So, it's still a huge problem. What you need of course in the profession is senior men to come on board and help you.

Absolutely.

And one of the great things that I remember very vividly is a wonderful Chairman of the Bar in the mid-90s, David Penry-Davey QC, who later became a High Court Judge, and I always remember I was then very active on the Bar Council dealing with sex equality, or equality generally, but principally sex equality, and David, I remember, coming to me and saying look, you know, I'm seriously unreconstructed and I need to understand this, and I was cynically of the view, when I first heard this, that he just wants to – because he'll be giving lots of interviews and appearing in public spaces and having to give speeches - he just wants to make sure he doesn't say all the wrong things and end up, you know, in difficulty in the media, but actually I was very, very wrong. I underestimated him and I told him so later on, you know, because he really genuinely wanted to understand more about discrimination and disadvantage, particularly for women at that time, and we had many, many conversations together over the months that I worked with him, and I actually saw him understand. He began to understand and then we moved into what can I do, what should we be doing about it? And I can just tell you one story about David, because there used to be a Woman Lawyer Forum, very active – I don't even know whether it's still going – but it was very active in the 90s. It was started by a woman called Margaret McCabe who was very instrumental in getting this to be a very good annual event, and the leader of the Law Society and the Chairman of the Bar were always invited to give speeches, and in this particular year when David was Chairman of the Bar, the President of the Law Society was a very controversial character that your more mature listeners will remember, whose name was Martin Mears, and he'd said a number of highly sexist things before he came to this event, but at this event he chose to use his time to give a speech on how women had made it, he didn't know what all the whinging was about and we should just get on with it and stop moaning about our lot because equality had arrived years before. Now, David had a prepared speech, which had probably largely been written by his assistants because he hasn't got time because his diary would be horrendous, but he just put it to one side and came to the lectern and spoke without notes for about 10-15 minutes and gave a complete put-down of all Martin Mears' arguments and about Martin personally.

Publicly?

Publicly.

Wow!

And it brought the house down and he got a standing ovation, and I was so impressed because it took a lot of courage to do that, but he did it, and I shall never forget that because it's a classic example of how important men are in senior positions to advance the argument. And it's not, you don't always get that, you know, it's quite a rare occurrence which is why we always encourage more men to come on-stream and help us really, because men who support us, you know, can only – mutual advantage for men and women.

Absolutely. I mean I often say men and women in this argument are like left and right, we need both to drive and certainly both to drive change. Can I ask you about the independent enquiry into bullying, because in April 2018 you carried out the independent enquiry into bullying, harassment and sexual harassment of the House of Commons staff? We know what you found because we've read it, but I just wondered if you'd got any comment to make really? The report is there for people to read. Has it all been implemented?

No, obviously all I can say in terms of the report is what's written is what I found. I don't feel I can add to that, or enhance it in any way, or comment on any of its recommendations, but I am patiently waiting for all my recommendations to be implemented, because they were all accepted immediately.

Yes, they were accepted.

And the need for dramatic cultural change was accepted, and the need for better procedures and so on and so forth, so I'm still waiting.

Yes, now, with such a dynamic career, how did you look after your wellbeing? You know I'm big into wellbeing and I'm a big advocator. I wonder if you can share with us how you looked after your own wellbeing.

Alcohol!

Yes, I was going to say Prosecco, but I don't know if it was readily available …

No, I mean, you know, a glass of wine at the end of the day always helps puts things in perspective really, and the important thing is not to drink an entire bottle.

Absolutely, absolutely!

Because that affects your wellbeing …

Yes, it does!

… in other dramatic ways!

Oh totally. Were you doing Yoga or Pilates? Or …

No, I didn't, that wasn't, that was just coming on-stream, it's much more prevalent now and women understand these things. It didn't really, it wasn't, you know, people didn't go to gyms or do Yoga or stuff. A few did, but it wasn't mainstream in the way that it is now and that I see, you know, with my daughters-in-law doing that sort of thing. But, I would say one of the best things was just going home to the family because, you know, to be fair I have always been able to close the door and put the horrors of the day out of my mind and switch off. I know some people find that very difficult, and there were times when a difficult case or a difficult Judge or whatever were causing problems, but mostly it was just going home to a supportive family who, you know, weren't interested in the horrors of my day and would soon get me laughing and joking and just unwinding, and that really, you know, together with a glass of wine, is very beneficial.

Absolutely, I concur with that – a lot! And in your experience, what equalities or circumstances do women especially, or all lawyers, need to succeed in the profession? And by that I just wondered if you had any tips that you could share with us?

Yes, I do have some tips, especially for women. Never give up. Because I hear from a lot of women that they keep trying to achieve something or to do something, and they get knocked back, and it's hard when you're knocked back because you lose some of your self-confidence. For example, if you're applying for Silk or Treasury

Counsel, or a judicial appointment, you know, and if you don't get through you can just – your confidence can be sapped. But, you know, never give up. If you want a pupillage, if you want a tenancy, if you want to achieve, just keep striving. I think that's terribly important. That's tip number one. Try and keep your confidence. Secondly, I'd say – and this is linked to that really – that women should always support other women. I think that is hugely important and it's relevant to the first one because if you've got a network of supportive women around you that helps enormously – and men – you know, if you've got men supporting you as well, as I had, then you know that's terribly important. The third thing I'd say is always retain a sense of humour.

Absolutely!

I think that's a key because, you know, life is basically quite funny sometimes and you need to be able to laugh at it and at yourself.

Yes, fantastic. What are the three things you had in your career that you couldn't have succeeded without?

The Chambers I was in, because they were brilliant and supportive and helpful so I could have, for example, three periods of maternity leave and go back and resume a practice, and I'm very aware that that wasn't the case for a lot of women, so I do feel really, really lucky to have been in a supportive set of Chambers; my family, and I do feel the support of loved ones and loving ones is hugely important to your own wellbeing and your own ability to function in the workplace; and my own sense of determination to do what I wanted to do and not feel that, you know, anyone could stop me for what were completely irrational reasons.

Absolutely, absolutely. Now, I always ask this. Can you share with us who your favourite fictional lawyer is?

I think that would have to be Sydney Carton in a Tale of Two Cities, because I just find the whole concept of a brilliant lawyer with unfulfilled promise and a sad character who drinks heavily and who does all the work for the more senior lawyers in his Chambers who can understand immediately the important issues in the case and get to the issues and prepare a brief for his leader, completely compelling. There was something compelling about his character and the fact that he then falls in love with a woman he can't have and ultimately gives up his life to help her. What's not to like?!

I know, I know, we're going to have to read that again in our Book Club!

It's just so moving, and then you see Dirk Bogarde in the 1958 film and, you know, my adoration is complete.

Oh, absolutely! And I just wondered if you could share with us finally an inspirational quote that you live your life by, or a quote that you use often?

There are so many, but I think one of my favourites has to be Madeline Albright's. I've talked earlier about the need for women to support other women, and she famously said – and I think she's 100% right – that there's a special place reserved in hell for women who do not support other women.

Hear, hear! Oh, I love that. I absolutely love that, and actually you said that at our annual Women in the Law dinner. Wonderful. Dame Laura Cox, thank you so much. We really appreciate it.

Thank you.

Thank you so much to Dame Laura Cox, she was just brilliant. It was thrilling to hear about her determination and her passion for the law. A huge, huge inspiration.

James Brown

This month we'll meet James Brown from Hall Brown Family Law. He's a co-founder of Hall Brown in Manchester. He specialises in divorce involving complex family issues, with cases involving up to £100,000,000 and some very high-profile clients. James is named as a leading expert in the independent directory Chambers & Partners, and leading individual in Legal 500. He regularly appears across television and radio as well as giving regular lectures. I asked James if his career had turned out as expected.

Yes and no. One of the reasons why I chose the kind of solicitor route rather than a barrister route is because I thought I'd find law interesting - thank goodness I did, given the fact that I do a bit of it every day! – but I also wanted the opportunity to kind of run a business, have a team etc., and of course that gives me that really nice balance. I didn't anticipate doing it at the level of the kind of legal side of things that we're doing it. I never imagined I'd do kind of cases of this magnitude etc.

Yes, and high worth.

And that really was just a kind of a series of fortunate accidents. So, yes and no.

And what has surprised you most about your career?

This sounds like an advert and it's really not, but the thing that kind of on a day-to-day basis we are most surprised by is how fast we've grown. That's a current thing. I think previously what I'm slightly amazed by was the fact that there are these individuals out there you imagine they are terribly impressive, terribly confident, really know what they're doing, and you imagine senior lawyers to kind of have all the answers. What's been most amazing to me is to find that the

more senior you get the more – certainly the better ones of them –
don't have all the answers …

No

… and what they are doing is, I mean not making it up as they go
along, but certainly questioning themselves every single day, doubting
what they're doing next, and that's been a real – well it's reassuring –
but also a real eye-opener.

I'm sure. And why did you go into law in the first place?

I did politics at University and I found that very interesting, but I got
very involved in the Labour Party and became pretty disillusioned
pretty quickly with politics itself - no criticism there of anyone who is
involved. But that gave me an exposure to law and how it works, and
so, as a result of that, that's when I decided to do the law conversion
course and the LPC, and I went into law that way.

*So, why family law? Because actually family law is dominated by women for
starters.*

It is.

Because it's quite grim in the sense of divorce, contact and so on and so forth.

Sure. I think any litigation discipline, so a discipline where you have
got people falling out, you are at, you know, you are a distress
purchase because you are dealing with individuals who can't agree
things between themselves. It isn't how I got into it. The answer is,
initially, complete accident. I applied to a number of firms. I wanted
to work at a midsize firm, and the firm I liked the atmosphere of the
most happened to be the number one for family law in the country at
the time. As a result of that, every trainee did a seat in family law.
So, I did my first seat there and I thought I'm not going to do this,
you know, I'm going to do litigation or corporate, but actually I fell in
love with it instantly because you've got this funny balance of it is
very commercial, or bits of it are very commercial, but at the same
time you are genuinely – and I know this is not fashionable to say it –

but you are genuinely having an impact on people's lives. And the final thing is the variety. You know, I can be trying to understand a share purchase agreement in the morning, I can be dealing with someone who has discovered that their partner has had a relationship- or relationships in some cases - at lunchtime, and I can be dealing with rushing off to Court for an emergency application relating to a child by mid-afternoon. And, you know, that's the stress of the job is you genuinely don't know what any given day is going to bring, but that's also the drug.

Yes, absolutely. Now, what are the most significant developments in your field over the last 20 years or so would you say? I'll come to no fault divorce in a minute, no blame divorce.

Okay, we'll touch on no fault divorce shortly, but actually just as I was starting to qualify there'd been a very big case called White & White, where for the first time the Supreme Court recognised that the domestic contribution of the homemaker, so the person that stays at home, raises a family, runs the household, is equal to the commercial contribution, the financial contribution, and that really did drive a coach and horses through everything that had gone before.

Absolutely!

You know, one of my partners, Beth Wilkins, is 73 and she can remember the day where you were quite literally fighting for every penny to ensure that your client, if she was "the wife", and I know that's a stereotype, but of course in those days it was still very much, you know, wife was the homemaker, man was the income generator, whereas actually the law suddenly changed and the Court said 'well, hang on a second, why don't we start from a position of equality and work backwards rather than the other way around', and we are still to this day seeing the kind of ripple effects that follow on from that. What's most interesting is there is a bill going through Parliament at the moment by a lady called Baroness Deech which is almost going the other way. So, for instance, this bill would limit maintenance to only five years which, if you can imagine, could cause some real difficulties for some people, and there will be a get-out that if it's real hardship you'll be able to extend it, but I'd still say it's going to be looking assumption of five years unless you can establish otherwise.

Absolutely, and the majority of them will be women.

Quite right, who are going to, you know, it's still a statistical fact that that's going to most affect women. The other big, big change that we've seen is pre and post nuptial agreements.

Yes

They're still not contracts, but nowadays if you can tick the necessary boxes of things like independent legal advice, the agreement not being unfair, there being financial disclosure so you each know what the other's got before you sign up to a pre-nup, but nowadays the Court will say, look, I'm going to enforce that unless you can show me a good reason otherwise. But we are, who'd have thought it, we're you know one of the most romantic countries in the world it seems, given the fact that these things are pretty standard in most states of America. They're pretty standard across Europe, but for some reason we Brits seem to be holding back on them.

Yes, I know, and it is unromantic. I don't want to disclose all my handbags before!

No, I mean Heaven forbid! Right!

I know, I know! I mean I've been married a long time so, yes. Anyway, moving on, moving on. What are your thoughts then on the no blame divorce? I mean, what do you say to critics who claim it makes it easy to dissolve a marriage?

I would say two things. One is, you know I've been doing this job for 17 years, as a firm we've got about 500 clients at the moment. What I can say as fact on the ground is no-one takes this decision lightly. People don't wander in and say do you know what, over the weekend I had a great idea, I'm going to get divorced. So, the idea that if there isn't a hurdle to clear people will suddenly wander into it and do it is a nonsense.

Yes.

The second thing I'd say to critics is let's assume what I'm saying is right. Let's assume what I'm saying is fact, that no-one goes into it lightly. What you have to do at the moment is, if there hasn't been adultery you have to have blame, which means before you even start the process and, you know, dividing two households is difficult enough, agreeing how children are going to divide their time is difficult enough, but most importantly just dealing with the emotional fallout of realising that your marriage is over is difficult enough. It does not need a hand grenade, which is effectively what this is, of having to blame someone and coming up with four or five examples of what the other person has done wrong and labelling it unreasonable behaviour. I mean, it's outrageous if you think about it. We all know lots of people in family and friends etc. where actually no-one's really to blame. It's just two individuals who have grown incrementally further and further apart without realising until it's too late to turn back. And in those situations, do we really want to be blaming one another? No, we don't. So, you know, let's be adult about it. If we both accept that this marriage is irretrievably broken down, let's get on with it without there being unnecessary conflict.

Yes, or continuing. Thanks James. I just wanted to ask you about what further developments in family law you'd like to see. I know you've been a big campaigner in the FDAC Courts, and that's been something that you and Sam, your business partner, have been passionate about. But, is that one of the developments you'd like to see in the law? I just wondered if you had any thought about future developments of family law.

Yes, well I think FDAC's a really interesting example, because the FDAC Courts themselves are a problem-solving approach to family breakdown. So, put simply, Care Proceedings before the FDAC Courts started were binary. If you were a good parent, you get to keep your child, if you're a bad parent your child gets taken away. I know I'm oversimplifying but it helps to understand it in that way. There was a Judge called Nick Crichton in London who said he took, I think, his thirteenth child off the same mother because she had very serious addiction issues and he said look, enough is enough, there must be a better way. And he was the person who pioneered, alongside a number of other very creative legal brains, and said do you know what, there must be a better way. So, he developed this two-track system. One was the traditional care system, and alongside that ran these new FDAC Courts, and in the FDAC Courts get rid of the lawyers so, you know, that's a good step in the right direction anyway, and, secondly, bringing in true experts. So, bringing in an addiction expert, bringing in a Social Worker, bringing in a, for example, a plan in order to keep the mother protected, for example, in case it's actually an abusive relationship which is causing the problem. And, he effectively said look, let's design a plan that works for you. If you stick to that plan, I, the Judge, will be on your side with the ultimate carrot, which is you will get to rebuild your life with your child. But if you don't commit to that plan that we're all designing together, we bounce back to the other track which is, I'm really sorry, proper hard-core Care Proceedings. The ultimate sort of carrot and stick if you like. So, (a) it's an amazing thing and it's been hugely successful not only in reuniting children with their birth parents but, most importantly, the number of people who are still clean five years down the line, so even just as a solution to addiction problems it's been highly effective. For the bean-counters, it's been a massive economic success as well, you know, for every pound spent, I think it's £2.30 gets saved, which is, you know …

It's huge!

… a lesson to us all, right? But what I would say is, then taking a step back from that, the really amazing thing about it is not just obviously that it's successful statistically, the really amazing thing is someone saying, do you know what, maybe there's a better way here. Maybe rather than just the old-fashioned binary, head-to-head system, in that case State versus parent in order to protect child, well actually I think right across our legal discipline coming up with more creative solutions to relationship breakdown or even any discipline of the law which is involved in litigation, I think has got to be the way forwards, because we are dealing with a legal system which in some cases is 150 years old, and a process which is 150 years old, and of course it has to evolve step-by-step, but what I would say is look at that, that is a beacon of, do you know what, we don't have to do it that way, we can do it differently and it can really work.

And how did you get on with the campaign with Lord Mummery? He was a former President of the Family Division.

That's right. It was a complete accident. So, when we started our firm, we – and again, it sounds slightly cheesy – but we sort of think of it as the four C's is what Sam and I call it. So, C number 1 is commercial, being a, you know, strong commercial performer as a firm, because it allows us to do everything else. The second C is the clients, so providing excellent legal advice, always being accessible etc. The third C is colleagues, so making sure that we are, touch wood, you know, a good employer with the various benefits we employ and the ways that we work. But the fourth was community and, you know, there's lots and lots of law firms that sort of pay lip service to CSR etc., and there are lots of law firms who do it really, really well, and we wanted to be in that latter category. So, we've done a few things from, you know, supporting local charities through to we fund under-privileged students through law degrees at Manchester University, but we were looking for a big sort of standalone project. And, at the time of the FDAC campaign starting we were looking into setting up our own legal advice centre and using a proportion of our profits to actually fund a standalone legal advice centre.

Fantastic!

Yes, and interestingly, you know, there are some great examples of that in Manchester and right across the country. Where I met my wife was a charity in the East End of London at Toynbee Hall, and they were one of the oldest legal advice centres in the country which set up back in Victorian times.

Oh, right.

But anyway, we were investigating this and realising a couple of things. One is that we were very keen not to sort of take oxygen in terms of publicity or take food out of the existing legal advice centres that were doing it. Similarly, we weren't, we didn't just want to write a cheque to those legal advice centres because inevitably control is a thing for us and we wanted to ensure that the legal advice centre was being run in the way we'd want it to. And we were quite literally walking back from a meeting with one of these legal advice centres, having looked into it, and on Sam's phone up popped an appeal from Nick Crichton, the Judge we were talking about before who invited the FDAC process, talking about the national unit which runs the entire FDAC's system closing, and the fact that all, in inverted commas, they needed was £250,000, which the Government wasn't prepared to give them. So, we dropped him an email and said look, we're looking for a project, we've got some cash. What about instead of the cash that we were going to put into a legal advice centre, we send that in your direction, but what we also try and do is generate funds from other family law firms to make up the shortfall. He said, yes, great idea. Within 24 hours we were sitting in the House of Lords with this kind of action committee that he'd put together, you know, feeling like proper imposters, you know, sitting there! But, as it was, we then approached a number of family law firms, we were singularly unsuccessful in raising money from that source, who knew?!

Yes, I know.

Right, but some of those stereotypes exist for a reason.

If you're listening now …

Except, what I will say is there's a firm in London called Family Law in Partnership, they immediately committed and have been amazing ever since, but we got nothing else from any other law firms. So, what we said is, well do you know what, we've got lots of contacts generally who are decent people and who have some profit margin that they can spare, so we just raised it from other sources.

Fantastic!

Yes, there's an IFA organisation in there, there's an organisation called Addcounsel who deal with addiction problems but for high net worth individuals, and a number of private individuals who said, do you know what, I'm going to put my money where my mouth is, and we raised the money that way.

Fantastic! James, I want to ask you a couple of questions really about you. You know, James the Managing Partner if you like. You started your career in fact in London before you moved back to the North. Do you think the law still suffers from a North/South divide?

I think certainly family law does, no question; not in terms of the calibre of lawyers. About 30-odd percent of our work is from London because they are clients who recognise that they get just as good a legal advice in Manchester, but a significantly lower hourly rate.

Yes

Where there is a North/South divide in what I do is the Judge's attitudes towards, for example, women who are getting divorced, and it is — anecdotally of course, before the Ministry of Justice gets hot under the collar, but fact anecdotally — the Northern Judges are not as generous to wives as Judges in London are, both in terms of housing requirement, and I don't just mean obviously you need more to buy a house in London than you do to buy a house in Bolton, but more in terms of the levels of maintenance and how long that maintenance should last. You know, there is a look, get out there and earn, get out there and, you know, start working again, in a way that London Judges are a little bit more sympathetic.

Interesting, especially when we're talking about a Northern Powerhouse, a Northern Powerhouse Partnership, but there are, you know, divisions in the economy. The London economy is obviously faster growing than the North, so that's quite an interesting view. I want to ask you this. You've actually represented a number of very high-profile clients. I wondered what additional challenges did those cases bring?

Do you know what, I think probably the most interesting thing about high-profile clients is (a) I think there's a tendency to think there's a degree of magic there. I don't think there is. I think genuinely clients are clients and I think across the spread of high-profile clients you get some clients who are more demanding than others, you get some clients who are more challenging than others. But that's exactly the same as your, you know, non-high-profile client base as well. The biggest driver for challenges and wellbeing in our discipline is the emotional needs of any client in any given situation, whether they are high net worth, or not. You get an awful lot of transference where you have individuals who are upset about the difficulties that they are having, and very much look to blame you, which of course is an absolute human reaction. There's a fantastic book called Persuasion, and in there he gives an example of weathermen who get death threats, and they get death threats because people are so upset about the weather forecast, and they get death threats because people, that idea of shooting the messenger really does psychologically exist. And of course, as a family lawyer you are often the bearer of bad news and often get blamed for that. So, actually, it's not so much whether they are high-profile or not, it is what are their specific difficulties that they are struggling with, and therefore, you know, you managing them through that process.

Yes, so dealing with divorce, custody and other family matters must take a mental toll as you said. How do you look after your wellbeing?

So, I think there's a few things there. I think, one, we are very open with each other in the office, so we use each other as our first line of support. You know, it is very natural to come off a difficult phone call or come out of a difficult meeting and share it with the team. And you will then find that actually sitting around that room there's four or five other people who are not topping but they can come back with their own horrendous story in terms of what's happened, and that can help you feel better.

Yes

It's something that over the next 12 months we're specifically addressing, in that we are retaining a psychotherapist on a confidential basis who will be a hotline for our staff, so that they will be able to ring with the difficulties they are having, either with clients or indeed at home or with us, God forbid not with me, probably with Sam Hall, he's a nightmare! [Laughter]

He's not, he's lovely! [Laughter]

Because it's something, I mean, you know, law is really bad at it generally, so I think there's still a, you know, get on with it, what's the problem?! And I think family law in particular, you know, you are often dealing with some incredibly distressing situations, and it's all well and good having a supportive team around you, but actually professional help can often be what is most beneficial in trying to get in there before it becomes a problem is our big objective in the next 12 months.

It's great to hear your firm doing such brilliant things on wellbeing. What is the profession learning, do you think, from its youngest members? I mean, what new attitude or skills are millennial lawyers bringing to the profession do you think?

I think there's two main areas. One is a real embrace of technology. You know, it constantly amazes me that I can look across at a member of my team and she can be dictating a letter on digital dictation whilst uploading a tweet about the firm on her phone, and on the iPad scrolling through Facebook or Instagram in respect of what's happening in her personal life. I mean, I have, you know I'm one of those people like a child learning to walk …

Yes, that's me!

… I can walk, but if I talk at the same time I fall over! [Laughter] You know, I can literally do one thing at once. [Laughter] And it amazes me, but of course they will then often come to us and say, well what's the problem, why don't we have this in terms of a way of preparing bundles because it's so much quicker, you know, why don't we all get two screens because it means we are saving paper, for example, and that embrace of technology really gets driven by them. Because whilst, you know, Sam and I are in that funny cross-generation – I wouldn't describe us as Ludites, but certainly we're not millennials – You know, I remember arriving at University within the first year when we all automatically got given an email account, you know, and it was a breakthrough and we were like, goodness me, what's this?! So, you know, I think that's the first thing. I think the second thing is a general attitude. They are much better, even than my generation, of working to live rather than living to work. You know, mental wellbeing, being open about that, and the fact that, you know, they may well have multiple careers in their life as opposed to, you know, when I came through it was still very much you choose your career, you were perhaps allowed one new choice, you know, you made a mistake and you always imagined your mum explaining that to her friends when you were doing it, you know. You were allowed one mistake but then once you got on the path, you got on the path, and goodness me weren't you lucky to get a job in respected law firm, and goodness me weren't you lucky to be promoted?! Whereas now, it's the other way around. Now it is, you know, like a cat versus a dog thing, you know, rather than a dog being loyal wherever, which is probably what I was, nowadays, like a cat, it's like well unless I provide a better home for them then, you know, they're going to …

They're going to go off.

… They're going to go off next door.

Yes, absolutely, absolutely. So, what do you think is the one thing that needs to change about the way in which lawyers work?

Well, you see, I'm slightly old-fashioned about this. I think that we need to be better at being more responsive to clients, which I don't think is that great necessarily for our mental health, but I think we need to wake up to the fact that we are a service, whether we like it or not. We're going to be put under pressure by technology, which with the assistance of millennials is going to take a large part of our work away, the rise of AI is a very real – threat's the wrong word because if it's used in the right way it can be a support, but, you know, if it's used in the wrong way it could be a threat – and you know really what do we offer? Well, what we offer is a human brain, an emotional and sometimes actual arm around the shoulder for our clients, particularly in family law at a very difficult time. Well, you can't do that and say to yourself this is why we are better than technology, and at the same time not be available all the time. You know, there's still for some this attitude of, I am the lawyer, you will do what I say because I'm the clever one with the degree. There is still this desire to tell people the law. Well, clients aren't interested in the law. They want an answer to their question. So, I would say we still need to get better at being human beings who get properly understanding into what it is our clients needs. And yes, that carries massive stresses in terms of, you know, wellbeing for the lawyers, but ultimately that's the profession that we chose to do and if you want to be truly excellent at it I think that's the direction we all need to continue going in.

So, do you think that we generally enjoy a good work/life balance? Is it possible for lawyers to enjoy a good work/life balance?

I think it is difficult, particularly if you want to do it at the sorts of levels that clients often demand, and I would say are often entitled to demand. The flip side of that is - I approach it slightly differently - I have on my staircase some black and white photographs of family members, you know, grandparents etc., and in one of the photographs is my grandfather on my mother's side, and it was taken the day before he became a prisoner of war, fortunately he came out the other end. Next to that is a photograph of my grandfather on my dad's side, and he and his mates are standing in front of the Lancaster Bomber that they're about to get into at 22 years old. You know, get yourself into a tin can, fly over Germany, kill some people whilst being shot at by other people, and the other guy, you know, is about to be a prisoner of war for the next three years. Well, I tell you what, it doesn't half put your life into perspective when you're saying, do you know what, I've got a very difficult Podcast to do this morning! [Laughter] You know, you're sitting and you're saying, well, hang on a second, these dudes had to do this for us. So we all talk about work/life balance, I think it's not so much you should be expected to work, I think often for – certainly for me – it really helps me if I reframe my brain and I say, do you know what, I am absolutely blessed to be able to do a job where for talking and/or writing I get the paid the hourly rate – which is very reasonable of course – I get paid the hourly rate that I charge, and I get to make a living doing that. I'm not going down a mine, which is what my previous generations had to do, and I'm not getting in a tin can and having to go and kill children and be shot at. So, you know, for me the work/life balance is a bit more complicated because I sit and I say, well, you know, what a privilege it is for me to do this. And what a privilege to do it in a generation where, you know, I can work at home, which means I can have my daughter sitting next to me doing her homework while I'm typing out an email, rather than having to do it chained to a desk.

Absolutely. Well, James, I want you to share with us some of the innovations your firm has introduced which put your staff's life ahead of their work. You know I love this! Such as the missing Sports Day. I just love this. Can you share that with us?

Yes, okay. Well, the first thing, the first thing, is we try and actually sort of live our values. I know it's an Americanism, no offence to those who might shortly be moving to America ...

I'm erasing it! [Laughter]

So, the first is, we kind of live our values. So, what that means is, I drop my kids at school every morning, for example, never miss a sports day, never miss a Nativity play, so it's all well and good an employer saying, no, no, no, we're a flexible employer, don't worry about it, you do what you need to do. If they're sitting there from 7:00am in the morning until 8:00pm at night, FACT, people coming in and out will feel like they are being clock-watched.

Yes

So, firstly, by saying, this isn't just lip service, I don't get in until 9:40am because I drop my own kids. I will walk out at 3pm for a Nativity play etc. That's the first thing. And the really important message to say is, this isn't just lip service. We have a, you know, you get fired if you miss sports day policy.

I just love that.

Because, and this came about because we had a member of staff who'd recently joined us and she sort of came off the phone and she sounded, you know, kind of relatively glum, and Sam said, are you alright? And she said, well, no, it's slightly frustrating because my husband's going to miss our son's Sports Day. To which Sam said oh, I'm sorry about that, you know, what time does it start? She said, well, in an hour. And he said, well you'd better get going! And she was like, well, I wasn't going to go, you know, I'm still, I've only just recently started. To which Sam was like, so no-one's going to see your son at Sports Day? Get out now! And, you know, said if I find you sitting here in 10 minutes then you're fired! And it was a bit of a joke, but it became sort of a proper mantra of ours. Because, in the nicest possible way, we've all got emails now, haven't we? We've all got, you know, remote working, so what's the problem? You know, the worst-case scenario, someone else could deal with it if it's a true emergency. The worst, worst case scenario, just give the client a call back after, you know, everything's done and finished or whatever. Or, more likely, it can probably wait until tomorrow can't it? Let's face it.

Yes, absolutely.

But you get, what, five Sports Days that your children want you to be at.

Yes!

And then a few others that you impose yourself on, you know! [Laughter] Make the most of it! So, we do that, and then we have, you know, the flexible working, we have a strong maternity leave policy, including the automatic entitlement to return back to work three days a week for the first month after you come back, four days a week for the month after, so you don't even have to ask, and that's in addition to your, you know, entitlement to flexible working. We have a physio who comes in every other week. We do Yoga on the off weeks. In theory we have lower targets for our lawyers, although we've been so busy most of them smash those targets.

Brilliant!

Anyway, although that's something we need to work on and we're trying to recruit enough to kind of keep pace with demand so that we can get people back to hopefully walking out at a decent time.

Yes.

We give an update every week as to where we are up to, so that people know where we are. We're a proper open-plan office, because lots of law firms remarkably still put their partners in offices, which amazes me because it says, before you've even opened your mouth it says I'm more important than you are, which is ridiculous, rather than same desk, same computer, same phone etc. We do an away weekend for all of the staff that they can bring their partners to, that we fully fund. We have a 'never put your hand in your pockets' policy. So, if you're on a work night out, be it, you know, networking or otherwise, we will pay for your taxi, we will pay for your hair and make-up if that's what you want to do, we will pay for your drinks …

Wow! We need to work here! [Laughter] I don't do family law sadly.

Well, it used to amaze me that you'd go out selling the firm and yet end up £200 down and you were like, well hang on a second, there's something wrong there. So, it means you're saying to people, look, if you want to go out it's a decision for you, and if you want to do that, brilliant, but you shouldn't end up being worse off for it, that's ridiculous! You know, and what else do we do? Well, we're making it up as we go along, so, you know, we've only been going for three years so we'll find out whether long-term they are good decisions or not, but you know that's what we're doing at the moment.

Well, you're doing fantastically well, and your retention is amazing, so I'm delighted you're doing all these new and innovative things. And so, have you got a favourite fictional lawyer at all?

I do, I do, yes.

Can you share that with us?

So, I used to absolutely love and still love The West Wing as a TV show.

Oh yes.

And there was a lawyer in that called Oliver Babish, where the President had done something a little bit naughty, as in misled the electorate about the fact that he had MS. So, you know, query whether that's very naughty or a little bit naughty! But anyway, there's this amazing scene where Oliver Babish first gets involved, the White House lawyer, and he basically said, I will only take this case for you and protect you if you promise to do every single thing I say. Now, of course, you know at that point it's fictional because the President agrees, and anyone who's been a lawyer for any length of time says, I've yet to have a client who does everything I ask' do you know what I mean? [Laughter] We'd all have the perfect case if it wasn't for the client, right?!

Absolutely!

And, so, he is my absolute favourite, because finally there is this lawyer who managed to persuade his client to actually do and follow his advice! [Laughter] Whereas I think I'm running at a sort of 50/50 at best with my clients. They're like, 'well I'll do some of it but I'm not doing that over there'. [Laughter]

And is there a book that you've read that has inspired you or stayed with you?

Yes, I mean I, this sounds as though I'm a bit obsessed with American politics, I'm genuinely not, but actually there is an amazing book about the rise of Bill Clinton, called 'First in his class', by a chap called David Moranis, and it charts childhood up to his nomination to be the Democratic candidate. So, none of the stuff that follows, which of course we've all heard so much about, and none of the perhaps more damaging decisions that he made in his career, let's put it like that. But, there's two amazing things about the book. One is this man, and I know he's not a fashionable "hero" to have for obvious reasons, but he was a truly brilliant mind and this really shines through in the book, and this was, you know, bear in mind this was the author through this book that exposed a number of Bill's, you know, foibles in the first place and he was the first to do it, so it's a very even-handed – this is no hero-worship biographer.

Interesting.

And what comes out is he is brilliant, truly brilliant and, you know, born on the wrong side of the tracks – to use an over-used phrase. He had a, you know, abandoned father, very complicated relationship with his mother, and just through sheer kind of ambition and ability he rose to ultimately become President, but of course where the book leaves off to become the Democratic candidate for President. So, it is a, you know, for any kind of you know, and I think we struggle a bit with diversity, you know, in law, no question about that. So, I would say for any kid who is doubting themselves, you know, I would say, look have a read of this because it really does make you understand what, in theory, is, you know, possible.

Possible, yes.

But the other thing that comes out of the book is, and it's something I tell my clients time in time out, he made a whole raft of mistakes in his career, and usually due to his own personal weaknesses. Let's put it like that. And the book very much focuses on his early career and, when he made a mistake, he would apologise for it. He would apologise for it, he would "mean it" and people could decide for themselves whether or not to forgive him. And do you know what, more often than not, they did.

Yes

Now, if you fast forward of course to Monica, that was the first time he didn't apologise and guess what happened, he ended up being impeached. You know, and I say this to my staff, if you make a mistake just tell us because I bet you we can fix it. But if you try and obfuscate or hide it, that's when it becomes a real problem. But I also say it to some of my "naughtier" clients. You know, if you get caught out, own up, apologise to the Court and to the other party, and nine times out of ten we can probably fix it. But if you don't, that's when the real problem comes and you, you know, end up getting impeached or equivalent. It's a great book.

Yes. Fantastic. I actually want to read it. I've read a lot of Hilary's stuff but not much about Bill. And finally, James, can I ask you, have you got any quotes that you live your life by?

Only, to go back to what we were talking about before and the photographs, you know, I will often say to myself, you know, you're not going down a mine, you're not going to war, what is the worst that happens?

Thank you so much to James Brown from Hall Brown for his time.

Jaime Hamilton QC

Talking Law interviews leaders in law, and this month is no different because we have Jaime Hamilton, Queen's Counsel, who is a barrister in Manchester. Jaime, welcome. (St John Street Chambers).

Thank you, hello.

Jaime, what's your journey to the Bar?

My journey, I suppose, started when I was about nine years old and had an operation on my leg, which meant that I had an awful lot of time off school and needed to be entertained in the afternoons. So, at that time, not revealing how old I am, but probably in the late 70s, there was a series on ITV called Crown Court which was half an hour in the afternoon and it would be a dramatised trial from start to finish, and I watched it and I saw the people in the wigs and gowns and I thought to myself, that looks like the sort of job I wanted to do. And as I got older I realised that the skills such as I had, the abilities that I had, probably matched that job, and I also realised that I became fantastically interested in what makes up a Crown Court Trial, which other people involved and the facts of it. It's a lot less to do with the law, although I'm not saying that that means that criminal law is easy, the law plays a big part in it. But the reality of it is, it's about what people do, particularly what people do to each other, and over time I have become fascinated by that. We get a real insight into a slice of life a lot of other people don't get to see. We get involved in people's lives at the time when they're most desperate, whether they be the victim of an offence or the Defendant, and I am fascinated by the stories that it brings up. And so that, combined with what turned in to be a real thing of public speaking for me, combined the two things of being gobby and nosey, and I like it! [Laughter]

And did you know anybody who was a barrister or in the legal profession? ...

No, not at all.

... when you decided to, when you were watching the television programme?

No. My sister-in-law, she qualified to be a solicitor at about the same time I qualified to be a barrister, having made a slightly later change in her career, but up to that point, no, nobody in our family had been anything to do with the law. Certainly not on the right side of it! [Laughter]

And so, what was your journey to becoming, did you go to University?

Yes. I was at a local comprehensive school in Stockport where I did my then O Levels and A Levels and went to Aberystwyth University to read law. Then I went on from there to the Inns of Court School of Law, which was the only place that did the Bar course at that time in London, and pupillage first six in London. I mean in fact I had all 12 months pupillage in London but I left after my first six to take up a place in Chambers in Manchester for my second sixth.

Well, you've been at the Bar for 25 years.

26 years this year, yes.

Yes, so have you been here since?

So, I've been in 9 St John Street – 9 St John Street had just moved premises just before I joined them, and we've been in that building now for 27 years.

Wow, crikey! That's really impressive. Can I ask you then, in that duration you've remained a criminal barrister where others, and others that we've interviewed on this Podcast, have changed or become, you know, specialised in dual areas, why is it that you've stayed with crime with its ups and downs on fees and so on?

There have been times when I've been tempted to, and there have been times when I've been advised to. I'd like to think the advice was friendly advice and not Hamilton, get out of crime, you're no good at it! And it goes back to what I was saying earlier on, it's about the stories and the people and the facts, and so for me, being a barrister has not been the end game, it's being a barrister practising in crime, and I very much came to the view that if I wasn't doing crime I'd look for something else outside of being – it wasn't about being a lawyer, a barrister, it's about being a criminal barrister doing criminal advocacy and criminal cases. Even to the extent that, and I don't want to put off anybody who's thinking of instructing me in something regulatory, but I really see the joy of the job that I do is doing what I think of as proper crime, some people say dirty crime, in front of juries, day in day out doing the advocacy in a criminal case where wrongs have been done by people.

Well, can I ask you then, just flowing from that, what has been sort of your greatest case, if you like, and your greatest personal achievement?

One of the things that I think is greatly undervalued of practice at the Bar, it's not the great triumphs in the Court of Appeal, it's not the great triumphs necessarily always in a Trial. I have really enjoyed, and I am missing a little bit now I'm in Silk, it's the plea and mitigation that does the job and makes a difference, and there are so many people that will do a plea and mitigation without really thinking about it, without really trying to persuade the Judge of something, and some of my best days in Court have been when I have come away and I have heard the Judge repeat what I have said in mitigation. So, they're not glory cases, they're not the famous cases, it's the cases where you feel like you've really made a difference in somebody's life. And it's, one of the last things I did in my junior practice was a plea and mitigation in a committal for sentence for somebody who had been caught selling drugs at Park Life, and they had done everything they could. They were of good character and they had done everything they possibly could to already rehabilitate themselves before they came to be sentenced. All the guidelines would say they had to go into custody, and we persuaded the Judge to keep them out. And that sort of thing, that sort of intervention in somebody's life is a great success. So, I've been in good cases, I've been in the Court of Appeal, I've argued in front of Brian Leveson and had good days in Court, but it's the making a difference in people's lives which are the triumphs.

Which are really life-changing aren't they?

Yes.

Could I ask you then, why is it that you've taken Silk? Oh no, you didn't answer the other question about any personal achievements, because you've had several pupils.

Yes, personal achievements – and undoubtedly somebody would probably think I would say well it's taking Silk, but it's not, it's my three pupils. I've had three pupils. Louise, now Her Honour Judge Brandon, which makes me feel really, really old. [Laughter]. Robert Smith …

Maybe you are. [Laughter]

… I am old! Robert Smith, my middle pupil, who is about to become a pupil master/pupil supervisor himself, and Fiona Wise who is my final pupil. Anybody who is a barrister out there who's not had a pupil, I would say do it, because it's a fantastically rewarding experience. You learn so much from them and about yourself in doing it, and I've had the great thing of all three of them are fantastic and firm friends of mine, so the relationship that I developed with them is a very special one. And helping somebody and seeing it come into fruition where they have a successful career at the Bar and, you know, with Louise becoming a Circuit Judge, I couldn't be prouder of them, and I'd like to think I played a little part in their achievements.

Well, I think Louise is coming on the Podcast later. We'll ask her. No, that's brilliant, that's really, really brilliant to hear. Tell me, why did you take Silk then? Loving the Bar as you are, enjoying crime, what's the difference from being a junior to now taking Silk, being Queen's Counsel for those who are non-legal listeners.

Well, the big difference is – and I have for a quarter of a century I've been at the junior Bar, it's a long time, and it does involve a huge amount of time and effort. So, I mean, you'll know …

Totally

… as a criminal practitioner you are in Court every single day. You can have a diary that's got 20 sometimes up to 40 Trial in it, lots of which you won't actually be able to get to yourself, all of which you've got to manage and juggle, and it becomes a point where the pressure of the workload, just by quantity, is quite a thing. And, the year before I took Silk I'd actually been very fortunate that I had a couple of quite big cases that both required and afforded me to be able to take some time out of Court to prepare, and I realised that I quite liked that, I quite liked having the space to prepare the bigger work rather than, as I'd been doing maybe for the five years before in between a big multi-handed many defendant Trial, I'd been carrying on doing sort of the more knockaround Trials in between. And taking Silk means you get that pressure taken off you and then it's a different type of pressure because then you are preparing more serious work, sometimes more supposedly "complicated" work, but you get the time to do it, you get the time to focus on really honing what you need to do in the course of a Trial. Yes, it's a great thing. It's also very nice having somebody effectively saying yep, you're actually quite good at this job, because we go around a lot of our time ploughing our own furrow and, you know, you think, well, I must be doing it alright because I'm getting the work in, I'm getting the results, but nobody actually will say it to you, and it's one of the things I've always tried to do. If I see somebody do a good plea mitigation, I will say to them, that was good, you did well there. If somebody does well in a Trial, I always try and say to them afterwards, well done, you did that really, really well, because we don't get a lot of that sort of experience in our job. It's a very times singular job.

Yes, there are no appraisals.

No, and so taking Silk is, it's nice because you get that moment where somebody says, actually, you obviously do know what you're doing, and you also get to wear the tights and breeches on the day …

Oh God!

… and the patent leather shoes! Who could turn down that opportunity?! [Laughter]

Well, we're all very inclusive here! [Laughter]

And so that, it was a great moment when I got the email saying I'd got it and I could tell my loved ones that I'd got it, and I went round to see my mum and dad that night, who had no idea that I'd applied, and the moment I could sit in their front room and say to them I've just found out in March I'm going to become a QC, that was a really – worth everything.

Did you cry?

I came pretty close. I did have a little moment when my voice broke, and I think I had a little dampness around the edges of my eyes. I'm not actually admitting to crying.

Did your mum cry? Or were they just overwhelmed?

I think they were overwhelmed.

Yes, I can imagine.

I think they were absolutely overwhelmed and, you know, I wrote a blog about taking Silk.

I read it! We're coming to your blogs.

Yes, and I had a conversation with my mum and dad that night, sort of saying to them, what do you think? Because I didn't really know my grandparents, because they were, about three/four of them had died before I was born but, you know, I kind of know their story and I did know one pop. My grandad was a roofer and my other grandad was a labourer from Gorton, and it would just never have occurred to them that within a generation-and-a-half, effectively – you know, they were amazed when people went to University, and the idea that their grandson would be a Queen's Counsel would never have occurred to them. Never.

That's really quite some achievement, isn't it? A real achievement. Can I ask you then – I'll come to the blog in a moment then – just about diversity in the profession, social mobility, something that I'm passionate about. What do you think about diversity in our profession?

I think sometimes we can perhaps over punish ourselves, and I think we should recognise the steps we've taken. So, in my Chambers, when I joined Chambers there was about 30 of us and there were three or four women in Chambers, which is ridiculously low.

Absolutely.

And people in Chambers used to say to me, 'we don't have a problem recruiting women in our Chambers, look at our Chambers, Caroline Swift and Janet Smith, who went on to the High Court Bench, have been in our Chambers', which I think some people used to wear as kind of like a badge of our diversity. And I used to think to myself, no, that means we'll take on blokes who aren't good enough to be a High Court Judge, but we'll take on women only if they prove themselves to be truly, truly exceptional, and I used to think that's not an indicator of diversity, that's an indicator in fact of the opposite.

Yes.

But now, you know, kind of me and below, Chambers is 50/50. The recruitment has been very, very balanced and we introduce things like blind marking of application forms before a lot of people did, and we took real efforts to make sure we levelled the playing field, but there are still problems at the Bar. The issue of retention of women is something which we need to get much, much better at, but we can't do it on our own. Frankly, the judiciary will need to play a huge part in that because …

Why do you say that?

Because a lot of retention, particularly at the Criminal Bar, is about things like listing practices.

Absolutely.

And if the judiciary don't sort it out, we can't sort it out on our own. So, there has to be support for women in the profession, there has to be support for returning to work after maternity, there has to be a real sense in a Chambers – I mean, I'm completely aware of, you see a big, many defendant case, if it's drugs or gangs it'll all be boys.

Yes, or one woman as I often find, if it's me.

And you'll look in the Courtroom and you'll think there's 12 defendants here and yet, you're right, there might be one out of 12 will be a female. See a sex case and usually there's a woman involved in a sex case. And there's a real perception of guns, drugs, gangs, fraud is boys' work, and sex cases is girls' work, and I think in that there's a certain inverse snobbery that fraud work is quite often seen as better, more complicated, more difficult – and it is not! But, there's a real, I think, whether it's conscious or unconscious, there's a way that the work is distributed, whether it be through solicitors or clerks, which involves a bias, and the Bar has got to really do all it can to even out that bias.

Yes, I agree with you. But also, though, we need to deal with the fact that, just back on diversity, there is a notable lack of black and Afro-Caribbean barristers.

Absolutely.

Your Chambers is better - I have friends who are in your Chambers – but it's true isn't it? How do you think we can improve that? Is that through social mobility or access to the profession?

There's no quick fix to that now. It's got to be a long-term thing. I think one of the principal things is, one of the mistakes I made in many ways was, I was criminally naïve, I never did a mini-pupillage, I didn't have much in the way of work experience, but the one advantage it gave me was I didn't particularly realise that, despite what my teacher had told me that boys from this school don't become barristers, I didn't realise that boys from this school didn't become barristers and I thought he was just being daft! I didn't realise it was a thing. And it was only when I was perhaps coming to the end of University and I'd already set my heart on it and I'd set my path that I actually went to the Inns and I met a lot of people and I began to realise that it was not an Oxbridge-dominated thing, and there weren't actually going to be that many people from a comprehensive school. Now, because the law is so much a part of everybody's lives, you know, it makes great stuff of TV dramas etc., there's almost a way in which the law has become more open, so people know more about it, slightly more reinforces the 'it's all white, middle-class blokes'.

Yes.

So, when you look at the Supreme Court, you've got Brenda Hale there, who would be a fantastic role model for anybody. But if you look around the Supreme Court at the recent litigation over the prorogation of Parliament …

Yes, all the advocates …

All advocates, you've got three women who were the Supreme Justices, but then everything else is very white, very male and probably, looking into their backgrounds, very Oxbridge, and I think it's going to be quite important from this point on for the Bar to go out there and say to people who are seven, eight, nine, ten years of age that they need to have two things to come to the Bar. You need to have the ability and the desire to do it and, if you have both of those, the colour of your skin, your religion, your gender, the school you went to, your ability to pay, those things should not matter.

Absolutely.

And so, we've got to get that message out there to people, so they know they've got access to the profession, and then we've got to take the steps to make sure that that's true.

Yes.

And so, the people without money can have a route into the Bar. People who come from a lower socio-economic background can have a route into the Bar. And that people have both the safety of the knowledge that they will not be held back by who they are, what their accent is, and they'll also know they'll also have the support there, and so it goes back again to women coming to the Criminal Bar, they've got to know that there's a path through the profession which means it's as open to them as it is to a man.

Absolutely. Actually, very well put there Jaime. You've become Deputy Head of your Chambers, is that right?

Correct.

Don't say it like that. Many would say 'why would you want to do that for?' But it seems to me, part of what you're talking about, about access to the profession, are they some of the reasons why you've become Deputy Head?

Yes …

You can really shape.

So, I was Head of the Pupillage Committee a few years ago and actually took it on for a second time for the reasons that I'd – and I'd stood at a Bar event, looked around the room and I thought it's still very white.

I think that all the time! [Laughter]

It's still very, very white.

And male!

Yes, and I thought to myself, well I'm not going to change that in a year, but there are ways in which we can change it in 20 years, and the difference can be made. And the Deputy Head of Chambers thing is, I'm quite soppy about my Chambers. I'm a great believer in Chambers is obviously a mechanism where people get representation etc., it's a business, but for me also Chambers is a family, and it is all about caring for the business and the family, and people get into Chambers, some people are more involved, some people are less involved. I've always been quite involved because it means something to me and I want people in Chambers to obviously have successful careers, to obviously have opportunity available to them, but also to be happy in Chambers, for it to be a good place to base your practice from. And so, when I was asked if I'd be Deputy Head of Chambers, yep, I had a moment where I slightly probably raised my eyes to the ceiling and thought, oh what am I getting myself into but, at the end of the day, somebody's got to do it – but somebody has got to do it – and hopefully do something to shape what Chambers carries on being, which is part business, part family.

Yes, and the profession, you know, you've got a real opportunity to change the profession, well, shape the profession. Now, I wanted to just move on and deal with social media, your blog, and your Twitter followers. So, you're one of the few barristers, and highly thought of, with a Twitter account which has gone over 8,000 followers, I think, and not the Jaime Hamilton who I think is a barber, that's a different person in my research. [Laughter] But, your Twitter account is called 'A view from the North'. I just wondered if you could just tell us how you got into blogging, because you also write a blog?

I've always been quite active in, particularly in relation to things with the Circuit first of all, but then particularly with the Circuit's response to fee changes – I've always been quite vocal about it, I've been on various committees. And when the most recent, and I say kind of, it's one of the many things we can blame Chris Grayling for, is my social media presence, because when we had the Transforming Justice, I wrote a blog that I'd intended to post on the CBA's …

The Criminal Bar Association

Yes, the Criminal Bar Association's blog. And, for whatever reason it didn't quite fit in with what the Criminal Bar Association wanted to do at the time, so I'd written this blog and it wasn't going to get published on theirs, and that's why I started my Word Press Blog, because I thought, well I've written it, I might as well put it out there. And, having had no real inkling that this was going to be something that I had any interest in at all, I became a little bit addicted to it, and I like – writing the blog is one of the best things I've done in my career. I've really enjoyed writing the blog. The opportunity it's given me to tell a story, which is what an advocate's being about, just doing it a slightly different way. And then the Twitter, at the time I was on Twitter but I was on Twitter because I'm also the Captain of a cricket team called the Gentlemen Gardeners and we had a Twitter account, and I discovered that you could post your blogs to Twitter. So, I posted some blogs about the law to a Twitter account that was mainly about really bad cricket, and I did think it was a bit, a bit mean on the followers who were there for the bad cricket to have to also listen to me whinging about the law.

Yes [Laughter]

So, that's how I ended up starting my own Twitter account, 'View from the North', and Twitter, I think, is absolutely marvellous. And it's got its bad side to it, but it is absolutely brilliant. And when people sort of talk about career highs, undoubtedly my career highs involve Tanita Tikaram and Jacqui Abbott, who are two of my favourite singers, they both followed me on Twitter and I punched the air! [Laughter]

Are they still following you?

They still follow me. They might not do for much longer, but they still do follow me. I check in from time to time to make sure they are still there.

We'll tag them when we release this Podcast! So, Jaime, can I ask you about what you do for wellbeing? You mentioned cricket before. Our job is incredibly stressful, I wouldn't say more so the Criminal Bar, but mainly because of the type of work we're dealing with. Wellbeing is so important now, the Bar Council is talking about it, we at Women in the Law have frequent events on wellbeing and wellness, and I just wonder what you do as a let-out, or what do you do to relax, if ever there is an opportunity, bar cricket?

Yes, I mean, I'm relatively fortunate that I'm – perhaps laidback is the wrong word, but I'm relatively good. I spend a lot of time thinking about work. I've always been very good about stopping thinking about work, so I am able to switch off, and I just have always been able to.

How do you do that? Many of us find it hard.

I do a lot, I've always done a lot – looking at me now you wouldn't necessary believe it! – but exercise and going to the gym. Unfortunately, at the moment, I'm injured so thank goodness this is a Podcast and people can't actually see me. [Laughter]

We'll release a photograph!

No, don't show the photograph! [Laughter] But I – so doing something – there was a period of time when I did a lot of running, and I do the occasional half-marathon and stuff, and going out for a run was a great way of switching off. You know, frankly it would hurt so much – the running – that you couldn't think about work, and so I used to do a lot of exercise, and also music, I love listening to music. And if I listen to music – so, the car's a great place for me to switch off from work, I actually enjoy the commute home. You know, I quite like a long car journey, and if it's not listening to music it's listening to the test match, so when I was a junior, I used to enjoy being sent up to Carlisle for one mention because it meant I could drive up there at 10:30 in the morning, do one mention at 10:30 and then spend most of the day hiding from the clerks driving back along the M6 really slowly in my Astra, listening to the test match. And, so, it's just finding things that you enjoy and then making time in your life to do them, and that's the big thing, and that's where so many people fall down is that they do not make the time. And so I have a rule which I've broken more recently, which was never work on a Saturday. I would never – no matter if it meant I worked 12 hours on a Sunday – I always had to have one day in the week where you did not work. And it doesn't matter if you spent the day watching a film or doing nothing, just a day where you didn't do something. Creating time for yourself and hopefully doing something which you enjoy is absolutely crucial.

And you've got a little dog, haven't you?

I have, yes. Toby. Overall, probably these days, replaces running and, you know, it is, it's great taking the dog out for a walk. My favourite time for taking him out for a walk is before Court in the morning. The last thing I do before I leave the house is – even if it's just ten minutes around the block – take the dog out around the block, sets yourself up for the day, and you do things that you don't ordinarily do. You make time, because you've got a dog, you've got to make time to take her for a walk, and taking the dog for a walk on a beautiful, crisp, winter's morning, even if it's still dark even, it just makes yourself a little bit of time. You and the dog, it's not work.

And a great opportunity to think about cases though.

Yes, sometimes, yes.

So, Jaime, I want to ask you about - recently you were quoted in the media for saying it was appalling for work experiences to be unpaid, and it was plainly wrong. Now, I may have quoted that slightly wrongly there. And then that got you to offer two weeks of paid work experience with you, which was something personally that you've organised. Can you tell us about how that's come about, because I think we in the profession really applaud it and we hope that more people will do it, but how did that happen? Because it arose out of a Chambers in London.

Yes, on Twitter I had, on two occasions actually in connection with a Chambers and a firm in London, I had been critical of the fact that they were offering unpaid internships, and I just, I have an innate sense that unpaid internships are wrong.

Yes, they are.

A little bit of work experience, a day here, that's something different, but unpaid internships where somebody is getting the fruits of their labour for nothing, and effectively the employer is taking advantage of their desire to get experience to get somebody to do something for free is – and you're quite right with your quote – plain wrong. It just is. It is unfair and it also is, I think, a handbrake on diversity because the number of people that can then gain that experience is going to be very limited.

Yes!

If you're offering three months unpaid work in London, seriously, who can afford to do that?

Exactly!

It's brilliant if you're able to afford to do it. It's brilliant, frankly, if you've managed to work and save up money to be able to do that because you want that on your CV, but there are other people for whom that opportunity is not going to be available.

And it goes back to the low economic background point you were making.

And their ability to get a CV which gets them in the door to get the interview for the pupillage is significantly diminished. Having critiqued and been very critical of that and formed a very definite view it was wrong – I was perhaps on a walk with the dog I think it was – and I thought to myself, actually it's no good just being somebody that complains about what other people are doing.

Hear, hear.

And I got into a bit of a discussion with another barrister on Twitter who, they were making the case that it was something that was fine, and it was during that discussion and then thinking about it that weekend, I thought actually, it's one thing to complain, actually do something about it. Provide the opportunity for somebody who wouldn't be able to have the half dozen mini-pupillages etc. on their CV, and provide them with a one-stop – they'll get lots of experience, it will give them lots to talk about in interview, it will be a process where they can talk about the things that they did in order to secure the pupillage or the internship, and they're getting money, and they can afford to spend two weeks doing it. And it was well received, and it was, you know, it was very good, so Nick Clarke, another Criminal Silk in my Chambers, immediately said to me, 'I'm in for the same. I'll put the money up, they can spend two weeks being supervised by me'. Chloe Ashley, who is a barrister junior in Birmingham, she said to me, 'I wish I could afford to put the money up, but you've got my time'. Somebody else said, 'I haven't really got the time, but I can put the money up', so putting those two things together, three internships and the response has been very positive from students. I ended up having to read 210 to 215 applications, and I interviewed 11 and they were all fabulous, and all well deserving. And an interesting thing about it, which I hadn't really – well, I've had people from all sorts of backgrounds …

Yes, good.

All sorts of responses and, very interestingly, one area that I hadn't really factored into it, and more than one person who made the shortlist was from this background of women who have had career breaks and in, maybe late 30s/early 40s, have said, right, I've now raised my children, I now want to embark upon the career that perhaps I would have embarked upon differently if opportunities had been available to me when I was in my 20s/early 30s, and so quite a lot of women who …

Who are returners, effectively.

… who are effectively returners but setting out at maybe the age of 37/38 on a law degree and are saying, effectively, I've still got caring responsibilities, I've still got things, I can't be, every holiday, doing a mini-pupillage here and there. It's maybe, I've been able to come back to full-time education myself because my children are in full-time education. But that means come the October half-term I can't be doing a week's mini-pupillage somewhere, and the internship gives them the opportunity of two weeks paid, which helps, but also so that they're going to do an advocacy exercise, they're going to cover at least three areas of Chambers' work, so they work with colleagues in Chambers who support it and they'll be taking people to Court with them, local Judges are taking them for a day so the marshalling kind of element of there, local solicitors have also said they'll take them for a day, and certainly with interns that are helping with me, our recruitment, Tim Collins, who helped me with my Silk's application, he is going to give them a little CV clinic over Skype.

Fantastic!

So, lots of people organising, and that's the idea, so it's not just two weeks of following me around, seeing a case and kind of …

Making the tea!

Well, yes, and that can happen, and so I wanted it to be more than work experience. I'm not going to expect them to do any work for me.

No, but you want it to be meaningful.

I want it to be meaningful, I want them to get experience from it and give them something to talk about in interview, and then it's up to them. If they've got the desire and the ability to become barristers.

Fantastic! And also I saw that you've got the Secret Barrister who's going to come on this Podcast anonymously to give copies of his or her book to the applicants. Perhaps those who didn't make it.

Absolutely! Yes, so all 11 who ended up on the shortlist, and in fact I've been contacting them all today. So, we've identified the three who are going to be doing the internships with Nick, Chloe and myself. The other eight who haven't been successful in getting that, everybody on the shortlist is getting a signed copy of the Secret Barrister's book, which I'm very grateful to the Secret Barrister for. I've got them a copy of a Rumpole book, because every barrister needs to read a Rumpole book at some stage.

Oh, that's why I came to the Bar!

Yes, and also in fact, I wish in some ways I could do more, but all that made the shortlist – so the other eight that aren't doing an intern – they're all going to do, well I've offered them all a one-day work experience in which I will pay their expenses. So, wherever they are in the country, so they at least can get some experience, and again it's not going to be that they can't afford to do it because they can't afford to travel. They can come to Manchester or I can arrange through friends and colleagues somewhere local to them and I'll pay their expenses for it.

Fantastic! Well, if you're a Women in the Law listener and you're listening and you can assist Jaime, please get in touch via the usual email to us.

Another thing is, it's not going to be a one-off, I'm going to do it again. It's not just this one.

Fantastic! That's so good Jaime, because what a difference you're actually making by not just moaning but taking positive action. Just before we finish, we always ask, do you have a favourite fictional lawyer?

Well, having just talked about Rumpole it'd be too much of a cliché. There is a temptation to kind of say well it's going to be Rumpole, because I do love the Rumpole books, and my Chambers in my first six in London, 1 Dr Johnson's, was in fact John Mortimer's set.

Was it?!

Yes, so if you look at my Twitter page, my Avatar, my photograph is me on the day of taking Silk next to the Rumpole nameboard, because the Rumpole nameboard used to be up in Chambers and I tracked it down to the Chambers in London, and they very kindly let me pop in and just have my photograph taken by the board. But in fact, it's got to be Vinny Gambini, My Cousin Vinny. [Laughter]

It's a brilliant film. If anybody's not watched it, stop listening to this Podcast, go and watch it! It's funny and it really is genuinely, genuinely very funny. It has a fantastically strong female character in it as well, Marisa Tomei. But in fact, when it boils down to it, there are great lessons for the aspiring advocate in it. It's about how to stand up for yourself and your client in front of a Judge, how to turn round a hostile environment when it comes to the Judge, how to get the Judge on your side by the end of the case, how quite a lot of the cross-examination is actually – well it's obviously vaguely ridiculous – but quite a lot of it is, the foundations are in some pretty solid advice for the advocate about setting up the ultimate question and not springing the trap too early. There are some good lessons to learn in there. And also, I don't want to bang on about it, but you know Vinny Gambini is a lawyer with the wrong accent in the wrong Courtroom, and he shows it can be done. If that's not a lesson for the Bar and a lesson about diversity, I don't know what is. So, yes, it's Vinny Gambini.

Crikey! I think we'll have to go back to Ally McBeal!

Ally McBeal also very good! [Laughter]

What, you're only allowed one! Can I ask you then about some of your favourite books? Or just at least one. We always ask everybody this, well I always ask everybody, it's my Podcast.

Not a legal in any way text, but I love John Irving. I was introduced at Aberystwyth by a very good friend of mine who was an American student who was there for a year who I always thought got the very rough end of the deal because they had a kind of transfer between California and Aberystwyth, and some Aberystwyth students got to go to LA and some LA students got to come to Aberystwyth, but Chris introduced me to John Irving and I read The World According to Garp, and I could pick probably five John Irving books and make a case for why they're my favourite. But, A Prayer for Owen Meany is a truly wonderful model. If anybody needs something to read on their holiday, it's quite a long read but it's a fantastic, fantastic story.

What's it about? Actually, don't ruin it, our Book Club, we have a Book Club, so maybe just a summary.

A summary, it's about a boy who is different and believes himself to be different and it's all themes of religion and all sorts of different things, and it's a book that's written over a very long period of time. But the main thing about it is John Irving is possessed of a wonderful imagination, as most authors are. But it's also, I think it's one of the biggest skills of the advocate, you've got to have a very, very good imagination, and if my imagination is a tenth of what John Irving's is, and I've got no idea how he comes up with things like A Prayer for Owen Meany, and just the way that he describes the character is amazing. He's got a voice, he's got a stature, Owen Meany is a remarkable literary figure, but we all have it in us to do that. When we dream, you dream in amazing detail, giving voices and faces to people you have never ever met, and sometimes as an advocate that's what you're doing. You're giving voices and faces to situations you yourself have not experienced, and your imagination allows you to have the empathy required to either deal with the client, cross-examination, so I think imagination is an underrated skill of the advocate, and John Irving has it in spades.

Wow! Thank you. Jaime, one last question, what do you see as the biggest threat to Legal Aid, Access to Justice?

I mean the obvious answer is money and the constant drive by politicians to do the simple thing of cutting fees and availability but, and this is where huge kudos has got to go to people like the Secret Barrister, in order to get the politicians to invest in it we've got to always explain to the public why Legal Aid is important, why Access to Justice for everybody is important, and people get it. They don't get it necessarily when they're having the headlines screamed at them about hundreds of thousands of pounds either paid to a lawyer or paid in Legal Aid on behalf of somebody whose committed a heinous and terrible crime. But when you actually talk to people about the law, they're interested in it, they actually quite quickly realise that it's so much a part of the thread and the fabric of civic life, and so whenever anything ever goes wrong, quite soon there's a call for an enquiry. Quite soon there's a call for justice to be done and to be seen to be done, and that requires an – particularly in the criminal sphere – an even contest between lawyers of matching ability, irrespective of who you are. So, sadly, the case against in the Supreme Court against the prorogation of Parliament could only be brought by people of means.

Yes.

But that's the sort of case that should be able to be brought by …

Anybody!

… the bloke that works down the road, the woman who is taking her kids to school but is interested and bothered about what is happening, and the availability of justice to only people who can afford it or have the means for it, that's wrong. Justice is such an important part, and yes, I know it has to have its limitations, but it's got to be more of a principle than a budget exercise.

Hear, hear. Have you thought about politics?

No!

Apart from voting, that's what I always say!

Yes.

Jaime Hamilton QC, thank you so much for coming on the Talking Law Podcast. We've really enjoyed interviewing you. Thanks very much.

It's been a pleasure.

Ros Bever

This month you'll meet Ros Bever, a partner in the London and Manchester offices for Irwin Mitchell, and also the National Head of Irwin Mitchell's divorce and family law team. Welcome Ros! Hello Ros!

Hi Sally.

You are an incredible woman and I want to start from the beginning. Tell me a bit about your path into law, because you didn't start your career in the profession straightaway as I did, did you?

No, I didn't. I started out on construction sites and I quickly realised that that was not the direction I wanted to go in! After spending a winter clomping around in the rain with a hard hat on and a pair of steel-capped boots, I realised that I wanted to try and look at something else and diversify. So, I managed to secure a placement over the summer in a very, very good friend of mine's legal firm in Wakefield in West Yorkshire, and I quickly realised that that was definitely the career path I wanted to go down. I absolutely loved it from the start.

Wow! Now, was it a daunting transition to make then?

It was incredibly daunting. The very first day I started at the practice, I was sent to Court, and having not had any legal training whatsoever – and it was the days before wheelie bags …

Oh yes.

… carrying ten files …

Oh no!

… asking my opponent, how do I address the Judge? [Laughter] It was a little bit daunting I have to say. I also was equipped only with one of those pencils that writes in different colours … [Laughter] … and was sent out by the Judge to draft an order! Fortunately, as is often the case in the Northern Courts, my opponent was collegiate to say the least …

Absolutely!

… and gave me a tremendous amount of support, let's say, in drafting – it was prior to the introduction of the Family Law Act and it was under the Domestic Violence and Matrimonial Proceedings Act, it was a Consent Order for what is now the equivalent of a Non-Molestation Order.

Wow! Well, notwithstanding given how successful you are as the head of the team nationally, was it a daunting transition to make do you think, and would you encourage others to do it?

I would definitely encourage others to do it! It is a stimulating career. It is a career where you can, if you want to, be a team player, and you can work in a very collegiate way to achieve objectives that you want to achieve. I also think that the interaction with people is fascinating. Sometimes, you come across people that you don't really like, but you get a side of them that you might find a chink of something that you like in. You are working amongst colleagues usually who are like-minded, and one of the greatest things, I think, is that most lawyers have a fabulous sense of humour!

Absolutely!

You have to.

Yes. Well, yes, it's good for our wellbeing, which I'll come onto a bit later. So, just very quickly before we move on from that, was the fact that you started in a different career an advantage or a disadvantage, do you think? And what skills from your previous career did you bring?

I think from a commercial perspective I was at an advantage in many ways because I'd been accustomed to working in an environment where we were looking to make a profit, and it was a particularly difficult time when I was working in the construction industry, so we were tendering for jobs – I worked for a large construction company – and we were finding ways to tender out at a very sort of, at the minimal level, but then finding ways in which we could make money and make a profit, or even break even. So, from a commercial perspective, it was an advantage. From a legal perspective, as I described in the answer to your first question, it was an absolute baptism of fire, and I think that I was at a disadvantage in that I didn't really know anything about law. However, I do think it gives you a different perspective ...

Absolutely

... I still feel today that because I didn't do a law degree - I did what is now the GDL was then the CPE - there are gaps in my knowledge about certain areas of the law. However, I think that it's very important that you look at legal cases strategically as well ...

Yes

... and I think that when you are a lawyer you do not just have to be technically good or technically an expert, that's a given. You have to have lots of other qualities and thinking – I hate this phrase – but thinking outside of the box, for example, looking at solutions, and I think sometimes, if you go down the track of being a lawyer, you can forget about other things that you need to look at. You are dealing with, well, in my case, you're dealing with people, you're dealing with their life.

Yes

And you may stray into the territory of other areas of the law and other areas such as tax advice, for example – I am not saying I would ever give tax advice! [Laughter] – but what I would do is be able to signpost. Would I be able to do that if I had been just a lawyer from the outset? Of course I would, but I do think if you've done something else before it gives you a different perspective perhaps.

Absolutely, and I think that's a good way to broaden entrance into our profession, which often can look so narrow, particularly from maybe one particular class. Thank you! Can we talk a bit about mentoring and mentorship of women? Did you have any mentors when you entered the law? And who were they? Were they any good, informally or otherwise? Just what your view was about that really?

Well, I described when I went to work in the summer on a legal placement, and I was, I would say I was mentored by two incredible women who'd set up a firm – it was called Jones Goodall. It was Suzanne Goodall, who's now Suzanne Munroe, and Claire Jones, and they were beacons. They were not fazed by anything, anything at all. They were solution-focused, they had a can-do attitude, particularly in the face of adversity. Both of them had personal issues that they had to deal with, and they were, they were survivors, but they also really, really supported you, wanted you to develop, gave you aspirations. I would never have thought that I could qualify as a lawyer and I never would have done without them. It was also there that I met my closest friend, Sam Hillas …

Oh, we absolutely love Sam!

I've got to give her a mention, because we were both paralegals at the same firm, and we went through some times which were pretty stressful, living in what I can only describe as penury! [Laughter] And coppering up to put a small amount of petrol into a car!

Oh my gosh!

And we had great fun, but also, we learned a lot about the law.

Yes

We were taught about statute. We were given practical advice as well. At one point, I was living with Suzanne Goodall who is now Suzanne Munroe …

Oh my gosh!

... and her children and, you know, it was brilliant! It was a really great period of my life and gave me a lot of life skills and a lot of confidence in my own abilities.

Yes, that's so good to hear. Can I ask you this at this juncture, Sam, who I'm a huge fan of and she's at the Bar, she went onto the Bar and didn't, you know, go down your path of being a family solicitor. Did you ever fancy the Bar as opposed to remaining a solicitor? I know you're the big cheese now, but I just wondered if you ever fancied the advocacy part and that aspect that I'm at, at the Bar, as opposed to the other side?

I don't think I am the best advocate in the world. I find advocacy for directions hearings absolutely fine. I would find cross-examination very stressful and daunting. In addition, I do think that life at the Bar – my perception is in any event – is more of an isolated existence.

Yes, it is.

I very much enjoy working as part of a team, and one of the things that I find empowering is working within a team, particularly with a range of age groups, and there is always something that somebody very new to the team brings to the party, an idea that they have that they share with you, and you think, wow, I'd never have thought of that, [Laughter] so I think, for me, I like to work as part of a team. I do like to be a leader or ...

Well, you are a leader, that's why you're here!

I hope I am a leader, but I also like to listen to other people, and I try to ensure that there is collective responsibility to a large degree, but I think for me, if I were a barrister, I'd just spend my whole life texting, WhatsApping friends – I do that anyway! – but ringing them saying, oh I'm on my own. You know, I wouldn't want to just talk to the dog, or listen to what my mum was saying.

Yes, yes, interesting! Now, Ros, I want to talk about the family law sector and really about the last 20 years and your experience, and going back to what's been the most significant case in your professional career?

Okay, so, over the course of the last 20 years – I'll talk about my cases in a moment …

Oh yes, I love your cases!

… But, over the last 20 years I think undoubtedly the case of White and White absolutely changed the landscape. And I remember I was very junior at the time, it was really, really difficult to get your head around this complete change in the way in which financial cases were determined, and I think that it was absolutely right for the non-breadwinner, the homemaker – and I pause to say it is almost always the woman – for there to be a recognition of their contribution, for there to be the notion that there should be sharing. I think it was completely wrong to limit that person's case to need. So, White was undoubtedly the biggest change. I think Radmacher with the recognition of pre-nuptial agreements ….

Yes, can you tell us a bit about that? Some of our listeners are not always lawyers.

Okay, sorry. So, prior to Radmacher – Radmacher and Granatino – which was a very significant development …

Yes, it was

… in whether or not there was any recognition of contracts which had been entered into which would regulate what would happen on divorce. Most lawyers would say it's not embodied in the statute, it might not make a significant difference just because you entered into a pre-nuptial agreement. Post Radmacher almost certainly provided that certain tests had been, or certain key points had been considered, so both parties had taken independent legal advice, both parties had fully disclosed their financial circumstances, it was fair – I've not rehearsed this, Sally, so I'm giving you an overview …

Yes

… Most lawyers would consider that yes, a pre-nuptial agreement might be a factor, but after Radmacher it became a very much more significant factor.

A significant factor – absolutely!

And it gave the opportunity for those parties who wanted to enter into an agreement before marriage the opportunity to do so, and have SOME comfort, not complete comfort, but that may well regulate what would happen in the event of a divorce.

Which was revolutionary really …

I think it was …

… because it was big in the States, you know, and elsewhere. That case really …

I'm not, I'm not going to say I advocate it in all circumstances, because often it entirely depends upon which party you are acting for. If you are acting for the financially weaker party who has been, who's entered into an agreement which you cannot categorically say is under duress, but you suspect it is, I find it a little bit shocking at times. But I still think that people should have the freedom to regulate what should happen in the future, provided it's fair.

Yes, absolutely. That's so great, thank you for sharing that. Can I ask you then, what are your views about the Court? Do you think that – we've had James Brown from Hall Brown, I've interviewed him on this Podcast – and I just wondered if you thought there was a difference between Northern versus Southern Judges when it came to matters of awarding maintenance? Because in his view, he thought that Northern Judges were less generous!

I certainly think that there is a different approach between the North and the South. I find that traditionally Southern Judges are more paternalistic, and that's usually towards the woman or the financially weaker party, certainly in terms of awards of maintenance, be it the amount or quantum of maintenance or, more usually, the term of the

Maintenance Order. I also think that there has been a shift towards trying to get some regulation between London and the regions, but it's not quite there yet. At the start of my career, we used to, where we had a high net worth case, usually when I was practising exclusively in the North/North West, we would – and we were acting for a woman – we would consider issuing proceedings in what was then the Principal Registry, and we would do that because we'd think this woman's going to get a higher award, much more generous, in London than in Manchester.

Yes.

What actually happened, there was a change – I can't remember when it was, but it wasn't a massively long time ago – whereby you were inhibited from initiating proceedings in London and you had to go to your local Court. We all know that now. And so, you'd be sort of saying, no, we would have issued this in the Principal Registry. I do think there's still a difference.

Do you?

I also think it's very, very interesting. There's a hugely different approach to practising in the North or the regions and London, and I think that's driven by two things. I think that, firstly, and I think it's a good thing, there's a greater emphasis in London I'd say on the use of alternative dispute resolution mechanisms such as arbitration, and it's taken off, it's taken off far more successfully I'd say in London than it has in the regions, albeit that lots of practitioners in the regions are championing it as an alternative dispute resolution method, and I personally think it's brilliant. Also, the use of private FDRs for those practitioners who are listening, I think it is more common in London. I also think that there is more of an emphasis on the use of Counsel in London. I've noticed that there is a big difference. Here, I'd say, in the North West where we are at the moment, lots of practitioners would, as solicitors, would do their own advocacy at First Appointment, or certainly the preliminary stages, whereas in London you would use Counsel more frequently I'd say.

Interesting, interesting. I want to talk a bit about being a woman and then I want to move on to wellbeing and wellness. Has being a woman impacted on your career do you think? And where do you think we're going with more women in the workplace and the diversity and women in the profession, and encouraging men to take perhaps flexible work and agile working? Has being a woman impacted your career?

I think I've been incredibly fortunate. I had the ability to return to work with support from a full-time nanny. Had I not had a full-time nanny I really do not know how I would have managed. But I have to say that I had not been married to somebody who could afford to pay for the nanny, which cost at the time more than I was earning …

Because you have three sons.

I do, and I remember the stress associated with taking my youngest son to nursery and the nursery calling after I'd been at work for about an hour saying he was poorly and could I come and collect him, and crying in my office thinking I'm going to be sacked, or whatever.

Yes.

How things have changed. We now are in a situation where people do work flexibly …

Yes.

We have fabulous opportunities to be able to work from home – obviously we can't have our children with us …

No, no

… babies crying in the background, but it means that you don't have to travel into the office …

Absolutely

... blow your hair, put something decent on to wear, you can get straight on to doing your work. I also think that there is a shift towards men sharing, which empowers women.

Absolutely!

So, for instance, in my team at the moment one of our male partners, Nat Groarke, will shortly be going on a career break and he'll be spending time with his two young daughters, sharing paternity leave, which is fantastic! One would never have envisaged that that would happen. I remember when I had my first son, my husband returning to work after taking two weeks holiday, no paternity leave, during which time he had been contacted on a daily basis by clients and his team, his boss, you know, he was back at work. Two weeks holiday, no paternity leave, nothing, and there was an expectation that it should be the woman. Now that inhibited the woman's ability, in my view. But that's not just about how society treats women ...

No

... It's about how society perceives men becoming involved in childcare as well ...

Yes

... and that has held women back, and that shift is well overdue.

Yes, absolutely – well, I fully support that because that will then progress women in the professions, not just ours. Thank you, yes, that's a very good point well made actually. Now, wellbeing – if you had more time, what should you be doing, or young women entering the profession or in the profession be doing for wellbeing? Because burnout rates are high. We work long hours where, you know, we have imposter syndrome, perfectionism and so on and so forth. What would you be doing and what do you do? I know Laura Cox previously has said Prosecco when I asked her about her years at the Bar!

Well, Prosecco would be high on my list! [Laughter] I would say I am a very poor advertisement for wellbeing. I do not relax very much. When I do, it tends to involve online shopping ...

Yes! [Laughter]

… binge eating chocolate … those sorts of things. I think to a degree that relates to my personality. I am an all or nothing person. If I got into doing some exercise, which is certainly something I should be doing, I'd be one of those people who bought all of the lycra outfits, the best trainers, and did it until I was skinny and muscly! [Laughter] That's what I need to put on my list when I stop being a lawyer. So, if I really could change anything to have a better work/life balance and to think about my own wellbeing, I might change my personality. I wish I could be more like my colleagues, who do their job, you know, between the hours – I love flexible working – so they might work to suit them between 6:00am and 3:00pm and then switch off. What I tend to do is work all of the time. I don't think that's healthy. Do I like it? Yes, I do. When I give up the law – I will give up the law – and I will do something completely different. One of the things I'd really like to do is have an allotment and to grow lots of different herbs and lots of different vegetables and get really into it, that sort of thing.

Yes, what a great idea! I mean there is some research about greenery outdoor – the NHS have got a lot of stats on this and the difference it makes to your mental wellbeing, which is great!

I think I'd only have about six months at that because I've already thrown it all away!

Yes! [Laughter] Not growing fast enough!

Yes! [Laughter] There might be some bionic veg by then!

Yes. Any advice you'd give to a young person starting out in their career in the law, from all backgrounds, you know, black, white, minority backgrounds, women, men, because you know the law is – I always say it's a marathon not a sprint.

It is, and I think that when a new lawyer starts out, they have fabulous research skills, they're undoubtedly academically bright, gifted - they know the law. What you also have to do is stand back and get some experience, and you have to be open-minded, and you have to be solution focused. One of the things I think is really important is don't focus on what's gone wrong, because it goes wrong for everyone, we all make mistakes. What you should focus on is how do I get it right, there must be a way. Look for a way. And also, owning up and having humility. If you've made a mistake, the best thing to do is to go along to somebody else – I'm always in that situation – you know, no, this has all gone wrong, how can I deal with it? And having that confidence takes time. So, there's that. There's also not making quick judgments. You know sometimes we can't like everyone! But try and look for the best in someone rather than looking for the worst.

Yes.

And also, one of the things that I think is really important for new lawyers is, when I started out, if I did a piece of work, I would do the piece of work and I would take it usually to Claire Jones who I mentioned before. She'd get a red pen and she would cross everything out and rewrite the whole thing! [Laughter] And I used to go back to my desk, and I'd think, this is the end of the world. Now, if I see a piece of work and I rewrite it or amend it, I do see people feeling crestfallen about that. They shouldn't feel crestfallen. They should learn from it. Don't make the same mistake twice. Some young lawyers send a piece of work to you with typographical errors in.

Yes.

We've all done it! I do it now, I send them to clients sometimes and feel very embarrassed afterwards. But I would check, check, check! I think it's really important because it's the impression it gives.

Yes, that's great, great advice. So, who is your favourite fictional lawyer?

I really thought long and hard about this, and I did listen to James Brown's Podcast, which I thought was fabulous, James, by the way, and I thought can I really say who mine is? And then I thought, why not?! Ally McBeal!

Yes!

When I was trudging around in my cheap shiny suits at the start of my career, she was an icon. And no matter how chaotic her life was, she always won, but best of all she was a great team player, and she was normal and showed fragility, and actually I think most of us – most of us who practice in the law – we're all fragile, we're all human. So, yes.

Oh, I know, I love Ally McBeal. We might have to play the Ally McBeal music!

Oh, we should do!

I can't remember – was it Vonda Shepard who was playing a lot of that? Now, can I ask you about a book that you've read that has inspired you or stayed with you throughout your legal career?

I haven't got one that stayed with me throughout my legal career …

Well just talk generally in your career.

… but, when I was going through a particularly challenging period of my career, which was about two-and-a-half years ago, I read Alistair Campbell's book, 'Winners'. Now, I'd always not really been that keen on Alistair Campbell, but it really inspired me …

Really?

… because he gave examples from Stalin to Alex Ferguson to the Queen of how you can achieve success, and what success looks like to you. And he also gave me the inspiration to think about how I wanted to adjust from a role of being not just a fee earner, but a fee earner, a solicitor where the priority was my client – and obviously my duty to the Court – but also to change that so that I was looking at how I could perhaps look at my team as my client, and how I could adjust my mindset and try and achieve the goals that I had identified myself I wanted to achieve. And I read the book and I didn't like Alistair Campbell, I'll be absolutely honest about that, but I read it and I thought he gave a can-do attitude and I really liked it. So, that inspired me.

Yes, fantastic.

I also don't like the fact that when people achieve success they sometimes forget about where they come from.

I totally agree with you.

And, so to me, one of the best quotes - and I do try and think about it – is from Theodore Roosevelt who said, 'Keep your eyes on the stars and keep your feet on the ground'.

I love that.

And remembering that everybody makes a contribution, and every contribution that is made is equally valuable.

Thank you so much Ros, a partner in the London and Manchester offices of Irwin Mitchell, and also the National Head of the firm's Divorce and Family Law Team. This episode of Talking Law has been brought to you by Irwin Mitchell. Thank you very much to Irwin Mitchell.

Rachel Roberts

This month, we'll meet Rachel Roberts, who is Managing Partner at Stowe Family Law in Leeds and Huddersfield. This episode of Talking Law is sponsored by Stowe Family Law. Rachel specialises in all aspects of family law but has a particular expertise in dealing with the financial aspects of a marriage breakdown, as well as issues regarding children and the arrangements following a relationship breakdown. Hi Rachel!

Hi!

Welcome to Talking Law.

Thank you for having me on.

Rachel, I want to start off by asking you about your own pathway into the law. Why did you choose law?

Well I probably had a slightly unconventional route as I first left school when I was 16 and went off to pursue my first love, which was horse-riding and three-day eventing. I spent about three years doing that, but then from 19 decided to return and do my A Levels as I needed to find a career where I could earn some money. I picked law as an A Level just because it interested me, and fell in love with learning it, so it then seemed the obvious choice to go on and do at University, so I went to Northumbria to read law.

Wow! Was there a particular person who encouraged you, or any other lawyers in the family?

Not really. I mean I had a lot of family support but there were no other lawyers in my family. Actually, I was the first of my generation, the first generation to go to University.

Wow!

Dad was a businessman, mum was a stay-at-home mum, so I didn't really even know about the career paths available in law really until I got to University.

Yes. Can I ask you what preconceptions did you have then about the profession before you joined it?

Well, I was educated at a State school and I think, before I joined, I fully expected at all times to be surrounded by white middle-class people who'd gone through private education. I've actually found since University that's not the case. That's not to say I don't think there are issues in diversity within the profession of course, there are, probably more so at the Bar and probably more so in other areas of law. I think family law perhaps doesn't have quite the same issues as in other areas of law, but there's probably still more diversity than I thought there would be.

Yes. Is working as a family solicitor as you imagined it to be, or has it surprised you, or fulfilled your dreams? [Laughter]

I think – gosh, it's hard to look back when you've been in a role for so long – but I remember there being a really big shock moving from the academic side of things to actually practising it, and in the early days being quite surprised by how much time you spend holding clients' hands when you're a family lawyer as opposed to, you know, practising law per se. I'd also say I think the thing that still surprises me, which is something you don't really talk about at all at University or when you're studying, is the need for business development and to raise your profile. That's now a really big part of what I do on a day-to-day basis.

Yes, especially as Managing Partner.

Yes, absolutely.

Well, let's just explore that for a moment, if I may? I mean, what led you to family law? Why did you choose it? I mean, what aspects attracted you, and how is it you've progressed to become one of the few Managing Partners in the country and in the profession?

I think, I think like most family lawyers, I like to help people. I think most family lawyers are very sort of people people. You have to be to enjoy that really close personal contact with people at what's a very difficult time in their life. Before that, it was about enjoying studying. It was that or crime, really, and I realised as I finished studying crime, as much as I'd loved it, I wasn't cut out to be sat in a cell at 3:00am being a duty solicitor. [Laughter] So, family was the obvious choice of being my other preferred subject at University, and when I joined Stowe's – or Grahame Stowe Bateson as it was then – it was to be a family lawyer. I knew that I would ultimately qualify as a family lawyer, so I never really looked back from that.

Yes. Would you be able to describe sort of a typical day? I just wondered if you could explore a bit about what skills does a good family lawyer need to possess, do you think, in your opinion?

My day is a lot more varied now than it used to be, I think, since I moved into the management role, which is one of the things I actually love about it. So, I probably split my time, maybe 50% doing actual day-to-day practising of family law and 50% doing the other aspects of my role, so the business development as I've mentioned, managing the junior members of my team – although I do have another three partners who assist with that as well – managing the office budget and trying to keep us all on targets, and obviously trying to bring in work to the office. In terms of the skills that a family lawyer needs to have, I think it's not enough to be a really good lawyer in family law. You can be a technically brilliant lawyer, but if you can't communicate with your clients, you're just not going to be successful as a family lawyer. So, I think having a great degree of empathy is really important but also, which I think is quite hard to learn, the ability to detach yourself a little bit from somebody's situation and to be able to take a step back. I think that probably gets easier over time because you have heard a lot of stories and there will all be similarities and you learn that there's probably – there are always two sides to every story and there's probably an element of truth from both sides – so you learn to be a little bit more detached and to have a more critical view of what you're being told as you go along.

Of course, of course. Now, how does working with people at difficult times in their lives impact you? Because you're obviously dealing with the giving advice to people at their most vulnerable, emotional and sensitive time, and I just wondered how you avoid taking their emotional stress home with you, if you had any tips? Because you've got twins, haven't you?

I have, yes.

Yes, and just, you know, so you're not actually taking all that baggage home.

I think that family time really helps actually, because it's good to be able to switch off and spend time with them. Personally, what works for me is exercising is very key for me, keeping myself sane and meditation and yoga – the latter two because I'm not brilliant at switching off and resting.

Yes, yes, you and me both! [Laughter]

So, that gets me out of my head a little bit. But I think the profession is becoming increasingly aware of the impact of taking on people's stress on a day-to-day basis, and I'm lucky to work for a firm where we have Mental Health Champions, so there are people you can go and talk to that can signpost you to appropriate support if you need it. We've had a couple of people go through quite difficult things in cases this year, and we've paid for them to go for counselling to help them come to terms with, you know, the information that they've taken on, because you do become very, you know, hung up on the outcome for your client. It's hard not to. You always want the best for your clients.

Yes, vicariously, I suppose. Now, I want to ask you about family law is often viewed from the profession – within the profession – as having a bit of a high churn rate. Would you agree with that? And why do you think that is?

It's not actually something I've particularly experienced. Actually, in my team at Leeds the five longest standing members of the team have over 80-odd years' worth of service between us.

Wow!

I know! And then there are three or four other members who have five plus years. But I think perhaps if there is generally a high level of churn and people leaving the profession, part of that will be some of the inevitability that goes with the fact that we have a largely female profession – or certainly predominantly female profession – so people leave to have children and perhaps for whatever reason don't come back.

Yes.

And I think the other thing, it is a bit of a Marmite role, so what I love about the job is that close personal connection with your clients, but for other people they feel that they can't cope with spending so much time hearing people complaining about things going wrong in their lives. So, you know, I think it is a bit of a love it or hate it role.

Yes, that might sort of explain a bit of it. So, you are the Managing Partner at Stowe Family Law. Now, I've got in my mind Jessica Pearson from Suits.

If only I had her wardrobe!

I know, I know! [Laughter] Clearly the Americans have got a different view to us, and she didn't do family law, let's be fair. But I just thought, can you just - for people who don't know - what being a Managing Partner entails, and why did you take this route, really?

Well I think it sort of found me. So, I've been at Stowe's for 17 years now.

Wow!

I know!

No high turnover rate there.

No, quite! And we were bought out by an equity house about almost three years ago now. At that time Julian Hawkhead who I'd worked with since I started, he was the Managing Partner of Leeds and was going up to be Senior Partner, and I joke – and I've said this before at the Women in the Law events – that I found out I was Managing Partner when I read our Chambers & Partners submission which said that I was Managing Partner. There had obviously been some discussions beforehand, but nothing formalised. So I confess, when I first got the role I wasn't even sure whether I wanted it, because I didn't know whether it was the right thing for my family, or if I could do it, but it's actually been one of the most rewarding things I've ever done in my career, and I'm really pleased I was given the opportunity.

Absolutely! Would you say therefore when opportunities arise, for younger listeners really, take it.

Absolutely! And I think it's that thing of being outside your comfort zone that you have to get used to doing that, and I did spend a lot of the first year very far out of my comfort zone, but you kind of look back and realise two years later that you're doing stuff every day without thinking about it that felt a really big deal two years ago. So, I think it's taught me a lot about how to progress as a person, and that that's where your growth happens.

Absolutely. And can I ask you, you know, the figures for law firms, just 20% of law firms, partners are women in the UK. Why is the change still so slow do you think, and are you hopeful things might even out?

I think coming from a family law background, that doesn't feel as prevalent. For example, at Stowe's, when I last looked at the figures – and they do change because we're expanding – but 70% of our

Managing Partners were female, so we kind of turn the stats on their heads.

Oh absolutely!

And as I say, that's probably not uncommon in family law. I think it's much more difficult in a corporate law environment and I think it's a cultural thing, and I can only speak from the experience of my friends and, you know, peers that I know working in that environment. I think it takes time to change that kind of culture. If the Managing Partners that have been in those, or Partners that have been in those kind of roles have worked 10-12 hour days as a minimum, it's a hard sell I guess for them to see the younger generation coming through and doing a lot less. But I don't know, I think, I hope that over time it will change because it's a shame to lose lots of talent out of the industry because people feel it's not compatible with family life, which I think is the main reason why we see so few women at top level.

Absolutely. Can I ask you then, what do you think we need to do to accelerate that change? Or do you think time will even it out?

I mean I think that millennials who are coming through and who are perhaps going to be the next layer of partnership level have a very different outlook on life to perhaps what my generation and the generations that have gone before us have, and a much stronger work to live ethic perhaps, so I think if it's driven by that then that may change the culture, which will then in turn make it easier for women to have, to feel that they have the – can have the family life and still get to that level.

Absolutely. Now, there have been calls by various people for quotas for the number of women at partnership level. I just wondered what your thoughts might be, I mean, do you support it? Or, as it's been reported, some female lawyers fear the clients will assume that women have only been promoted to bump up the numbers? I just wondered if you could sympathise with that, if you have any views?

I think that's a worry, and that's potentially then a step backwards isn't it, if the perception is that people have not got there through merits. I also think that having quotas, unless you do something to provide the right working environment, is not really helpful because people are still going to feel that those roles are out of reach for them, for personal reasons. So, you know, unless the culture and the right working environment is there, you may not be able to fill the roles.

Yes, yes, absolutely. Can I ask you, earlier in the year the Financial Times carried out an article asking, 'Can you be a Partner in a law firm and a mother?', and we got loads of responses - I hadn't commented on that by the way - but on our Women in the Law UK LinkedIn page, and I just wondered how difficult is it? You've got two young twins and you're married, and you're obviously proof that you can be a Partner in a law firm and a Managing Partner. How difficult is it? And I just wondered if you had any tips?

There are times when it's challenging. I think I'm lucky because I work at a firm where I have a flexible working pattern. I start early every day which means I can do the school run every day – sorry, three days a week – and I try and make those couple of hours after school all about the children, whether it's activities or doing the homework, but it does inevitably mean that I often end up logging back on a little bit later. But I look at my friends in other careers and they're all doing that as well, so I don't think it is just because I'm in a management role, or just because I'm in a law firm. I think there's probably an expectation in a lot of areas of law – sorry, a lot of areas of work – where you are available perhaps more than you were ever expected to be. For me, I think I minimise that by being efficient. I'm very sensible with my time but, you know, I just think once you get to a certain level in any career, you know, it's hard to do it within your allocated time. You'll always end up giving a bit more, and that's what you're paid for.

Yes, and you've been a brilliant Ambassador for Women in the Law in addition to that role …

Thank you!

… which is great. And you've been very keen to develop a culture in your own firm, haven't you, of agile working and smart working, and is that built on that ethos you've been talking about?

Yes, absolutely. So, for me I work from home at least one day a week normally, which makes, it saves me kind of an hour-and-a-half of travelling and messing around getting to and from the office. It's quite a relaxing day for me then, and it gives me chance to catch up without being disturbed as I am in the office. I don't really mind if people want to work at home. Some people work at home because they find it quieter and more peaceful and they can get more done. For some people that live further away it gives them a day when they haven't got to battle with the M1 or the M62, and from my point of view, whatever makes their life easier is more important. I think a happy team is a more productive team, you know, and that's more important.

Absolutely. I mean millennials anyway want to work from home to brew beer and train for a triathlon! [Laughter]

Nothing wrong with that!

No, no, no! All inclusive! We talked a bit about wellbeing earlier, which we're passionate about at Women in the Law UK, and you mentioned meditation, and I just wondered what do you do for your own wellbeing? What else do you do?

I think exercise mainly, but I also love to cook. I find that really relaxing, so I cook from scratch pretty much every day, just because it's kind of pottering around the house and doing that is how I switch off. I'm not a great one for sitting down and watching the telly. And walking. If I sort of need a bit of peace and quiet then I quite often get out for a walk outside, get some fresh air.

Fantastic, yes, I support that. What are you most proud of in your career? You've been in the job now for 17 years, the first in your family to go to University. I just wondered if you could reflect for a moment on what you're most proud of in your career.

I think probably how much I feel personally I've progressed since I took on the Managing Partner role. So, I think doing that and giving that a go when it felt like a huge step for me. And I feel proud of, you know, the team's doing well, we've got a successful office, I'm told by the Exec team that they're happy with how I'm performing, so that's probably my biggest achievement, I think.

Brilliant! And what advice would you give to young women, and men I suppose, who want to rise to the top?

I think two things really. The first is, it's never too early to start building your network and to meet as many people as you can. It ever surprises me where I get worked referred to me from, and it's not always the traditional links that you expect them to be from. And the second I think would be to find a mentor who will push you out of your comfort zone. I know when you and I first met, Sally, and you said to me that you were going to help me raise my profile, and I remember feeling vaguely terrified at the time.

Did I say that? [Laughter]

Yes, you did! [Laughter] But with a few of your less than gentle shoves it's safe to say I've done some things in the last year or so that have, you know, pushed me out of my comfort zone and have been really good for me.

Fantastic, because you're a great speaker, you know, you're brilliant. So, can I ask you then some fun questions, if I may? And I love asking these. Who's your favourite fictional lawyer?

Well not just Jessica Pearson for her wardrobe!

Oh yes, I didn't know that!

I think Alicia Florrick who's – I don't know if you've ever watched The Good Wife/

Oh yes, yes!

So, it's about the wife of a Senator who comes back to law after having her children, so, I think for two reasons. One, you know, I appreciate the difficulty of managing your family and a career. But secondly, my parents divorced when I was about 21, just in my first year at University, having gone through a bit of a difficult financial time, and mum hadn't worked for you know 25 years, and she went back into the job market and she was – I mean I will say that she wasn't somebody that particularly was driven for a career, but she nevertheless you know at nearly 50 she had to start from scratch, and as a very bright, capable woman, she was kind of doing initially warehouse work and then admin work ...

Blimey!

... and she did. I mean she studied a law degree actually part-time as well but never got to use it, which is a shame. But I think it gave me the kind of determination that I always wanted to know I would be alright and could support myself, and I see that in Alicia Florrick, and that's why I quite like her as a character.

I didn't ask you about role models before. So, your mother would be a role model then?

I think so, I mean she was a wonderful mother. I lost her a few years ago, so she's not around now, but yes, she was a wonderful, wonderful mother. I think she probably regretted that she'd let her career go quite so much when it became so much more difficult in life, but you know ...

Yes, thank you for sharing that. Alicia Florrick, yes, great! Can I ask you about a book that has changed you?

I find this really difficult because I'm a massive reader ...

Yes, you love the Women in the Law Book Club, I know you do.

… any opportunity, and I will read kind of anything from autobiographies to crime to chick-lit to anything. But I've recently been reading a bit of Brene Brown's work, I don't know if you've heard of her at all.

No, I haven't. Is she an American author?

Yes, she's a Shame researcher actually I think, but she's written a few books sort of around vulnerability really, and it's about how you will think of vulnerability as always being a negative thing, but actually how being vulnerable and allowing yourself to show up in life as your authentic self is one of the bravest things you can do, and I just really enjoyed reading her work, and it's really resonated with me.

Oh brilliant, I need to read that. Then finally, have you got a quote that you live your life be?

There's a really lovely quote by Maya Angelou where she says – and I apologise, I may have paraphrased this slightly – but it's something along the lines of 'I have learned that people will forget what you said and what you did but they'll never forget how you made them feel', and I just think that's a really nice way to think about your interactions with people, and particularly now I'm in a management role because I realise that what I say or the way I behave towards somebody very junior can really impact their day, and I would like them to all feel that I do that in a positive rather than a negative way.

Yes, absolutely, I love that. Oh gosh, that's a good one! I wish I'd thought of that! [Laughter]

You can borrow that. [Laughter]

Rachel Roberts, thank you so much, I really appreciate you coming on.

My pleasure, thank you.

A big thank you to Rachel Roberts who's the Managing Partner at Stowe Family Law in Leeds and Huddersfield. This episode of the Podcast is sponsored by Stowe Family Law.

Miriam Gonzalez Durantez

On this month's episode I'm thrilled to speak to Spanish international trade lawyer, Miriam Gonzalez Durantez, Lady Clegg. As well as practising law, Miriam is also the Vice Chair of UBS Europe, a company that provides investment advisory services, and she is a founder of the international charity, Inspiring Girls. Hello Miriam, welcome to the Women in the Law Podcast. We're delighted to have you with us. Can we start from the beginning? Many people will know you as an international lawyer. I suppose lay people, not in the law, will know you as Mrs Clegg, but we at Women in the Law UK know you for being a fantastic international lawyer, and I wanted us to go back from the beginning and ask you, I'm fascinated by why you chose the law, and how you became so successful, essentially from a small village in rural Spain to an expert in international law.

Well it was by chance, really. I never managed to become a lawyer in private practice, I never planned that, it simply happened. During the time when I was starting, I had chosen humanities simply because I started in my village and my whole primary and secondary education, and my mother was the chemist teacher and physics teacher.

Oh right!

So, I was determined not to be with her as my teacher, [Laughter] and I chose humanities. And as a result, when I finished humanities, I thought about the possible careers and degrees to study at University, and law seemed like a rather broad option that would not close many doors. I didn't really know what I wanted to do. And it's fair to say that at the time many women of my generation, you know, they didn't really know what to do, and they either have a very clear vocation and had studied humanities, they could do a law degree, precisely because it keeps doors open, so that's how I ended up with a law degree. But I have to say that for many years I wasn't at all practising as a lawyer, I was a trade negotiator and then an advisor on foreign affairs, so it was only late in my profession in life that I went back to private practice.

Ah, I see. What was the difference between that work and when you went to private practice? Some of our listeners are students, so, you know, when you were dealing with trade negotiations, for example, were there skills that you used then when you went into private practice?

Some of the skills are similar, like being able to deal with huge amounts of information and distil what is important to you or not. But then I think that in private practice the analytical skills are particularly important, especially in the kind of work that I do with sanctions, investigations and so on. While in the world of trade negotiations and foreign affairs, there is much more of the strategic understanding, in particular in the trade negotiations about being able to have the instinct as to where the other part would be moving, so that you can sort of choregraph it, [Laughter] and a trade negotiator is the one who makes the other side feel that they are winning when they have not.

Yes. What was it about international trade that particularly fascinated you? And was it a very masculine world?

I have always been drawn towards international issues, probably precisely because I come from a small village and I was born when Spain was still a dictatorship, and the generation of my parents was very keen on telling us all that, you know, if we studied hard we could do whatever we wanted, and that rather than having that endogamic look at the country that predominated during the dictatorship in Spain, that we should be looking outside. So, they all encouraged us to travel and to look abroad, and I think that that is why I have always been an internationalist. And pretty much everything that I have done in my career has been an international angle, and even now that I do quite a lot of political commentary in Spain, I am constantly trying to do the comparisons between the country and other countries, so that has always been the motive of my career. And yes, it is quite masculine. I think that the trade worlds, trade law worlds in particular. And I set up one of the first specific trade practices in the city of London. It was particularly dominated by men because it tended to be done beforehand by corporate lawyers who happened to do a little bit of sanctions here, a little bit of export control, so it wasn't really their main role. And, as you know, the corporate world has traditionally been mostly men. Now, it's changing a bit, but probably not fast enough.

Yes. Often, you'd probably be the only female voice around the table. Did you ever struggle to be taken seriously?

Well, that happens still now. And it constantly surprises me that, you know, the 21st century, there's still so many occasions that I am the only woman at the table. And also, which is, I think much more significant than normally, I am the only one at that table who realises that I am the only woman. [Laughter] So, I think that we all need to do much more about highlighting whenever there is a real lack of female presence, because sometimes people do not even notice. And I have a struggle. I think that most women have a struggle at some point to be taken seriously. We all have plenty of anecdotes when we have gone to a meeting with some men and they assume that they were the bosses when in fact the boss was – that last half a second really for everybody to understand what is the hierarchy there. I normally advise people not to let the anger silence you. Make sure that everybody hears you. Don't become silent. Don't become aggressive. Just, you know, take it naturally, and normally, within a few minutes everybody understands what is your value - if you have value, because you have to have value.

Yes, absolutely, absolutely. Can I ask you, can you remember a case or a job that shifted things in your career, or shifted your reputation?

Not so much a case, you know, although I have had crucial cases for me. Obviously, the kind of work I do, very related to compliance, I would not be able to talk about it or I would have to kill you.

I know, I thought that! [Laughter]

Something that really made a big difference to me was Brexit, and up till then I was doing a lot of work for corporates and for countries, and trade was considered a little bit specialised advice. And then suddenly Brexit happened and put trade squarely within the everyday agenda, and it meant that reputationally it became much more of an open kind of work, and lots of people started asking about the kind of advice that I provided, and I have to say that that is happening in the US as well, mostly thanks to President Trump who has put trade again on the agenda. So, it has been quite interesting to find that I started doing something quite specialised and now it is rather fashionable to do trade law.

Well, let's hope we get more women doing it! [Laughter] Just on that point, how has the move to the US been? Have you, you know, rebuilt your career? We know that you're on the board of USB and so on, but I just wondered, you know, how that's transcended moving your family across, and how you're finding working in the US?

Well, for me it was quite straightforward, because being an international trade lawyer I was always used to working from wherever, and the amount of work that I have done from airports throughout my professional life, you'd be really surprised to hear! [Laughter] So, that hasn't been so much of an issue and I continue doing pretty much the same kind of advice, and sometimes even for the same clients. The time difference is brutal, and you have to adapt to that and to the fact that when you put together the deadlines with the time difference, you need to be even more organised than you were before. And the other big difference for me has been to understand the market here, which is a rather closed market but is very, very exposed to European Regulation in particular, and there is a lack of understanding of how that regulation is developed and how it affects them, you know, what can be done multi-laterally, and that is – I'm finding that fascinating really, because it is companies mostly with huge ideas here. They think very, very big, but there is quite a lot of lack of understanding of some of the regulation in other parts of the world, so you know, it's a great challenge and I'm thoroughly enjoying it.

Absolutely! Gosh, you're so clever. You're amazing really. I don't know if I could do it.

Everybody can do it!

Everyone can do it. Actually, that's a big plug. Come on girls! And I'll come on in a moment to Inspiring Girls Global, but can I just ask you this before. You're of course — your husband is of course a former leader of the Liberal Democrats and was formerly the Deputy Prime Minister, Nick Clegg. I just wondered how his political success affected your career as a lawyer, and how you coped with the additional pressures that public scrutiny added to your life?

Well, I tried to keep things rather separately from the very beginning, and I was lucky in a way that when Nick became part of the Government, there had already been other women, namely Cherie Blair, who was working and had a husband who did an even more prominent job. So, in a way I was the lucky one! [Laughter] I had seen how she had coped with it, and I tried to impose very clear barriers on the kind of free time and how much was expected from me in the political world, and I think probably because I was very open about it at the beginning, and to be fair also probably because I'm Spanish and I was considered the foreigner. [Laughter] It worked rather well, and I never really had any big issues. You accept that you have to submit yourself to a system of conflicts, and for me it implied that I had to tell all my clients that I would need to give their name to the Ethics Office so that everybody could check at any point whether there could be any tiny possibility of a conflict. But you get used to that very quickly, and obviously if the clients have a trust relationship with you, that is normally never a problem, and for me it was never a problem. And then you accept that the rest of the public is scrutiny and having from time to time, you know, a naughty journalist who would aim to dig into something or so which is not appropriate, you just accept it as part of the territory. And provided that you don't get too worked up, it doesn't affect you.

Yes, well I ask that question because Cherie Blair, who's been on this Podcast, talked about the challenges of fulfilling the diplomatic appointments expected of the wife of a politician whilst sustaining a challenging career in law. So, I just wondered how it was for you and whether, you know, you were ever pressured to step back from your career and available to support your husband I suppose. So, anyway, that's why I was asking that question. Now, I know you've got three boys - I've got two boys and a daughter – and you've got a successful career. How do you look after your wellbeing? How do you juggle? And really, is the structural legal profession good for supporting mental and physical wellbeing for people who work within it?

Well, there's lots of questions!

I know! [Laughter]

I deal with it badly, basically. Because when I am in one particular place I am quite diligent about spending time running, and for me that has been a lifesaver really because it's not only good for the body but it's particularly good for the mind, and my best ideas tend to happen either when I'm running or when I'm doing something related to the house like doing the dishes [Laughter]. You know, some of those routine moments in order to be able to think properly, and I do kind of weights and have started doing Pilates, but it is also true that whenever I have to travel my whole schedule goes out of the window! Re-start again, but the beginning of restarting that process is always painful to find the will to get into the routine again. And no, I don't think that the legal profession by and large is good about the wellbeing, physical and mental, of its workers. And sometimes I think that we are still set in an old-fashioned industry, and you see people piling up the hours. You know, at the end of the day, many of us save time, which is a surprising concept in this day and age, and it's like if many have not evolved into thinking we should be looking at ourselves and, you know, the more integrated the teams, the better, the happier the teams, the better and the healthier the teams, the better. I think there are many other industries that have done that, that work on updating themselves much more than us, and for us it is still a bit of homework.

Yes, absolutely. One of your children, like my own child, was diagnosed with cancer and needed a transplant, and I just wondered how you coped workwise and as a family with that? When in one's life career is everything but then life and something big like that when you have children, I know with my son, you know, it happens, how did you manage to cope, and how did the family manage to cope?

Well, Antonio didn't need a transplant, but he needed chemotherapy, and when that happens, obviously your job takes a very secondary role but it's also true that you become rather pragmatic. And I remember thinking we cannot simply give up everything because we don't know how this is going to develop and what kind of resources we are going to need to deal with this, so you're constantly trying to think about how you keep things going but obviously changing completely your priorities while that is happening. And for me, you know, I had to accept it and I had to accept that during a couple of years it was much more difficult to keep my practice at the level that I had, and I was super lucky because I had a really, really good team that knew me very well and to make sure that things go on. But there is no doubt that when big things happen in your life related to health, you know, sometimes you have to make compromises and, you know, I would make those compromises anytime.

Yes, yes, me too. Thank you for sharing that. Now, can I ask you about your charity work and the amazing, Inspiring Girls. What is Inspiring Girls and why did you set it up?

Inspiring Girls is a very simple idea. It's about connecting female role models with girls, and showing to girls, all the 12-14 years old girls, all the many things that women already do, so that they can choose freely what they want to do themselves, and also so that we can inspire them and help them to go in whatever direction they want. And we showcase all sorts of women. It's by no means only the CEOs of the big investment banks. It's those and also women who are starting and in any kind of job, and all women, young women – whatever it is, we really believe in the whole concept of diversity and also showing all the possible options. All that it requires is one hour of your time per year, and we make it super-simple now because you don't even need to go physically to the schools, but we have a tool now to be able to do it remotely using technology, and also to reach out to pretty much every girl with access to internet in the world. But physically, we are in 15 different countries already, and we are hoping to reach 20 this year, 2020, which is a good number!

Yes, absolutely, good number! [Laughter]

Exactly! And I wanted – I'm the founder and the Chair of it. I originally had the idea because I saw some research from the Girl Guides that if you are into gender issues, they are a really good source of research because they have access to lots of girls. But more than 55% of the girls said that they felt themselves that they did not have enough access to female role models and I thought, you know, how absurd because I on my own know thousands of amazing women who are not in newspapers, magazines, glossy magazines, television all the time, but they are amazing! So, I would love to show them to the girls, and that's what we did. And, you know, I was completely surprised to see the enormous success that it had from the very beginning, and whenever we go to a country we continue having the same reaction, and I'm convinced that there are so many people eager to help and that the only thing that they need is somebody telling them, you know, here, this is what you can do, in concrete terms, and they go and do it!

Yes, absolutely. And who were your role models?

Well, I grew up in a village in the middle of nowhere in Spain really, and there were not very many women working there. My mum probably was one of the ones who was most determined to have a career and having to defend that she wasn't disrespecting my father by doing so. So, obviously my mother and my grandfather also had a tremendous impact on me by insisting, you know, that I should study and do well and so on. But then when I was a Foreign Affairs Advisor, one of the women who really had a big impact on me was Anna Lindh who was the Foreign Affairs Minister of Sweden …

Yes

… who was sadly assassinated, Eurosceptic actually, and she was young and there were not many female ministers around, and I remember that she came – you know, all the ones who were there power dressed and so on, and there came this woman just with trousers and looked almost like a teacher, and she didn't even have a briefcase, she had a backpack, and I remember just drinking it all, mimic her and so on. And she had young children, and it was when I started having young children, I remember her telling me, you know, you have to set your boundaries. If you cannot do cocktails in the evening, just say that you have a 'no evenings policy', and the first time I say to an Ambassador, 'I have a no evenings policy', I sort of closed my eyes thinking, oh my God, this is the end of my career, and nothing happened! Nothing happened, everybody accepted it, so she was actually very, very influential on me.

That's such a good policy. I'm going to remember that! [Laughter] Can I ask you, you have of course three boys, how do you view men's role in the fight for equality?

Oh, I think that is absolutely crucial, and to me this is the main thing that has changed over the last few years, probably because of the "Me Too" campaign. That was such a big moment that many men started thinking, you know, some of this behaviours that we have accepted, was it okay for us to feel that this was normal, and I think that that triggered many men just thinking about equal rights and feminism more widely. And for me, you know, that has changed the whole thing, because now it's a transversal movement and now it's just a question of time how we get there. Whenever something becomes transversal in society, you know, of course it always works, and at an anecdotal level, when I started Inspiring Girls it was only women really who came with their companies and so on, telling people about the campaign. Then kind of two to three years later we started getting the fathers of doctors coming, and now it's amazing! You know, we have all sorts of men, fathers of doctors and fathers of sons, and men without children, and they all want to participate, and I'm thinking now constantly what can we do for them to do, because they keep saying, how can we help, so we need to give them things to do.

And what sort of, what lessons do you teach your boys then in all of this? Is there anything? I don't know if we teach the boys any different. Apart from making my boys take their food to the plate, to the sink and try to get them to stack the dishwasher, but it becomes a problem then. Are there any lessons that you teach your boys?

That's a problem for teenagers, whether they are boys or girls! [Laughter] Generally, I don't go around just lecturing my children about, you know, feminism and equality and so on. I think that they see it in the house and they get it through osmosis almost now because whenever there is respect – and even Nick and I, you know, we don't do 50/50 every day, and I do fundamentally much more of the house, that's even when I have been busier than he has been. So, there are lots of things that you could point to, thinking, you know, this can be done differently, but the basic respect and considering each other as equal, and suddenly one needs to do something and the other one steps in and so on, I think that that is the main thing that they see. And in my experience, not only my children but that whole generation, they really have equality in their DNA. They cannot understand the discriminations.

Yes

It is us who bring the discriminations to them. So, the best thing that we can do with all that new generation is not to interfere too much really, because they are much better than us when it comes to equality.

Absolutely, absolutely. Can I ask, what are you most proud of in your career?

Well, I'm very proud of having kept the family together throughout the years when Nick was under intense public scrutiny, and I think that we are very proud as a family to have come out of that and then out of a very serious illness without being bitter people. Like, we have always retained a sense of happiness and sense of humour, and I think that that is probably the best thing that we can leave to our children.

Oh, I love that! And how is your son now?

He's very well, he's very well, thank you very much. He's recovered and, you know, have to make always a bit of a mental effort not to feel victim of the health that you no longer have, so you have to work mentally on some of that. And I myself, you know, I imagine that you know it probably better than I do, but you lose a little bit of the trust in the body, and you know you normally looked at your children and you knew whether they were well or bad, and then when you have an experience like this, you think, oh perhaps, you know, they look well but I don't know, they may have something terrible inside, and so you mentally have to work on it, but we are really, really lucky because he has fully recovered.

Absolutely, absolutely. Have you got any advice for young women who want to rise to the top?

Well, I think that it's always very important not to hide your ambition, and not to feel guilty about your ambition. Not everybody wants to go to the top of whatever it is, but if you want, and you really have that ambition, you don't need to be constantly, you know, apologising for it. It's absolutely legitimate to do so. You obviously need to put that together with hard work, and it's not okay for everybody to want to go up there without being able to, you know, put the effort that it takes to get there, but I normally keep meeting lots of women who, you know, you can see they are eager to go further and there is a little bit of, oh you know, I'm sorry that I want to do this. It's like, don't be sorry for this, you have every right to want to be at the very top of your profession, and I hope you do.

Yes. Can I ask, is there one thing that you want to change to ensure that the legal profession remains relevant for the next decade maybe? You know, we celebrated 100 years of women in the law last year, just in December. Is there any one thing so that we remain relevant?

Well, for me I think something that is really important is to bring back integrity to the centre of the legal profession. I think that because it has become very much of a business with big companies around, too much focus is being put on generating money almost at any cost. And at the end of the day we have the same rules that apply in pretty much every other job, which is that we need to do things with integrity and never cutting corners, and never stepping over the breadline, and that to me, whether you're a man or a woman, continues to be the most important thing in the legal profession. And then, more generally, I think that we just need to start modernising the profession. It is not okay that there are still so many lawyers who feel forced to go to an office from 7:00am till 10:00pm/11:00pm/whatever, working their weekends, and sometimes you say, like, what exactly are you doing there that you cannot do somewhere else with a computer? You know, it's just – why can't we just modernise this profession so that we can make it a little bit more human and we don't lose all the talent that we are losing, particularly women I think. Many women abandon when they become senior associates and they cannot make it to partner before they have children, and it's such a pity because it's fantastic talent for the profession.

Yes, absolutely. You, of course, have written several books. You know, how did the writing come about? And then I'll ask you who your favourite fictional lawyer is, and your favourite book.

Well, I have done three books. The first one was pretty much about something I was working on, which was the World Trade Organisation Telecoms, so that was pretty straightforward because I was a co-author and it was just about, you know, downloading my knowledge of those negotiations basically. And then, very oddly, I did a cookbook. People ask me if I'm mad when I tell them this. But I run an internet blog with my children on cooking, and I did it in a hidden manner when Nick was in Government. And I was very, very keen to internationalise Inspiring Girls, and I needed some money to do that. So, somebody came out with the idea of, why don't you put your blog into a cooking book, and then we sell that and with that money we can start Inspiring Girls, which is what I did.

Wow!

And some ideas and some anecdotes to make it a bit more relevant and so on. And I have to say, with all that money we've managed to launch in the first four countries. I'm really very grateful!

Wow!

And then the very last thing that I have done, which I have just published, is a book on liberalism and politics, and I sort of taken ideas to go forward in Spain from the political view, and that to me it has been a pleasure writing it because I love politics and I love my country, and I never understand why countries do not start copying each other much more and getting the good ideas from one country into another country. So, it has been wonderful to put that together and I was, and I became a bestseller and, you know, I was really delighted with the whole process.

Well, I've tried to order that book. It is in Spanish, so I've asked some of my Women in the Law UK here lawyers, albeit, you know, we're in Manchester as our headquarters, lots of Spanish people here, to try and translate. So, I hope it arrives soon. I don't know if it is – is it in English? Have you got an English version coming out?

It's not, and it's very much about the Spanish system, so I'm not sure how it would go down. [Laughter]

Well, we've got Man City and Man United here so, you know, it'll go down very well! And do you have a favourite fictional lawyer?

Well, you would not be very surprised because pretty much every lawyer that I know thinks of Atticus Finch.

Oh yes, yes.

If you read that. I don't know whether it is or not, but you read that normally as I did during your teenager years, and those books always have much more impact on you than anything else that comes afterwards. But, actually, I think that that focus that he had on integrity, that is something that I believe very much.

Absolutely. And do you have a quote that you live your life by? Do you have a quote that is meaningful to you?

Not a quote, but I believe a lot on the keep trying, and I just stand up again and you just keep trying, and when you come to my age, and I am 51, you realise that, you know, nothing is linear. So, you have good moments and bad moments, and sometimes you put an enormous amount of effort into something and you think that you deserve something and it doesn't work out, and you feel at that moment that, you know, this is going to be a disaster for the rest of your life. And I'm finding that, you know, the energy and the effort taking one more step, just try one more time and see what happens. You don't need to map out your whole life, just one more time. That to me has always helped me a lot, and sometimes you are surprised when you look backwards to see that things that you wanted and since, you know, are so important in your life, actually it was for the better. So, just keep going.

Miriam Gonzalez Durantez, Lady Clegg, thank you so much for talking on the Talking Law Podcast.

Helena Kennedy QC

On this month's episode, I'm thrilled to speak to Baroness Helena Kennedy QC of the Shaws. We started by talking about her long career.

Oh listen, I've been a barrister since 1972, so we're talking about 48 years, you know, we're talking I'm a real old bird, you know, so ...

You're not, you're wearing a fabulous jacket, some wonderful pearls, you don't look like an old bird to me! That's amazing.

Well, I mean I qualified when I was 22 so, you know, there we are. And I qualified at a time when there were very, very few women at the Bar. It was 6%, you know, that was 6 out of 100.

Is that all?

Yes. And I went into practice. I mean, probably the qualifying was maybe about 9%, but quite a lot of women, you know, married or whatever and just didn't even do pupillage. But what made me even rarer at that time was that I was from a working-class background. I was from a very, very different background from most of the, well from, I think, except me, all of the women that were studying with me, you know, around that time. I came from Glasgow, I was from a working-class family, brought up in a tenement until I was 11, and ten in a Council house. I went to the local schools, Catholic schools, we were very much part of the Catholic community in Glasgow. So, you know, we were not well-off people. We were people who, my father had periods of unemployment, and I remember as a child there were difficult times and my mother did waitressing and things to kind of cover the bills. But my parents were thoroughly decent good people and they had a strong sense of social responsibility and giving something back, and they were very good Catholics and not dogmatic. I look back on it and I think they were really fine people. My father was in his Trade Union, and a lot of that was about industrial injuries and things happening to people which would have left them very hard up if there hadn't been a strong Union to advocate their cases. And so I became very aware of the whole sort of social circumstances which meant that people's lives could suddenly be stricken. And I was good at debating at school.

Yes, I was going to say …

And I enjoyed that. It was very much part of the Scottish tradition that you debated, you know, and I remember I did Latin and Greek at school. I was pretty clever, and so Mr Lovell who taught us Classics – it was a mixed school, boys and girls, a Catholic State School – and I remember him. He really brought me on as a debater from when I was about probably 12, and I remember him saying, you know, you'll be on the side of, you know, the death penalty, and you, John Brown, will be on the side against the death penalty, and I was saying, no, no, no, I'm against the death penalty – because of course this was, you've got to remember this was in the 60s, the early 60s …

Oh gosh!

… and so it was the very time when, you know, the death penalty was ending, you know, where they were putting legislation through, and my family were against the death penalty and so I'd heard my parents discussing it, and so I wanted to be on that side, and he said, no, no, no, debating's about learning how to put your feet into the shoes of other people. And so, in a way, it was a preparation for being a lawyer.

Yes.

The subject I truly loved at school was English. I loved English and history, and I was pretty much a humanities person from the off. And I thought I would go to University to do English, because I imagined the idea of being able to just read all those books that I desperately wanted to read, but I was diverted into doing law.

Yes, I was going to say why law?

Well, what happened was, I mean I always tell the story about the fact that I certainly was aware from my father talking about industrial injuries and so on about how ordinary folk just, you know, had difficulties in getting good lawyering. But I also was aware that once my mother suffered an injury where we lived in a poor area, I mean, which when we moved up to Pollokshaws - and Baroness Kennedy of the Shaws ...

Oh, I see!

Yes, it's part of the place where we're from. Well, at that time there were a lot of very old houses and stuff, and my mother had her head split open by a slate that fell off a building that was neglected. It almost blinded her, and I remember people saying to her, May, you should go to some lawyers because they shouldn't have let that building be in that state, and so forth. And my mother, who was a douchty woman, I mean she wasn't frightened of many things, but she said, I don't want to, they'll charge us a lot of money and we haven't got the money to pay a lot for a solicitor, and she was frightened to even go there, and she had to be persuaded to go to a solicitor. And that stayed with me, that idea that for many people the idea of engaging with the law is just so, so not open to them, and it's not something they would instinctively think of doing. And the cost is a serious consideration, and my God we should think about it now as Legal Aid has been decimated.

Yes.

But I came down and got a summer job when I was 17. I came to London and I worked for the summer holidays. And I worked in an employment agency. I saw the ad in the newspapers, and I was a Girl Friday in an employment agency in the City. You don't have Girl Fridays nowadays, but I mean I used to basically be a sort of runner and getting people lunches and things, and then I used to be answering phones and all of that. And I became friendly with some students who had holiday jobs, and some of them were guys who did, sort of, you know, office work like filing and that sort of thing, and a number of them were students who were at the London School of Economics. And you've got to remember, well, you might not remember because you're too young and many of your listeners will be too, but at this time, 1968, was a very important time. The Vietnam War was going on, students around the globe were actually very upset at the idea that we might be, you know, at risk of falling into yet more wars. Our parents had fought in the Second World War, my father had, and so we were very much against the idea of war. We were also very much against the idea of, you know, making decisions for people rather than leaving nations to decide for themselves what kind of systems they wanted. And so we were all kind of against the Vietnam War, and certainly at school we were against the Vietnam War, and so I met these students who were sort of all studying and they were at University and they were politically aware, and I thought I want to be part of that. One of the boys was studying law, and I remember thinking, that does sound like something I ought to be doing where I can make a difference to society, and so that was why I made the choice. And I think, it's very interesting nowadays because I often have these conversations, most of us choosing to do law, of course there's the business about being someone in a profession, and that's very appealing and the kind of, if you like, security and the status and all the good things that come with that and, you know, hopefully being well paid, although too many are not well enough paid nowadays and people don't realise that. But I wasn't interested in the money or the status or anything, I wanted to make a difference, and I think that most people choosing law, they know that good law makes for good societies, and good legal systems make for decent societies, and they come in with good intentions. And I don't want lawyering to be seen as being just a business. I want it to have that sense in which it's a vocation and that we're contributing to something bigger. And even if it's in a small way, that that's our purpose in becoming lawyers.

Do you know, that is such a brilliant summary, because I really applaud that. What do you think about people wanting to study law and practice law as you did?

For me, coming into the law was really a vocation. I wanted to make a difference to society. I wanted to be acting for people who had little voice within the legal system. And even if people become commercial lawyers, I do believe that for the majority of people becoming lawyers it's because they do want to make a difference, and they do recognise the importance of law as being one of the fundamental aspects of a society, and that, you know, adherence to the rule of law is so important that most of us become lawyers, not just to become business people, you know, and making money, but actually because we want to make that contribution. And we have to constantly remind the world of that and to remind lawyers of that, that they're more than businessmen and women that actually contribute into something bigger and that we have to keep that sense that we're in part of vocation, part of a profession, where ethics of a high standard are so vital. Our willingness to represent people who sometimes are abhorred by the rest of society. You know, we have to keep reminding people that being a lawyer is not about just being a business person.

Absolutely. I mean, I totally, totally agree with you. And for you as a feminist, because you've written some wonderful books which we've all enjoyed. We read one of your books, your recent book about whether or not British justice is not against women but …

Does it deliver for women? I mean it's a kind of obvious thing but when I started seeing this back in the 70s it wasn't obvious, and what I was saying was, who made law? And basically, you know, our institutions, our nations have been run by men, and the nature of our world was that power was in the hands of men, and those who made law, made decisions about what the rules of society were, were the guys. And the absence of women from law-making has meant that law often doesn't deliver for women. And so even now when we're increasing the numbers of women within systems, within institutions, unfortunately they're often not in the places where law is being made, and often we've not been challenging the nature of law itself. Because sometimes it's the actual law, the black letter of law, that fails women because it's been drawn in a way that was reflecting men's lives and not the lives and reality for women. I mean, the most obvious example for me was around issues to do with self-defence, you know, in domestic violence or in any circumstances, or in circumstances of sexual violence like rape. Somehow there was this expectation that people would fight like a lion, defending their honour or, you know, that women could walk away or leave the home if they were being battered, and you would hear Judges saying – and prosecutors saying – you know, well why didn't she leave if it was so terrible? And so the assumption was it was being exaggerated, when in fact, you know, you've got to look at were the rules made with women in mind? Were they made recognising the kind of, if you like, the power balance within relationship, and within sexual intimacy how often that might go awry, and who was making the decisions as to how it should be? All of that stuff. And when I started practising at the Bar back in the 70s, I knew of class stuff. I knew what it was like to be a girl from a working-class family, and I knew that the problems that confronted working-class people. My mother was someone that people came to with their problems. My father was a Trade Unionist, he worked in newspapers, despatching as a despatch hand, getting newspapers distributed around the country, and so they were people who kind of did things for other people. And so I knew how things were around class and I had a fairly strong political sense about, you know, how class operated in our society and who did not have power.

Yes.

But I also learned suddenly, because it was that moment, was how women's lives were affected by a system which disempowered women. And I became a feminist at a time when there was that second wave of feminism where suddenly we were shining the spotlight on this, and we've got to remember why that was. It was because in the United States there had been the Civil Rights Movement in the 60s of course. It grew out of a long period of challenging to slavery and so forth, but the fact that there was still a kind of apartheid in America and that black people were second-class citizens and the Civil Rights Movement led by people like Martin Luther King, but by white progressive people joined in to say this has to stop, and recognising that privilege. So then women started saying, hold on, what about us? In a similar way that black people have been treated as second-class citizens, women too are kept in subordinate positions.

Absolutely!

And so that gave rise to a lot of the change that we now are still grappling with, but we've seen a huge difference. And the same thing happened of course in Northern Ireland. Catholics in the community in Northern Ireland started saying, you know, hold on, we're also second-class citizens here, and so, you got the Civil Rights Movement in Northern Ireland. And so, there was an unleashing of that around the world of people saying we've been colonised. Imperialism has placed us in a secondary position. And so, there was more and more of this voice rising, saying, we demand to be treated in a manner to be absolutely recognised in the dignity of us as individuals. And although the Human Rights Declaration – you know, human rights had happened after the Second World War – it was really in the 60s and then into the 70s that organisations like Amnesty International, Human Rights Watch, took sort of roots amongst young people wanting a different world. And so, I was part of that generation. And so, I wanted to be a lawyer who was involved in those things, and so I started looking at how does law deliver for women? And I of course often went to Court for women, you know, shoplifting in Marks & Spencer or something, and you started looking at the lives and the circumstances that had driven women to these things. And so, I then started writing about that and I also started looking at how the profession itself was so discriminatory against women.

Yes.

Chambers said quite clearly, you know, we don't take women, or once the Sex Discrimination Act came in, people didn't say it so loudly.

What did they do? Because I remember on a previous Podcast with Dame Laura Cox, she talked a lot about this, you know.

Yes, I mean it was so interesting. I mean, Laura's of a similar generation to me. First of all, the Sex Discrimination Act made it clear that you couldn't be saying we don't take women, which of course they had done up until then. I mean when I was looking for a pupillage they were saying 'we don't take women'. It was very hard for me to get a pupillage. And of course women, most of my friends, of the women that, you know, my friend Hilary Heilbron or whatever, they came from different kinds of backgrounds where they had connections, and Hilary and I have discussed it recently. I didn't have those connections, I wasn't from that kind of background with, you know, anybody in the law who was connected. So, I had to really bludgeon some poor man into taking me as his pupil, and he warned me that I wouldn't have an easy time, and I didn't! And so we ended up, I mean, it was very interesting because they then had to not discriminate, but they would say to people, 'are you engaged?', 'are you planning to get married?', or whatever, and so in interviews apparently they used to ask people that. I didn't have that experience myself, but I knew women who had, and it was interesting. The women who had succeeded often made great sacrifices, remaining childless or remaining single, or whatever, and Chambers liked that. That was fine. They wanted what they called spinsters, you know, the spinster successful woman, or women often that sent their children off to boarding school very, very young, the very privileged women that I knew who were older than me. The way they managed was that their children would had gone away to school.

So, how did you manage though because you've got three children? And you were married!

Well, I didn't have my children until I was in my 30s.

Right.

And so, I had three of them, I was 33, 36, 39. [Laughter] How's that for planning?!

I know!

Anyway, and the thing about that was that by that time I was doing rather well, I was doing big Trials and so on. I was earning decent money. I married a guy who was a doctor. So, between us we were earning decent money and could afford decent childcare. And so, you know, that is about being privileged. I don't pretend that it wasn't because of being older and earning decent money, and there are women now who are struggling because Legal Aid has been, you know, decimated …

Decimated absolutely.

… and it's not right that people who have spent years learning their trade, learning their skills, shouldn't be paid properly.

Yes.

But to go back to the business of what happened with Chambers, when I finished my pupillage there was no question that I was going to be taken on by the Chambers. They didn't want women. And the clerks in Chambers had a lot of power because they got 10% of the earnings of their barristers, and so they didn't put opportunities in the way of women.

Yes.

And so, I looked around and with some friends we decided to set up a new set of Chambers.

That's revolutionary!

It was revolutionary actually, and I feel that I should actually write about this because there were six of us – three men and three women – and one of the women was a gay woman who was an out gay woman, you know, which was pretty rare in the 60s.

Yes, oh crikey!

She was a lesbian and she was openly a lesbian and didn't make any secret of it, and we very actively made it clear that we were very keen and we should be joined by people who were from regional minorities and so forth. And so it was a set of Chambers which is now Garden Court, and it started off as Stone Buildings and we had a little annex, and it happened because I pinched the little card that was on a notice board on Middle Temple Lane saying, 'Rooms available in Lincoln's Inn, suitable for annex. Apply here.' And so, I whipped it off the noticeboard. I moved the glass along, pulled it out, and so we were the only applicants for the rooms, and we got a junior clerk from a set of Chambers, but we made the revolutionary change in that we paid him a salary.

Rather than the sort of percentage that existed?

That's right, we didn't.

Wow!

We said no, and the reason we said no was because we knew that it put too much power – if you're getting a percentage of somebody's income then you're going to choose people that you think are going to be earning and so they always chose, you know, posh young men.

Yes.

So, we paid him a salary. And, of course, it also provided him with security.

Yes, of course.

And then we slowly grew, and we moved to Fetter Building in Inner Temple, then we moved to Garden Court, and now Garden Court exists as a huge set of Chambers in Lincoln's Inn.

Oh yes, and an annex in the North in Manchester.

That's right. And so that came out of that moment of saying we are different, and we were people who also wanted to do work that was often not very well treated by clerks in sets of Chambers. We wanted to represent juvenile offenders, we wanted to represent the law centres which were just opening up at the time. We wanted to act for Legal Aid firms in places like Hackney or up in Kilburn or, you know, in parts of London which were really working-class areas then.

Now there are no areas of working class in London! Then, we also did a lot of work for Chiswick Women's Aid, which was the first refuge for women who were battered, and we started doing that work for those women. And so, we were in at the beginning of the community law centre movement, of the refuge movement, and we started doing all of that work. Now, I earned very little money. I lived hand-to-mouth, but I really, really learned my craft, and it was wonderful. And I think did a lot of public order cases because there were lots of demonstrations. We saw the rise of the National Front at that time, and a lot of cases involving racism. We did lots of cases around basically where people were demonstrating against insidious things that were happening in society.

Absolutely.

And so, that was how our work was. And then I became pretty well-known as a civil liberties lawyer.

Yes.

I used to volunteer for the National Council of Civil Liberties and for different organisations, and then …

And then you did some high-profile cases.

… Well I started then. I moved into doing a lot of the Irish cases.

Right.

By the time I was in my late 20s I was doing some of the Irish cases as a junior barrister, being led by more senior lawyers, and I worked a lot with Michael Mansfield - who wasn't in our Chambers, he was in Cloisters - but he and I worked a lot together and then I became someone who became recognised as a lawyer who was good at dealing with high-level terrorist cases. And then I did them not just in the Irish circumstances, because it came out of the Irish troubles, but also out of – I did work on the Middle East involving Palestinians who went on Trial, and we did some cases involving, I mean, I eventually did the bombing of the Israeli Embassy, but I did the Guildford Four Appeal and the Balcombe Street Siege, and so we did a whole range of high-level work. And then, after 19 years practice, I became a QC.

Wow!

I was involved in the setting up of three different new sets of Chambers.

Yes.

The second one was Tooks Court, which I did with Mike Mansfield because I co-defended with him a lot in Irish cases. We became good friends. He then said he wanted to set up a new set of Chambers and asked if I would join it with him, and I did, and Len Woodley who was the first black QC at the Bar joined us …

Wow!

… and we had a lot of young, black lawyers come in when we set up, and it was really to provide — to break this logjam which was that black lawyers were having a very difficult time and basically, you know, they were having to set up sets of Chambers where everybody was black.

Yes. I hate this term but "Ghetto Chambers"

Yes, because traditional sets of Chambers that had existed forever were not welcoming to black advocates, and why would you want to go somewhere where you didn't see any other black people? So, we really developed Tooks Court and I was there for a number of years and then I really wanted to start doing more work in the international domain, and Geoff Robertson always did quite a lot of work in the international sphere, and he and others who were at Dr Johnson's Building were talking about setting up a new set of Chambers, and I went to Dr Johnson's Buildings. I was there for about a year and then we set up Doughty Street Chambers, which is where I still am.

I see!

Yes, that's right. So, I've been involved – I like setting up new things, I like being creative about where you take the legal system next, and Doughty Street was very interesting because not only does it do a lot of international criminal work and things in international Courts, but it's also very modern in that it started saying, you know – we hot-desked before people did that, we also had a library and a librarian. We also brought in people who were researchers and had academics who belonged to our Chambers in quite a connected way. And we also …

Which is very different.

… yes, and we had management. Instead of having a traditional clerking system - we always paid salaries but, you know, they'd get bonuses if things went well in a year - but we always paid salaries because we believed that you had to break this thing which is, you know, where your career could be affected by somebody thinking well, I'll push this case in her direction because it'll get us a lot of money, rather than letting the barrister say no, I'd rather choose a case that's not going to pay me well but where I believe that the substance of it is so important.

Absolutely.

And we also had people, you know, who – we basically had a management team – and so it was much more professionalised, I think, in the modern way and using new technology and things, and Doughty Street now is, I think, one of the well-recognised Chambers that does human rights.

Totally! And you've got Tunde Okewale there, Amal Clooney, Caoilfhionn …

Caoilfhionn Gallagher …

Henrietta Hill – all these wonderful people, women!

Lots and lots of women!

Lots of women!

I know, I know, fantastic!

And lots of minorities, which I think is amazing, and that's down to that vision.

We had a clear vision about what we wanted to do there, and it's fantastic and it's great fun and I love my colleagues, and I learn so much from them all the time, and I'm always hungry to keep on learning. But one of the things that I would say, and I would always say it when I'm talking to women coming into the law, is do other things. I mean, you're, Sally, doing other things because, you know, you're broadcasting and stuff, but it's about doing other things.

Yes, let's talk about that.

It enriches your practice.

Do you think so?

It makes you better at what you do. It means that you're also connecting with people who are not inside the law. You're not just with your own crowd.

Absolutely.

And so, I was always interested in the Arts and had lots of friends in the theatre who directed and did different things, and lots of actor friends, and so, I ended up being on the Board of the Hampstead Theatre when I was still quite comparatively young. From that I went on to being – I chaired the London International Festival Theatre – and then I ended up becoming the Chair of the British Council around the world at the point when Labour went into Government in 1997.

Wow!

But before that, I had chaired Charter 88 which was a Constitutional Reform Group where we were arguing that there should be a

Freedom of Information Act, whether there should be a Human Rights Act, whether Parliament should be reformed and so on.

Brilliant!

And again, that was why I ended up in the House of Lords. And so, other things open up to you when you do things outside of your own sort of safe space and your own particular cases, and so, I always did other things, and so it has opened up doors for me which I think have been important. And part of it of course was that from the late 70s I was very concerned about the position of women, and I championed that and I went on to the Bar Council, being a pain in the arse, but at the time I was considered very problematic and a boat rocker, and some of the people would say to me, stop rocking the boat and, you know, women will get there in the end. And I said, not fast enough for me, pal! And I really think you sometimes have to stick with what you believe in and be principled about it. And then it's become mainstream. I mean, now it's not unusual to talk about the law in the way that I talk about the law, but there was a time when I was considered a complete iconoclast. I used to appear on Women's Hour …

Yes, we enjoyed you doing that.

… Yes, and I used to be invited to make television programmes which were around the law. And it's important we talk about the law in ways that it doesn't turn it into some mystified subject. The law is about our lives, it's about the stuff – it's about all of our human relationships with employers, with landlords, with our neighbours, you know, with our lovers, with our partners in life, and so the law is everywhere. You know, some people would say it's too present, but it's about regulating relationships both internationally and nationally, and so we've got to be able to put it into language that is accessible, and so I've always believed in talking about the law in a way that makes it readily available to everybody else. And so, I started doing quite a bit of broadcasting and occasionally writing articles in the Press, and then I wrote 'Eve was Framed', and at the time, let me tell you, it was considered …

I love that book.

… it was like I threw a hand grenade. It's now nearly 30 years ago.

I know! I think there's a new published cover.

Yes, that's right. It's like I threw a hand grenade into the legal system because Judges came out saying, you know, this is completely untrue and we don't even notice that people are male or female and we treat people equally and all that kind of thing. Well, I was actually saying what does equally mean? You know, you actually have to look at the life of the person in front of you, and if you want to do justice you have to contextualise, you know. There's no point in treating a woman the same as a man if she's the mother of three kids and she's been abandoned by their father and she's the person that's having to try and make a life. And so, you know, so much of that stuff has entered, as I say, into the mainstream, and now we're sort of, you know, having to keep pushing it because some of the changes that we thought would make the difference haven't, and also we know that for women as professionals the juggling is hard, the business – it often falls to women to be the people who kind of organise …

The main carers.

… and are the main carer, and that has to be taken into account. And so, we're often talking about trying to change the working environment so that it is better for people who are parents who look after their elderly relatives or whatever. And the thing I love though is that now, you know, young men will say to me, I've got to get back home because, you know, the people who are my juniors in cases or whatever, so that's fantastic.

Which is brilliant, it really is! And does that make you think, oh right, we have actually progressed?

Well, we've come a long way, undoubtedly. I mean, it would be a pretence to say that we haven't. We just have more battles to fight. And it is terrible that domestic violence remains a blight in our lives, but let me tell you, Sally, I now am the Director of the Institute of Human Rights for the International Bar Association …

Absolutely.

… and here it is, it brings together Bar Associations from 180 countries around the world.

It's huge, it's huge!

It's huge, it's huge, and huge numbers of lawyers in it, and of course many of those lawyers are commercial lawyers, but not all of them …

Yes.

… and there are employment lawyers and, you know, I'll go out to places and domestic violence is a blight – there isn't a place in the world where women do not experience, you know – of course it happens the other way around occasionally and so on, but we're talking about the position of women in society and how we've still got a long way to go globally.

Yes.

And, you know, one of the wonderful things is that, you know, I was just recently in Pakistan and a young woman comes up to me and she said, do you recognise me? And she's a woman who actually did some pupillage with me and she now is out there and she's a Junior Minister in the Ministry of Law and Justice.

Wow!

And we're now plotting the expansion of Courts which are going to be Courts specifically to deal with gender-based violence.

Well that's amazing!

They'll be basically to deal with the problems that women face because, you know, across Pakistan there's been real issues around, you know, forcing women to marry the people who rape them. A failure to address violence against women. And so a lot of that has got to be about training prosecutors properly and so the IBA, the International Bar Association's Human Rights Institute, is working with her on doing that. And we do that kind of work all over the world, and we do incredible work training lawyers and Judges about human rights, and at this stage in my professional life I'm rather liking that I'm getting the chance of, you know, looking at systems rather than looking at doing the individual cases.

Absolutely, absolutely.

Obviously, Khashoggi was an example of my being the legal expert on that, of Jamal Khashoggi's murder at the hands of Saudi.

I mean that was, that's not the only high-profile – I mean I'm thinking Julian Assange and Myra Hindley …

Yes, I did act for Myra Hindley when she tried to escape from prison some years ago.

When she tried to escape, yes.

No, I've done lots of really – my life in the law has been wonderful and I thank God for the fact that I've had such, you know, opportunities and I've experienced good things in my life. It hasn't been all plain sailing …

No, of course.

… but I've really loved my professional life. But I want other women to have that same joy, and young men too, but I want it to be different for them. I want their struggles to be alleviated because we aren't there yet, you know, and I want to be an enabler of that kind of change and, you know, so that's been part of my life's work.

And having impact. Helena, I want to ask you about work/life balance, and then I'm going to ask about your favourite fictional lawyer, and the script that – you wrote Blind Justice, which is a fantastic production if nobody's seen it.

Well, you're all too young you see! This was back in the 80s. I put together a drama series with a wonderful playwright, Peter Flannery, and it was a television series about, at the heart of it, a woman lawyer and her colleagues in a progressive set of Chambers. A set of Chambers rather like the ones that I'd been in. It was fun doing that and of course it was about terrorism and the difficulties of doing terrorist cases and the hostility that there is from the get-go and assumptions of guilt and so on. But also then the, you know, cases involving racism, cases involving violence towards women, and so it was a fun thing to do and so it's made me look at drama as one of the ways in which you can really change attitudes, and often you can say things in drama and in creative writing that you can't do elsewhere.

Yes.

But that was an interesting thing to do. Another interesting thing that I've loved doing is that I've been involved in Higher Education, Further and Higher Education. You know, I've been the Chancellor of a number of Universities and I also was the Head of an Oxford College.

Yes, Mansfield College.

I didn't have that kind of Oxbridge education but I, all I can say is that going to Mansfield, which already had a very good record in providing opportunities for young people from State Schools, and we drove it up! We were at 92% of our young, you know the people who come to Mansfield College come from State Schools up and down the country. It made me very proud that we did that. And also, while there and being the Head of the College, creating an Institute of Human Rights at Oxford, which it never had one.

That's fantastic! I went there last year. They invited me …

Oh fantastic!

They were wonderful. I mean, I met a girl from St Helen's … a wonderful, wonderful group of people.

Well quite a number of our young come from Liverpool and come from all over, because we've got special links with State Schools up and down the country but, you know, I want to encourage people listening to know that, that it's a great place and a great place to do law. But the other thing I wanted to just mention is that, you know, we can – people get their inspiration from watching things on telly, and so you were going to ask me about, you know, lawyers that I ...

I was! Your favourite fictional lawyer and your favourite book

... my favourite fictional lawyer, oh I loved Maxine Peake in Silk, and I have to tell you ...

Was it based on you?

No [Laughter], no, all I can tell you is that Maxine Peake, I had the great joy of meeting Maxine and becoming friends with her because we did a thing for charity where I defended Lady Macbeth ...

Was that in Gray's Inn?

No, it was in the Royal Courts of Justice, and Bob Marshall-Andrews, another QC, represented Macbeth, and that was Matthew McFadyen, and lots of fabulous actors were in it, and Judge John Deed was the Judge, and Maxine was Lady Macbeth and I did get an acquittal and I got her off! [Laughter] Anyway, it was great fun and she came and spent time with me and so on, and at that time the writer of Silk was already starting work with her on that, and so she and I had lots of conversations around the business of her playing that role, and I loved it and I thought she was terrific in it.

She was terrific in it.

And she also encouraged lots of people to think you can be a working-class person and come into the law and make a success of it and make a difference to people's lives, and you can remain your own person and you don't have to turn yourself in somersaults into becoming some sort of, you know, person remote from your being and who you really are.

Absolutely.

And I've never tried to get rid of my Scots accent, I've not done that. And I've never ever not talked about the fact that I'm from a working-class background. I am proud of the fact that I, of my background and I think it made me aware of lots of things that perhaps the law needs to be conscious of, and so we need lawyers from as many different backgrounds as possible, and that's why I'm sitting here with a gorgeous, wonderful black woman who's a barrister and a successful one. It's a great joy to me too. And that's the thing ...

Thank you.

... the law needs to be enriched by people from many different backgrounds, and that's not to say that you know there aren't plenty of, you know, good middle-class folk doing great things in the law too ...

Absolutely

... but we just need all of that stuff, and we will make the law serve our communities and the world better if we have that diversity.

What a great, great place to end on! But, I've got two more questions.

Okay, fire away.

I just wondered what you do for, you know, we're always pushing wellbeing, women shouldn't burn out, do too much. Have you got any tips, anything that you can do because you do so much? You're a great advocate, you sit on all these great Boards ...

Sally, this morning I was at Pilates. I go to Pilates twice a week! I try to do Yoga if I can over the weekend, you know, if it's possible, but I now have three grandbabies ...

Oh wow!

And so I like to get the chance of spending time with them. We were yesterday playing Snap with our four-year-old granddaughter [Laughter] and …

Did you win?

Sometimes I win [Laughter] and sometimes she wins! You can't always let the other one. They've got to know that sometimes losing is fine and you have to do it with dignity. [Laughter]

Amazing.

And, yes, I love the theatre and I go to the theatre a lot. In fact, I'm going to see Maxine Peake shortly in The Welkin which is on at the National which is about all women's juries, all women's juries.

Absolutely!

… back in the 17th century, and I've written a piece for the programme notes for that. And I'm a great reader of novels and so I love reading novels.

Well could I ask you then, because you know you've written a lot of novels, you write a lot. What's your favourite? Do you have a favourite book or novel?

Well, one of the great ones of course as a kid was To Kill A Mockingbird, and it feeds on that idea of, you know, of fairness, that justice comes out of that visceral thing that every human being has, which is about what is fair.

Absolutely.

But, a book that I would recommend to everybody who cares about human rights and so on is, I love Philippe Sands book, East West Street, which is not a novel but which is a lovely piece of history about his own family. Beautifully written by a great human rights lawyer, but about how modern human rights came into being. I can think of many books but I'm also an avid crime reader [Laughter] – crime writing reader, and so many of them of course nowadays involve lawyers.

Yes, they do. Baroness Helena Kennedy, I know you said just to call you Helena, thank you so much for talking law. I've really enjoyed talking to you and we look forward to seeing you soon.

Thank you.

Robert Rinder

This Podcast is supported by Wesleyan Financial Services, providers of specialist financial advice to members of the legal profession. Wesleyan's team of dedicated experts have been helping law firms and their employees achieve financial wellbeing over many years, providing personal and commercial financial advice, in-firm seminars, and online guidance. Strategic partners with The Law Society, Wesleyan is proud of its partnership with Women in the Law UK. If you are looking to make investments or financial plans, talk to a qualified financial advisor. For more information about Wesleyan, visit wesleyan.co.uk, or to arrange a financial education event in your firm, or a no obligation financial health check, connect with Sarah Deacon, Wesleyan Area Manager on LinkedIn.

Now, on to my guest this month, Judge Rinder. I started by asking him, given his many talents for singing and dancing, writing, why it was he started a career in law.

You know, I ended up in the law really through a series of accidents. I went to University at a time of real privilege, and that privilege was that it was free, and so I left with £1,100 worth of debt. I went and did politics and modern history, with no real intention of doing the law. I mean, it was a possibility, certainly, but I didn't really know much about it. And then kind of what happened is, I really thought I'd become an actor because I'd been in the National Youth Theatre, and I've told this story several times, but I was up here in Manchester …

Yes!

… You know, I'd really deliberately chosen to go, you know, and that was because my heroine, the person who changed my life was my teacher, Jackie Grice …

Wow!

… and, you know, I'd not been really great at school. Certainly, until I was sort of 15, I was a little bit ahead, you know, and I'd given kind of childhood my undivided indifference. And then when I was about sort of 15, she looked at me and said, you know you're quite clever, and from that point she sort of became not just my role model but my sort of everything. And she'd gone to Manchester, so I thought that sounds great, and done politics and modern history. I came here. It was the 90s, you know, it was a fantastic old time. The first play I auditioned for in Manchester, I thought I'd done rather well. I think, you know, it was The Front Page was the play, and I'd read Fahilde, and I thought, oh that looks alright. I mean, I was never a great actor. I was in the National Youth Theatre, as I say, and there were some famous people. I thought, hmm, I could probably tread a board or two, but then the next person came along and read and I thought, gosh, that's the real deal, like touching the face of real talent, and that was Benedict Cumberbatch!

Oh my gosh!

I know, and so after that point I thought, not much point really! [Laughter] You know, I knew I'd never have a career beyond, you know, Heartbeat and the odd fifth rate part in Emmerdale, if I was lucky, you know, a walk-on job. And I ended up getting involved with debating, and that was my entrée into law. You know, my debating partner and I became sort of quite good at it fairly quickly. He was infinitely better than me and I, I suppose, was elevated to his standard. He raised the game and we started winning Intervarsity competitions.

Wow!

Right. I mean, he was really good. And then at that point, sort of the people that we were in each weekend at these competitions, the milieu if you like, the kind of next thing, the ipso facto was that you would become a barrister, because all of the law schools were debating. We used to debate against Inner Temple, a couple of them have now become High Court Judges, which is interesting to see how their careers have gone on.

Yes.

And so, I sort of thought well, okay, I'll have a go at this. I sort of crept, or really, I suppose you might say I slept-walked – is that the past participle of sleepwalk? – my way into it. You know, it's so different now. I didn't have a driving ambition but that was because I was free not to have that driving ambition. You know, I wasn't saddled or, you know, suffocated with debt. By the time I'd finished University with £1,100 worth of debt, I was free enough to be able to make some choices.

Yes, absolutely.

So, I went to City Law School, because I thought well, I'll do the law conversion, and I applied for criminal Chambers because that's what most of the people I debated with had decided to do, and I wanted to be clear at that point. I think I'd been to Court once. I'd certainly never seen a criminal Trial. I'd done zilch work experience, you know. Granted this was last century, but God it really does expose just how different things are now. I applied for a pupillage at the Chambers of the late Sir Desmond de Silva ...

Oh wow!

Right, and of course it was just like debating. So, a plea in mitigation, which I'd never seen but I'd sort of read about at that point, was just like making submissions, you know, triaging your best points and then selling the argument to the Tribunal. And so that went down rather well, and the interesting thing was they took five pupils at that time ...

Wow!

... right, because you could, and the result of funding pupils has been an interesting one, and no doubt we'll come onto it in terms of its impact on diversity.

Yes

But it is an interesting thing that in our year they took five of us, two were funded, me and my now very close friend – I say we were funded, we were paid £7,500 for six months.

Crikey, it's more than that now. [Laughter]

Right, it's a little bit more [Laughter] and then, you know, you're on your own. You eat what you kill in your second six months. The other three were not funded, and the other three are still in the law. My friend and I are not, and the other three are doing incredible things.

Wow!

One really very senior at the Revenue, one who's got a stellar career dealing with proceeds of crime …

Wow!

… and it was interesting because all three of them I think now, looking at how challenging it's become, how utterly challenging and difficult it's become to get pupillage, almost certainly wouldn't get it nowadays.

No.

You know, I came from what you might loosely describe as a traditional background. I look the way I look, I sound the way I sound. Sure, it's a creation which I invented by the time I was 13 in opposition to the working-class upbringing I had I suppose, to some extent. I am my own special creation, you might say! [Laughter]

Well, you're very, very much admired!

That's one way of putting it. But that was the thing, and you know I got a first, and so I ticked the boxes.

Absolutely! But that was through hard work.

Yes, that's true but, you know, anyone can read a book and do well in exams. And yes, I suspect possibly now I'd edge or elbow my way into a pupillage, but I had no experience. I didn't know what Court looked like. I wasn't able, meaningfully or effectively, to demonstrate that I had a passion for the career. You know, I just knew I wanted to be an advocate, and that was, you know, large when I ended up going to my first Trial as a pupil and I couldn't understand why it was that the Prosecutor and the police officer were reading out the interview. I thought that was very strange. Apparently, that happened in every Trial! [Laughter] It was actually Sarah Whitehouse who was doing that Trial. I think she's now in Silk.

She is actually. I think she's Treasury Counsel actually.

She is Treasury Counsel. I remember the case, so I'm sorry Sarah. [Laughter] You know, but the thing was, the extraordinary thing was that the passion came after I started.

Yes, yes.

Again, that was a gift, so I could meander my way into this gift of a career. And then it was probably about seven or eight months in when I was doing my own cases, and it's two-fold, there's a kind of macro and the micro. You know, the micro stuff is a little bit egotistical, you know, you get your first client off and there's a little thwack of endorphin [Laughter], you know, I won my first Trial. It all went downhill from there, but I did, and I thought oh this is great! But then there was this moment, for me a genuine real deal epiphany, which was that I suddenly had this moment of appreciating how important the job was. I never came with a deep-seated mission, the idea that I wanted to a Prosecutor or Defence Counsel.

Yes.

And I can't actually remember the case, I'd be lying if I said I could. It was a series of cases where I realised that I was, I realised – it sounds so silly now perhaps – that I was standing between the individual and the State, and that mattered. And then I really thought back to my grandfather who was a Holocaust survivor. That really mattered to me. He lost his four sisters and his brother, and his parents were murdered in the Second World War, and he survived the camps and came to the UK in 1946 along with 1,732 others to Windermere - they've just made a film about it – and he convalesced here. And this is really - England was gifted to him, and that's how he felt, and he felt this passion, you know, it permeated through him, it was like the golden thread. You know, sometimes, well, trite lawyers use that as their closing submission.

Yes, yes.

But for him it was woven into the tapestry that he was cloaked in. You know, and I never thought much about it. It was like, you know, dot drawing. When he used to take my brother and I to Speakers Corner - this was back in the day before Twitter when, you know, cruelty had a face and you could at least know who was saying these vile things -

Yes

And we would stand and listen to the most cruel and appalling antisemitic bile. I'd never get it, and he'd say, ah, you see in this country, he would say, this man can say what he wants. And, you know, to be present alongside somebody who had quite literally touched the face of tyranny ...

Yes

... who absolutely understood that the rule of law wasn't something, it was absolutely everything, everything to him. You know, he loved the country, and above all else he loved that he lived in a country of laws. And, I think as I represented more and more people, I became more and more passionate about that, and about chiefly defending, and I ended up defending in some, you know, some extraordinary cases. Even when I first started, you know, there are memorable ones. I represented the National Front once.

Wow!

You can imagine that, being a good, gay Jew!

Yes, exactly! Yes. [Laughter] That's quite difficult, I mean, you know, we talk about the cab rank rule at the Bar, but was that difficult? Did you think about that at the time?

No, not for a second.

No, exactly, because often we just do the cases.

Right. Completely, there was no part of me that wasn't totally shielded, cushioned in the idea – not in the idea, in the absolute fundamental importance and truth that even that person, whatever their political stripe or view, didn't just deserve a defence but that was critical, necessary, everything, everything. You know, when he used, you know, the F word and the Y word, I know, and I thought to myself – that's when he said to me, we're really glad you're here because all that solicitor does is send me, well, I'm going to use the bad language, and I said, well I remembered thinking I should do jazz hands and say oy vey. But, you know, the other thing of course that it taught me, which was a gift later on, and I suspect a lot of defence, a lot of criminal lawyers, in fact lawyers in general probably feel this, certainly criminal lawyers, you know, these were not happy humans.

No.

You must have experienced this. Anybody that's got residual energy in their life for cruelty, unkindness, hate, and wants to do that anonymously on Twitter, let alone to family and friends, isn't a happy individual.

No, no.

You know, you're sitting up all night, you know, chain-smoking Parliaments and wearing a Momo.

Yes, yes, you're absolutely spot on.

So, whenever I meet that kind of unkindness, which is just about the worst thing I can say about somebody I think, they're unkind. It says everything. Unkind. You know, I never think that they're happy people, and that always cushions the blow of their unkindness.

Yes, yes, I think I would probably say other things, but I know that we've got students who listen to this Podcast. Can I ask you then about how it was you had a hugely successful career at the Bar, how it was that you've come to leave and become hugely successful on our television screens and on our radio?

Well, I'm going to say luck, luck, luck, to both things and, you know, you might be overstating my huge success at the Bar. I mean, I did okay, but I had a lot of luck, a lot of role models and, you know, a lot of people helping me along the way, and the thing I love about the Bar most is that it is – oh God, brace yourself for this word – collegiate.

Yes.

You know, it's my Learned Friend and, boy, did I have friends that pushed me and elevated me and made me better. You know, I had luck early on because I did one case. I was defending in some Magistrates Court and there was a very influential solicitor, Mohammed Nasra, I hope he's listening, you know, and I think I'd given a police officer a hard time – I can't even remember, my Pupil Master was rather good at this sort of thing, it was never about the questions it was always about positioning the water – just because it would annoy the police officer and so you'd get the upper hand. This is of course back in the days when eyewitnesses mattered, but nowadays forget about it, it's all technical by the time you come to Court, you know, it's much more challenging and less fun than it used to be.

Yes.

And he then instructed me on a series of really high-profile cases in Birmingham when I was only about four years call, and once you get your break in that way the luck continues to build and come.

Wow.

And so, yes, I did a number of these cases. By the word 'did', I mean, I was privileged, I learned, God, I learned, I learned, I learned so much from, you know, brilliant Silks who have led me – too many to name but, you know, mentors, people like Sallie Bennett-Jenkins in my Chambers and, you know, Jane Humphryes at 3 Raymond Buildings. You know, I think of Sallie, she'll probably remember this, the last case I did, the last criminal case, was in 2010 and was a murder Trial, and I would always try, if she was available – she's always far too busy – to get Sallie to lead me. And the reason for that was, by the time 2010 came along, as we were just discussing, you know, the reality was or is that, you know, the technical evidence, let's call it that, the objective stuff was pretty overwhelming, you know, you had CCTV evidence, you had telephone cell site evidence, computer evidence. So, let's face it, by the time your client was facing that murder charge, you know, it was a much greater uphill struggle. And what Sallie ,who'd been Treasury Counsel, and by the way also having had six children, triplets, twins and one – I sometimes go and troll MumsNet and pretend I'm Sallie Bennett-Jenkins just to see what people will do [Laughter], to see the rage hit you! You know, anyway, she absolutely understood and taught me, oh did she teach me, she taught me to always remember the victims, to be sure, but also the Defendant's family, and she would find time always to explain with such care and such emotional intelligence and range what was happening, to include everybody. It's a funny story, when she was leading me on one of these cases, the clerk in the – I can't remember what Court it was at the Old Bailey – came over and said 'Mr Rinder', I said yes. She said, 'Do you know it was so lovely the way you were looking at Miss Bennett-Jenkins'. I said, well, what do you mean? She said, 'It reminded me of the way Nancy Reagan used to look at Ronald Reagan'. [Laughter] And apparently during her closing submissions to the jury I was just sat behind Sallie looking in total bewildered awe, going, yes! [Laughter] So, you know, luck really. And then in about 2006, you know, the kind of commercial turbulence, I'll call it that, of the slower and cruel unnecessary and frightening death of Legal Aid began to really bite, and I became sort of interested in proceeds of crime stuff, so I wrote this little tome about money laundering.

Yes

And I became sort of interested in that. Really because it struck me that that was how, you know, finance – well, that was how terrorist and all criminal swill got about - you know, that we needed to be focusing on the money. Also, I was quite sort of naturally talented at that sort of thing, and I never say that about myself, but I can open accounts – I'm useless in my own personal finances – but I could open accounts and very quickly tell you whether they were kosher or not.

Yes, interesting.

It's an interesting thing. I don't know but I suppose I had a sort of affinity for it. So, I ended up doing this book and then kind of did back-to-back money laundering cases. I moved Chambers - at that point, the Head of Chambers was David Waters QC, that went on to become the brilliant Orlando Parnell, and is now Johnny Laidlaw. I mean, and I'm incredibly proud of my Chambers, just how not just kind they have been but, you know, it's interesting when you go to a place where everybody is the best at what they do, it's interesting how you find, you know, almost no – what's a good way of describing bitchiness? – well, I just did! [Laughter] There's none of that stuff.

Yes.

It's a lovely environment. Because they are gainfully employed.

Exactly!

It's just great.

Yes, and you don't need, you don't need it, you know. What's the point?

Right. I'm surrounded by, you know, people at that level. Every single person there was just fantastic – IS fantastic! And, you know, I had a criminal defence practice. And then in 2010, some people may know because the Trial is still ongoing ten years later, the Government of the Turks & Caicos came a-knocking!

Yes

Now , I say they came a-knocking, I, when I went to interview for this job with Helen Garlick who was the previous Director of Overseas Corruption at the SFO, I didn't where the Turks & Caicos was. The only reason I'd heard of it was because I used to watch Miss World! [Laughter] I know it's not PC, but this was when I was a child, and I used to keep records of it! [Laughter] And it's true, and there was always Miss Turks & Caicos.

That's right! [Laughter]

Right. So, I thought, that sounds like a good job! - and it was an interesting opportunity. And the interesting part of it was that I had very much become a poacher turned gamekeeper because this was the first, the first serious prosecution I'd ever been involved in, and the idea was – and it was a real gift of an experience – was to go out SFO model-style where barristers work alongside the police officers, really to build a case. And my practice up to that point had chiefly been looking and prodding at weaknesses in large cases to try and, well, win abuse of process arguments. It's very hard to do, but I used to enjoy that kind of aspect of technical law. And so, I went to the Turks & Caicos Islands and worked for the better part of four years off and on there …

Wow!

… alongside, at the time, you know, police officers that had certainly never met anybody like me! [Laughter] And you could tell the sort of curious look that they gave me and, you know, a lot of them had been police officers who had retired many years ago, and at first they were dubious, but I always forgive that as long as they gift me the opportunity of letting me show them what I can do.

Yes, absolutely.

And they did, and we became really great friends. And having built this prosecution and worked effectively alongside, you know, these partners, these police officers, I then came back to do a case in Croydon. [Laughter] Now, there's nothing wrong with Croydon ...

No, no

... I'm sure it's lovely at the right time of year, and sunshine can make anything look beautiful, but when I came back to defend in this case – there's a lovely Yiddish phrase, the koyech – I'd lost the guts to go and defend. I hadn't become a prosecutor necessarily as such through and through, but when I had a client where the evidence was overwhelming and every day I was instructed to go and run this abuse argument or that abuse argument, you know, to do this job you have to get up and believe in it 100%.

Yes

You have to delight in the importance of what you're doing and, if you don't, you know, the emotional capital you have like little financial currency, little finite amounts of coins perhaps, those bankrupt fairly quickly, if not very quickly. And I used to get up every morning and trudge my way from North London to Croydon and just feel totally and utterly depleted and miserable and out of love, and especially out of passion with the job, and you can't do it.

No.

You have to believe, believe in it. It doesn't have to be perfect every day, it doesn't have to be perfect every week or even month, but you have to believe that there's a possibility that around the corner there's going to be a good case and it's going to matter, and I guess I'd lost that. And around that time, luck – luck, luck, luck –

Wow!

I was just, for fun, writing show formats, I was trying to bring back Crown Court from the 1970s.

Ooh!

Right, you're too young to remember that surely?

I know, but I've heard so many of my guests here - they've told me. and I've actually been watching it. It's pretty good.

Right, it is pretty good I think! I tried to bring it back – mainly because I've got a lot of out-of-work actor friends and I thought it would just be perfect for them! [Laughter]

Well not Benedict, he's not out of work ever!

Well, he's doing alright, but you know ... sexiest man in the world? [Laughter] I mean, it's different when you've known someone from when they're 18 I suppose! [Laughter] You know, they all had keys to my house because I was the first one to buy a house.

Oh right!

I know, what can I tell you?! Anyway, so I guess, you know, it was luck. I ended up writing this show format and went to flog it, along with this production company, to somebody at ITV. I had no idea who she was, and I never care about that sort of thing, I'm just myself. And she read it, and she looked at me, slightly perplexed, and said, 'That is the worst thing I've ever read!' I thought, fair enough. It made me laugh! She was perfectly right of course. And I thought, well, that's funny and, you know, I like somebody – because she's forthright – and I thought, that's great, and she's honest which, you know, as I came to discover in TV, is a challenging thing to find, you know, they find language and have meetings.

Oh yes

It's very unloyally, you know.

Oh yes, we want a conference and get on with it!

Exactly, they just like meetings, you know. And also, as a barrister, you're somebody who ultimately makes the decision.

Absolutely, and then they're for you. You're the leader!

Right! There, it's musical chairs in television whilst, you know, they kind of work out who's going to be responsible for the thing if it goes wrong; and take the credit if it goes well. No criticism to you, telly folk, but you know who you are. That's how it goes. [Laughter] She said it was dreadful and I came away really liking her. I love that sort of thing. And I discovered she'd written these novels which she self-describes as chick-lit – I don't really like that way of describing that sort of literature because I think it's fun and great - well, it was an education to me, put it that way! You know the expression, you might read the brochure, it doesn't mean you're going on a package holiday!

Yes!

Well, it was a lot of learning, and I wrote a review of her book, and lovely to meet you. And she said, randomly, there's a guy in Manchester, he's not met anybody, he's quite keen to do a Court show, it would be an arbitration, do you think you could do it? And I said, yes, I'll go up to Manchester, why not? And I met him, and this was the strange thing, she turned out to be the Head of Daytime …

Wow!

I had no idea how unusual this is, but usually from the germ of possibility of a show to getting it on telly it takes years because they have to, you know, market test you and people have to say, you know, you look like Max Schmeling, we don't want you on telly and this sort of thing, [Laughter], what are you thinking? You know, no, no, no, that sort of thing, and of course it didn't happen in that way.

She commissioned 20 shows with just us doing like a two-minute pilot thing!

Wow!

Well, she was – IS an extraordinary maverick. Her name is Helen Warner.

Interesting. I know a lot of the role models and people - you know we are predominantly a women's organisation but we have loads of men - that actually a lot of women have had a huge impact, not influence, but been role models in your career, which is interesting.

Completely the case.

Yes, did you have quite a, you know, a forthright mother? I know you talked about your grandfather …

Yes, to say the very least! I was brought up by a single mum. A single mum who found herself a single mum when I think I was five and my brother was seven and, you know, I never like to describe her, I try to use her language, but she, you know, describes herself as a Schtetl Frau, that's sort of Yiddish for, you know, being a small-town person who really had little formal education. And she went back and trained, re-trained, became a financial advisor …

Wow!

… and within ten years ended up running a big publishing company. And my grandma would pick us up from school and feed us, and my aunt was round the corner, you know, surrounded by and enveloped by incredibly strong women also who have gone on again – brace yourself – real journeys, especially my mum. You know, she's gone on a cultural journey, an intellectual one, a spiritual one, and grown - which is the greatest gift of all – as we have. You know, the greatest privileges of all of the privileges we have, and there are many, but in my case it's to be loved by somebody who did so unconditionally, and when she said she wanted me to be happy, really meant it. Now, it helped of course when I became a barrister [Laughter] and wondering how delighted she'd be if I'd said I was becoming a body piercer or something! I'm sure she'd have said, 'as long as you're the best one, darling', but who knows?! So, yes, strong women. And I didn't believe a word that this woman was saying back to Helen, because it's on telly, so we're making a TV show, yes, yes, blah, blah, blah, and I ended up taking an instruction in Jersey. A very interesting case where it was for the Jersey Independent Care Enquiry.

Oh right!

And as you know, there's no separation between the judicial and the legislative branches of Government.

Yes.

And a colleague of mine in Chambers had been advising who's now a High Court Judge, the brilliant Bobbie Cheema-Grubb.

Oh yes, yes, she's amazing. She came last year to speak at our Annual Dinner. She's wonderful.

She's completely wonderful. The thing about Bobbie, or Bobs as I call her, is that, you know, I've known her for years and years and it doesn't matter what we're talking about, I never feel I do well in the conversation. [Laughter], you know, it's just a – yes – you know, and Brenda Hale, Lady Justice Hale, you meet her, I just walk away - some of you will know this reference from Dirty Dancing - I always when I see Bobbie Cheema-Grubb, I always walk away thinking oh I carried a watermelon. [Laughter] I mean, I just didn't do well. Please think I'm clever Bobbie! Anyway, so she'd been doing this particular job and I sort of took over from her, and it was fascinating because – because they don't have separation between the legislative and the judicial branches of Government – they needed someone to manage the disclosure process, so I started doing that. And I flew to Manchester and there was a Court with my name on it, and I thought, what is going on? Right. Oh my gosh. And, you know, these were arbitrations and real deal arbitrations …

Yes, yes

... you know, case number one, a woman was suing her wedding photographer, and I thought, oh my goodness, my opening remark was, you know, 'Madam, I've very glad you've brought your mother here to support you' – 'That's my sister'. [Laughter] Case number two – and of course I had to give full judgment, right – case number two, and this was a really important one – you talk about strong women, you know, the person who was really the -well, she was at the start of the show - her name's Kate Broadhurst, she's the Executive Producer of my show – all the people that run it, apart from Tom, are all women, and Kate's hugely influential in setting the whole thing up ...

Interesting

.. and she's from the Black Country. And I'll never forget it – they're not supposed to speak in my ear because we're regulated by Ofcom - so where I say there's a judgment coming, they can't say anything to influence a judgment. They can talk about evidence coming up and that sort of thing so we can curate a television programme ...

Oh right!

... but in general terms they're certainly not allowed to interfere with any of the evidence that I'm hearing, except on this one occasion where, you know - talk about privilege by this stage - and I'd been dealing either defending in or prosecuting cases worth millions, sometimes billions of dollars - I'm finding myself in front of two people saying something like, 'oh well, this case is worth £100, that's not a lot of money'. You're not supposed to speak in my ear, and the voice from the Black Country comes, 'do you want to rephrase that, you sound like a right posh 'bleep''. [Laughter] Of course, she was right, she was right! And of course, that's been yet more privilege layered on more privilege. Perhaps the most important actually in terms of my career, believe it or not, which is that I've been given this unusual chance, this opportunity, to hear, to experience, to see, to touch people's lives and to meet people from communities that I never would have met.

Yes.

To understand what it means to fill in a Universal Credit Form. I can't do that.

No

And I'm no intellectual slouch. I'm not a genius, but boy is it tough. To see case after case, thousands of them, where £1,000, £500, can be the underlying reason for the toxic break-up of a family. To see case after case of – usually it's a female partner, in fact in 99% of the cases – where they've had no access to Legal Aid in a family dispute and they've just been left and unhelped entirely with thousands and thousands of pounds worth of debt and no way of pursuing their partner for maintenance payments, in family disputes, you name it. And the privilege of meeting people from those communities, you know, I think above all else gave me, or has given me a sense of perspective, both of my own privilege – especially my London privilege …. [Laughter]

Coming up North!

Right, but not just North, no, no, because the cases come from all over …

Yes, yes, they do.

But also, just that sense of the lived experiences of communities. Millions of people whose lives I knew little, if nothing, about.

And has that, you know, I was going to ask you a question about diversity which we always ask, but that's broadened the, I suppose, the diversity of people that you dealt with post the Bar as opposed to pre the Bar, do you think?

It's a difficult one. It depends what you mean by diversity. It's such a complex question.

Yes, it is.

You know, when I was growing up, and I've discussed this with friends, for me, living in London, if people talk about intersectionality and then they kind of, you know, dive under the table with embarrassment, I don't think you should. I think it's quite important. But it's a kind of useful way of kind of, I guess, assessing how people have experienced the world and how they've come to be who they are.

Yes.

Right. I don't think at all it's an oppression Olympics, that's just a way people want to dismiss, you know, people who have had more challenging experiences.

Yes.

But, when I was growing up, and I feel sure that this is the case for a lot of my friends, and to some extent perhaps it's true now, I think – I'm not sure, I'm never sure – but I think in our country the most important, most damaging and perhaps the most critical of the intersections is class. So, when I grew up, right, I mean, it's nonsense, you should never trust anybody that says, oh I don't see colour.

I agree.

So ridiculous!

Yes, it is.

Right, but the question is the extent to which it mattered. And certainly, my mum would be way more happy with us playing with a Nigerian doctor's family. I mean, go and play with them!

Yes. [Laughter]

It was great! As opposed to, you know, the family down the road whose dad's been in prison ...

Oh yes.

… and didn't have books. You know, that was the aspiration. That mattered a great deal more than anything else. So, in terms of diversity, I mean, I suppose I've seen a different if you like range of people from different backgrounds, and I'm still convinced that the most challenging dynamic to overcome is the class that you are born into. That affects everything much more profoundly than any other, and then you layer on other things, to be sure.

Yes

But, for me, I feel that that's at the kind of centre of some our challenges, and it's especially true now. You know, I see case after case of students crippled with £50,000 worth of debt, you know, I see families who could have solved their problems if they had access to some kind of network. If you think about all of us, right, you want to talk about privilege, right, you know, I have a mentoree, she's an incredible young person, you should meet her, she's doing so well, she's got a bunch of pupillage interviewees, I'm so proud of her. You know, she comes from a background, she's first generation, she's done brilliantly at University, she knew absolutely no-one to get work experience. You see it in television too. You know, in London you see far too commonly shiny-haired examples of nepotism. Not necessarily because they're any worse intellectually, it's just that they've jumped through perhaps the same hoops as other people, but they know somebody through one or two or even three degrees of separation who've given them access to work experience. You know, it's true on every kind of outcome. I've seen case after case of a mum struggling, struggling to get perhaps their kid who's got educational special needs and challenges, statemented. Well, the difficulty is that at every hurdle somebody's told them no, and in some instances when that no looks like the face of authority, perhaps white authority, the response is 'okay'. Not because the mum doesn't want to fight, because she'd got nowhere to go. Right?

Yes

And that's the story of so many people who are disenfranchised. I think we'll discover, I don't know, but I intuitively suspect that's the story of Grenfell too. The story of you starting up an organisation, you not being sure, but you not having the muscle, the might, the capacity to say no to authority.

Yes, yes.

And so that, that's the reality against the backdrop of dwindling Legal Aid.

Yes, which I know you're still very passionate about.

The lack of access to power. What does that say about who we are? What does that say about a country that my grandfather loved because everybody had equal access to the law?

Yes, yes, and to justice. Interesting. Can I ask you Rob a couple of questions really, I know we always ask these, but what do you do for wellbeing? I mentioned that Women in the Law saw you singing at the Bridgewater Hall in Manchester with the BBC Breakfast Team.

I know, let's not go mad, that was a disaster!

Well, no, I had a bet that, you know, people saying 'can he sing, can he sing?', and you were wonderful, and I wondered, is that one of the things? What do you do for wellbeing and relaxing?

Okay, well I think you might be overstating your case a lot! [Laughter]

I was there! I was there!

Were you?

Yes!

Oh my gosh! You didn't put cheese in your ears like they used to do in Allo, Allo!?

No, no. I was there. There was a huge gospel choir. Wayne Ellington invited me.

Oh, isn't he wonderful?

He is so wonderful, and it was wonderful.

Well, I was invited to put bums on seats, I thin, but there you are. It was not long after Strictly, so people would show up and watch me do anything!

Yes, well maybe dancing is – is that what you do for relaxing, because you were brilliant on that?!

No, again, I mean I think that you're biased. You have to declare your bias! [Laughter] I was not good, I just loved doing it. Because of all of this free stuff you get for the dubious something of being on the telly. Free dancing lessons! Free access to your family history. I mean …

Yes, that was particularly interesting.

… gift after gift after gift after gift, you know, which is why I've got zero time, zilch, for people in the public eye, especially so-called celebrities who grumble when people stop them in the street and ask them for selfies. I think to myself, you know, pull yourself together or get a good job – or get a real job I should say! You know, talking of Strictly, you know the hard part of that is people kept saying to me during the whole thing, 'oh you must be working so hard'.

Yes

And, of course, the hard part is that most of my girlfriends are barristers, many of whom, you know, are working mums, and it's like working hard? The difficult part was that it's not exactly easy to conscript your friends into feeling sorry for you. I remember phoning my friend, Gudrun Young, who's a, you know, a brilliant barrister who had two kids - I think she went back to do a murder Trial about nine days after her first was born.

Oh gosh.

Right, and I telephoned her, you know, and said, how's things? And she's got, you know, one kid screaming, hanging off her arm, and she'd been up all night reading evidence in some hideously complicated Trial, running off to Court with sick down her leg and, you know, everyone screaming, and I can hear this hullabaloo in the background, and I'm saying, 'well, I can't get this cha right!' [Laughter] All of the press going, 'oh yes, he must be working real hard'. Yes, real hard, it's a nightmare! Anyway, so what do I do for relaxation?

Yes

Exercise. That's everything to me. So, I mean, I can plonk on most musical instruments badly, really badly, you know, I'm pretty useless at that. But I am, you know, I love exercise. You know, when I was at my most depressed, exercise was hugely important to me and I, you know, I put on a lot of weight in my 20s, decided to enter a triathlon and got super fit for it and then kind of integrated it into my daily life. And then, about seven years ago, another brilliant barrister, Adina Ezekiel – I'm not sure if you know the brilliant Adina?

No, I don't actually.

She's amazing! She's sort of, I don't know, she's sort of terrifying and fabulous in equal measure, just everything I love! She took me to Barry's Bootcamp where I go most days.

Oh yes, he's so tough!

I know, but I love it because at the end it's difficult but it's the one good news story you can tell about yourself for the day. It's something you can, you know, tick off the list so to speak.

Oh well, the clerks in my Chambers go and – I tried it and I was hopeless, so I've stuck to Bikram Yoga.

I tried that, I did that every day for a month once.

Yes, did you?!

Yes, years ago.

Wow!

Too sweaty, plus it had carpet, I wasn't too sure about the whole sweating on the carpet thing.

Oh yes. I mean, do you know I had the same conversation with Maxine Peake!

Oh really?! [Laughter]

The same thing. But no, it's good to know because we encourage people to avoid burnouts in the law, to do different things.

Well, I was burnt out, and that's really important and actually now my Chambers has got much more – I'll put it in this way – mindful about wellness, and they've created a space and it's become much more kind of present in the lives of barristers. I'm still a member of my Chambers.

Brilliant, brilliant!

But you know -

Might you return? Sorry to interrupt you.

I don't think I could, you know I'd, like I say earlier, I'd lost the joy and delight of it and, you know, I love doing my Court show. You know it's interesting because colleagues have come to watch the arbitrations …

Have they? There's never any tickets!

Well you're welcome anytime. I had my Head of Chambers come and sit in the background and he's, you know, brilliant at everything, but especially he's – in fact he was doing a health and safety case at the time and I had a health and safety case in front of me. It was a nightmare! It was absolutely terrifying! My mouth went dry, it was a disaster! But, you know, the interesting thing is that when lawyers do come, they often get really into it. By getting into it, you know, you might see 15 minutes of a case but very often the arbitrations last for an hour let's say, and if we've got a landlord and tenant dispute I have to go through all of the law ...

Oh yes.

I know, I mean that's the bit where they never broadcast.

No, no.

Mainly because the audience is in a coma by the time I've dealt with the relevant statutory instrument that I'm dealing with! [Laughter] But, yes, I think you'd be surprised. I really am, you know, there's never a moment where I shut the door behind me thinking will this be funny for telly? Even where the cases are, you know, on the face of it, a little bit pantomime, I'm genuinely trying to apply legal principles.

Absolutely!

... and that's why the, I suppose the show has survived and why I suppose I wasn't murdered by my colleagues, because at the core of it there is real legal integrity, and boy do I care about that.

Yes, and actually you explain it so it's understandable to lay people, and I think that's part of the success of the show.

Right. But it's all of our jobs. I mean, you know, you know that as a barrister or, I'm not sure if you're a Pupil Master?

Oh yes, yes, teaching ....

Right, it's everything.

Yes, it is.

You don't often get that, especially now I think in pupillage interviews, you know, where people come along and ask themselves the question, how would a barrister sound? You know, and you feel it. I don't know if it's got worse but, you know, oh they took the vehicle to the public house. Do you mean the car to the pub?

Yes, yes, we have to – [Laughter]

Right!

We have to correct that in advocacy training.

Right, all the time. But, you know, it's an interesting thing. I don't know whether there's a connection here, but when I started at the Bar, intellectually, you might say in terms of academic credentials, things were a lot more diverse. You know, the great, so to speak, many of them went to Universities now which frankly wouldn't get you a look in, in the Chambers that they're now Heads of!

Yes

In many cases, they didn't go anywhere near a University. You know, I'm thinking of Orlando Pownall, one of the greatest advocates I've ever seen, David Waters …

Oh yes!

… Stephen Kamlish. You know, these are – none of them went to University!

Wow!

And yet they're amazing advocates, because they themselves had to understand legal principles, make them decipherable to themselves, and so they understand how to explain it to ordinary people.

Yes

That's what matters. It should matter to all of us …

Yes, it should.

Unless you do Trusts, in which case, you know, it's important that nobody understands it! I mean, it's just part of the fun of it! [Laughter]

I know, gosh, Trusts Law, I know, I know! Do you have a favourite book, and also do you have a favourite fictional lawyer?

Right, so my favourite fictional lawyer – the book one's impossible to answer, I mean it's just impossible! [Laughter]

Too many, too many!

I mean, I don't know where to begin! Also, it changes as you get older. You know, it used to be Giovanni's Room by James Baldwin, and that's changed over the years, you know. It's so difficult to know. I worry, you know, if I'm ever asked that question. You know, I've been on various shows about books and it's so difficult to choose.

Yes.

Sentimental Education maybe – I don't know! But, well, lawyer, that's an easy one. I mean that's a dead easy one! It was Anna from This Life, played by Daniela Nardini. In fact, This Life, to anybody that's of my sort of vintage, you know, kind of late 90s/early 2000s call …

Oh yes.

... did more for, I guess, promoting, well, or suggesting to people that they went to the Bar, inspiring them perhaps. You never saw any Court by the way!

No, I know! They were always late for Court.

They were late for Court and, you know, they were having this kind of fabulous but sort of baroque squalor life in this cool style just delight with one another. They were also gorgeous, you know – Jack Davenport as Miles.

Oh, I know.

But Daniela Nardini, who I've subsequently met.

Have you?

I know, and I blushed from head to foot. It was the first time, I have to say, a woman's ever made me do that, but I really did. I was just overwhelmed, she was just so cool, and they were grown-up and they lived this fabulous life and they did a fabulous kind of job which seemed to kind of matter at the same time, as they were vulnerable and chaotic and, you know, that's what I wanted to be, that sort of grown-up, you know.

Yes.

God, I loved her! She was amazing.

She was amazing. I know, and everyone had cut their hair like her, as well! Suddenly, we all had the same – although I was thinking the other day, what about Ferdy? Do you remember Ferdy?

I remember Ferdy? He came along –

Was he a courier?

He was a courier. He came along a little bit later and he was having sex with Warren. I remember all this stuff! And of course, Egg played by Andrew Lincoln ...

Oh yes, yes. He was my favourite.

I know, I've met him as well. Couldn't talk! I know, because the people that when you were young who are famous are the people that make you blush. Not people who, you know, are famous that you meet when you're a grown-up. You know, you meet Clooney or Cumberbatch, I mean, once the initial flush of recognition has disappeared, they're actors! You know, you're in a coma after the first few sentences! [Laughter] What do they bring to the table? But, meeting Andi Peters, well! [Laughter] I mean, that was the moment I needed to sit down!

Gosh, well you must have met everybody now, really. I mean, people want to meet you.

I suppose. It's such a gift but, like I say, when they're famous from when you're a kid and they say that they like you, I mean, that's just the best thing ever! I met Floella Benjamin, Lady Benjamin ...

Oh, did you?!

I know! That was just too much!

Did you get a selfie?

I sort of wanted to but I think we were sort of in the House of Lords and it felt a bit much, and I would have said something inappropriate because I've got no small talk, so I'd have said, 'let's go through the round window' and, I don't know, it would have gone horribly wrong! [Laughter]

I love that! Oh gosh, you're so brilliant!

No, you're brilliant!

We could have you for like two hours. It's been so wonderful for you to come on our Podcast.

No, it's been a joy, and thank you so much for having me, and these Podcasts are really, really important. It's an interesting thing, you know, when I, I think got called, it was the first year that it was 50/50 women to men. I think it was about that year.

Oh right, yes.

It's about 20 years ago now. But it is an interesting thing as I've watched, you know, the trajectory of people's careers, how I've seen a number of women kind of disappear over the years.

Yes, the retention has not been ....

Right, and especially you know friends who after they come back from maternity have challenging years, and especially the lack of support at the Bar for that. It's improving a little bit but, you know, there's so much talent that's been lost over the years because of that. I mean real talent.

Yes

Also, for a long time it was super embarrassing because I used to go and do cases – well, I did alongside American lawyers and there's a chance my show might go to America ...

Oh right!

... and they would say, you know, how many Supreme Court Judges are women, and you'd say, one, and for most of my time I would say none!

Yes, yes.

I mean, that's not a kind of virtue signal kit, it's just straightforward embarrassing.

Yes, yes, it is.

You think now of the range and depth of talent out there, you know.

I totally agree. And do you think we could do more? I mean, that's partly why we set up Women in the Law, just to give a bit of encouragement. You know, if someone listens to the Podcast and thinks actually I'm alright, you know, I can switch off, or I've taken comfort from the, you know, download. Do you think we could do more, and what could we do?

Definitely. There needs to be structural changes. I mean, the Bar sort of worked, well, the Bar is fine and the model is okay and it suits some people, but most of the people it suits, let's call it what it is, especially nowadays, are people of financial privilege.

Yes.

You know, the reality is that my young mentoree – she's just exceptional. You know, I met her when she won a mooting competition and she was ready to go to Court there and then!

Wow! I'll invite her on!

She's so fantastic. Proud of you Shasumita, keep going, good luck in your pupillage interview this week. I hope she's done well, I'm so nervous. I feel like a dad!

I know, I bet you do! They're like children.

I know.

They're just, you know, when you – especially when they're young. Oh, fingers crossed. Tell us how she gets on, because everyone will be rooting for her.

You know, I think about her, and she's in tens of thousands of pounds worth of debt. You know, if she finds herself in a situation, let's say she decides to have a child etc., I just don't know how sustainable the career is, and frankly she has, I mean, not just clawed her way up to it, she's fought, she's battled every day, she's done everything that's asked of her. The least we could do would be to rethink the structures that do everything possible to support women to, you know, to achieve their full potential.

Oh absolutely! I've got three children and I know how hard it is, and that's part of what we need to be doing. You're spot on, you know, having positive role models as well, just to encourage as well as the structures. What a great suggestion. Well, I hope the Bar Council's listening.

I'm sure they listen to me all the time! [Laughter] I mean, I can't get – you know, sometimes during the proroguing case, I mean, Lady Hale if you're listening …

She's next! She's the next interviewee!

Well, I'm so sorry I didn't return any of your calls. I know how desperate you were for my advice! [Laughter] It came in - on the same day as the proroguing case I had a case where a woman had brought her dentist into Court and I wanted to know where in the country it was. I said, 'Madam, can you tell me where you got your teeth done?' The answer was, 'In my mouth'! [Laughter] I thought, goodness me, I could have been sitting there alongside other greats in the Supreme Court … [Laughter]

I'm going to have to re-watch all of them now.

Some of them are great.

They're so great. Thank you so much for your time.

No, it's been a real privilege.

Will you come back on?

I'd love to come back on! This has been joyous.

It's been wonderful having you and thank you for sharing some of the personal stuff. Can I ask you, when is the film coming out about your grandfather, and the documentary you've just made?

Right, so I did a 'Who do you think you are?' last year, and, you know, they were very kind. It won a BAFTA.

It did, it was very emotional.

It was such a gift to be given that experience, and I've made two further films where second-generation survivors go back and discover their stories. And, I also go back with my mum to Treblinka where my family were murdered, to go and say Kaddish, the memorial prayer, and it was, without question, the most profound moment of my life, for reasons which, I hope when people watch, they share in.

Yes, thank you very much.

Thank YOU very much, it's been a delight.

Thank you so much to Judge Rinder, what an awesome, awesome guy, and what an interesting background.

2 WELLBEING

Introduction

The subject of wellbeing and mental health in law is close to my heart. We at the bar work long ours on complicated issues. Burn out rate is rising and we need to learn better self care for our own mental health. It remains the subject of interest in many of the podcast interviews but also of the webinars and seminars I give and have chaired pre and during covid 19. Managing ones wellbeing remains as crucial as ever especially during the lock down and covid19. Lawyers remain isolated whilst working from home. Students whilst studying from their rooms and not at campus physical lectures. Now more than ever, we all need selfcare and to manage our wellbeing.
In this chapter are some tips I have and I have sought the assistance of an ex solicitor now a counsellor for her tips also. *Thank you Susan Carr* for your assistance with this chapter.

The subject of wellbeing in the law, particularly in relation to mental health, is something that is close to my heart. I have a strong sense of justice and fairness, and so was naturally drawn to a career in law especially after watching TV portrayals of courtrooms. Any illusions were soon shattered when I shadowed both barristers and solicitors, but this didn't put me off reading Law at the University of Nottingham. I then completed my legal practice course at Manchester Metropolitan University.

After qualifying I worked for several years as a commercial litigation solicitor. It was during this time that I experienced a depressive episode, for which I sought counselling. I had never considered therapy as a potential career but realised that I may have some of the qualities necessary for this line of work. I did not immediately retrain as I wanted to give law another chance but when I went on maternity leave, I felt that this was a good time to change careers.

I qualified as a counsellor in 2012 and have worked both in the NHS and the charitable sector. I now have my own private practice working with individuals and businesses and am an affiliate counsellor for a number of Employee Assistance Programmes.

What is mental health?

According to the World Health Organization

".......mental health is more than just the absence of mental disorders or disabilities. Mental health is a state of well-being in which an individual realizes his or her own abilities, can cope with the normal stresses of life, can work productively and is able to make a contribution to his or her community." (WHO, 2018)

Statistics show that one in four people in the UK will experience a mental health issue each year (e.g. McManus et al). However, there can still be stigma around mental health, and it was not something that was talked about when I was a solicitor.

There is nothing to suggest that those working in the law are immune from mental health difficulties (in fact surveys such as The Junior Lawyers Division's resilience and wellbeing survey suggest otherwise) so what prevents open discussion about the issue?   It may be the fear that admitting that there is a problem could be viewed as being weak or vulnerable.   But this reinforces the stigma as it is only through speaking out that mental health issues can be addressed.

How can we challenge the stigma around mental health?

This may necessitate a widespread change across the profession, particularly at leadership level, but there are things that can be done on an individual basis, such as:

- looking out for colleagues who may be having difficulties.

- recognising our own prejudices about mental health

- becoming more informed about mental health issues

- avoiding the use of labelling and language such as "mad", "loopy", "crazy" etc

- being open about experiences of mental illness so that it is not hidden

It is important to challenge some of the myths about mental health, such as:

Myth: Mental health doesn't affect me

We all have mental health in the same way that we have physical health. Just as we would go to the gym and eat well to look after our bodies, there are things we can do to help look after our minds, such as going for walks, relaxing, and talking about our emotions.

Myth: Mental health issues are a sign of weakness

Mental ill health is not about being weak; there are lots of factors which contribute to mental health difficulties.   Conversely, Dr. Tim Cantopher notes how being "strong" could be a factor in some forms of depression (Cantopher, 2012).

Myth: Mental illness can't be treated

There are a wide range of treatments available including both medication and talking therapies and many people are able to live and work productively.

Myth: Mental health is static

Mental health is not fixed but is on a continuum, with good mental health at one end and mental illness at the other. We can move up and down the continuum depending on different circumstances. Thinking about mental health in this way helps to explain how anyone can develop a mental health issue but that recovery is also possible.

Factors which affect mental health

There are several different factors which may affect our mental health, such as:

- Personal lives and relationships

- Bereavement and loss

- Money, work and housing

- Life changes

- Health issues

- Traumatic life events

- Uncertainty

The legal sector is a highly pressured, competitive environment, with a "long hours" culture in which presenteeism is encouraged, so it is easy to see how mental health can be affected. According to Lawcare, in 2019 the top three reasons for contacting their helpline were stress (26%), bullying (12%) and depression (12%) (Lawcare, 2012). Let's look at each one of these in turn.

Stress

Stress is the response felt by your mind and body in relation to an event or situation. It can be both positive and negative in that a small amount of stress can motivate you, but when it is sustained or is coming from multiple sources then it can affect your wellbeing. Stress is individual in that what one person finds stressful may not trouble someone else.

There are different ways in which the body can be affected by stress, for example:

- Physical symptoms: breathing more quickly, racing pulse, increased heart rate, sweating, nausea, muscle tension.

- Emotional symptoms: feeling angry, irritable, upset, nervous or depressed.

- Behavioural symptoms: difficulty sleeping, over-eating or reduced appetite, increased use of drugs/alcohol.

- Mental symptoms: lack of concentration, forgetfulness, negative thinking, indecisiveness.

In terms of managing stress, the first step is to identify the particular factors which are causing you stress. Next, look at each individual issue and try to break it down into more manageable chunks. List all possible options and choose one to try. Make an action plan of how you will carry out this option.

It can be tempting to put things off when you are feeling stressed, but this can actually make the situation worse. Don't put off until tomorrow what you can do today! Also try to manage your workload; avoid working long hours or taking on extra responsibilities. Although it is not always easy, learn to say "No" and if possible, delegate tasks to others who may be able to help. Prioritise what has to be done today and don't be a perfectionist – sometimes "good enough" will do.

When we feel stressed, we may not find time for hobbies, but these are the things that will help to relieve stress. Exercise, meditation and relaxation/breathing techniques can all help to reduce stress.

Bullying

Bullying is not just something that happens in the playground and stops once we leave school. It can exist at all stages of life and has been identified as a serious problem in the workplace. The legal profession tends to be conservative and both the partnership model and the emphasis on billable hours can lead to a culture of competition and pressure in which bullying can thrive.   It is likely that at some point in your career you may come across a bully - whether it is one of your own colleagues or a solicitor, barrister, judge or client that you are dealing with.

What counts as bullying varies but it is generally accepted that what matters is how the behaviour is perceived by the victim.   Examples of bullying include overt actions such as being shouted out, name-calling, being unfairly blamed or criticised and being left out, as well as more covert actions such as being excessively monitored or given an unmanageable workload. Bullying tends to be recurrent rather than being a one-off event.

Bullying can lead to a loss of confidence, anxiety and low mood and it can have an impact on both work and home life. Although bullies often prey on the weak and vulnerable, they may also target colleagues who they see as successful, competent and popular. Their behaviour can intensify if the victim is resistant or impervious to their attempts.

What can you do if you are the target of bullying?

Remain calm – the bully wants to provoke a reaction and so try to resist the temptation to scream, yell or fight back as this may lead to the situation escalating.   Where possible, talk to the perpetrator explaining what they have done and how this has affected you.   Ask for the behaviour to be stopped and outline what you plan to do if is not e.g. "I will speak to my line manager if you continue with this conduct".

Keep a diary or record of all incidents (no matter how trivial they may seem) as well as copies of any documents e.g. emails.   If there are any witnesses, ask if they would be willing to write down an account of what they have observed.

Report it - if the bullying persists speak to your line manager or HR and follow the relevant procedures for making a complaint/raising a grievance particularly if your employer has an anti-bullying policy. You may also want to obtain some independent legal advice in relation to your rights and options.

Build relationships– when you are being bullied you can feel isolated or you may instinctively withdraw from interactions with others. However, it is important to have a good social network both at work and home.

Bullying can make life very unpleasant at work and in some circumstances, you may feel that you have no option other than to resign, but this should be seen as a last resort after all other options have been exhausted.

Depression

Depression is a mood disorder, which varies from person to person, however some of the common symptoms are listed below:

- Physical symptoms: feeling tired or lacking in energy, loss of appetite or over-eating, aches and pains.

- Emotional symptoms: feeling low, empty or hopeless, feeling helpless, finding little or no pleasure in life, feeling prone to tearfulness, experiencing feelings of guilt or shame, lack of self-confidence and self-esteem.

- Behavioural symptoms: difficulty sleeping or sleeping too much, cessation of hobbies, avoiding social events, self-harm, increased use of drugs/alcohol.

- Mental symptoms: forgetfulness, difficulty concentrating, negative thinking, suicidal thoughts.

There are many different causes of depression and it is not always easy to pinpoint the trigger. Some common reasons are trauma, stress, loss, childhood experiences, biological conditions, side effects of medication, drug or alcohol use, and chemical changes in the brain.

Whilst there are some things that you can do to help yourself, there are times when you may need more support. Your GP can prescribe medication and there is now a wide range of anti-depressants available.   There are also numerous therapies on offer such as counselling, CBT, art therapy, and psychodynamic therapy to name but a few.   It may also be helpful to join a self-help group by sharing how you feel and listening to the experiences of others.

If you are feeling suicidal then you can contact Samaritans (116 123) or attend your local Accident & Emergency department.

<u>Looking after your mental health</u>

In the same way that there are things that we can do on an everyday basis to look after our physical health, there are also things that we can do to look after our mental health (some of which overlap).   A good place to start is the "Five Ways to Wellbeing", developed by the New Economics Foundation, which are Connect, Be Active, Take Notice, Keep Learning and Give (Aked et al, 2008).   In addition, our mood is also affected by sleep, what we eat and drink and how we talk to ourselves, all of which are considered below.

Connect

Humans are inherently social creatures and so we naturally require interaction and connection with others. This helps to give us a sense of belonging, feel valued and accepted and over time build a support network that can be called upon in times of need. There are lots of ways in which we can connect on a daily basis:

Speak to a colleague instead of sending an email

Meet a friend for coffee/lunch

Join a new group

Talk to someone on the commute to work

Connection is also about talking and listening but doing this in a meaningful way. Research carried out by Time to Change highlighted that when asked "How are you?" over 75% of people would reply that they were fine even if they were not. Accordingly, they launched a campaign to "Ask Twice" as simply asking again "Are you really OK?" shows that we are genuinely interested and ready to listen.

Similarly, think about how you respond to the question "How are you?" as being open about your feelings is good for your mental health. Talking can help you to release tension, see the problem in a different way, realize that you are not alone and identify possible solutions.

Be active

We all know the importance of exercise in relation to looking after our physical health, but it is also great for our mental health too. Exercise releases chemicals like endorphins and serotonin that improve your mood. It can also increase energy levels, so we feel more motivated and less lethargic. Regular exercise can boost self-esteem not only through weight loss or improved muscle tone but because it can create a sense of achievement increasing self-confidence.

Exercise does not have to mean the stereotypical idea of getting sweaty in the gym as there are lots of ways to get active, such as:

Taking the stairs rather than the lift

Going for a walk or run (especially outside as there is also evidence that being in nature improves mood)

Playing sport

Having a dance around the kitchen!

Take notice

We can spend a lot of time thinking about the past, replaying events and conversations, or worrying about the future, preparing for the worst to happen, rather than being present in the moment. However, paying more attention to the world around you can help to improve your mental wellbeing.

Mindfulness is very much about taking notice as it involves being present and fully engaged with whatever we're doing. There are two parts to mindfulness; formal meditation and the informal practice of "everyday mindfulness".

So how do you take notice? Let's think about having a shower, which is a good example of a time where you may be present in body, but your mind is likely to be elsewhere.   Try to focus on how it feels by using your senses:

Sight. What can you see? Watch the water create a whirlpool as it drains away.

Smell. Try and notice the different scents in your shower gel or shampoo.

Touch. What does the temperature of the water feel like?

Sound. What can you hear? Running water, music, your own singing!

There are many activities in which you can try "everyday mindfulness" such as eating, making a drink, walking, gardening, cleaning, listening to music, or cleaning your teeth!

Keep learning

This is not just about formal education or continuing profession development (although it can be). It's about being curious, trying new experiences, acquiring additional skills and expanding existing knowledge. Learning stimulates the brain, boosts self-esteem and helps to build resilience.

Learning can be in relation to an existing interest, such as playing an instrument. Or it may be about doing something you have always wanted to do (e.g. learning a language).

Here are some other ideas:

- Do an evening class or online course

- Join a book club

- Listen to podcasts (Talking Law is a good one to start with!)

- Take on a new responsibility at work

- Try a new sport or hobby

Give

Giving doesn't just benefit the recipient - it can also help us to feel positive about ourselves. This is because feel-good chemicals such as serotonin, dopamine and oxytocin are released.   It can create a sense of purpose and belonging as well as improving connection with others.

Giving also means that we focus on others, so we are less aware of our own issues. This can help us to gain a different perspective. Furthermore, it can encourage other acts of kindness thereby building a happier community.

There are many ways that you can give whether that is by donating to your favourite charity, volunteering for a community project, or simply giving someone a smile to brighten their day.

Sleep

Getting a good night's sleep does not always fit in with the lifestyle of a lawyer, with the pressure to work all night to meet that deadline or waking up sweating because you've realised a document has not been filed at court.   However, sleep is important not just to our physical health but also our mental health.

We may all have the odd sleepless night but when lack of sleep is prolonged it can lead to tension, irritability and low mood and can affect both concentration and our ability to make decisions. Sleeplessness and sleeping too much can also be symptoms of depression and anxiety (as well as factors that can contribute to these conditions).

The amount of sleep we need varies from person to person but on average eight hours of good-quality sleep is required to function properly. So how can we get a good night's sleep?   Here are some tips

- Establish a bedtime routine

- Going to bed and getting up at the same time each day (even at weekends) will help set your body clock.   Try to wind down at least an hour before bedtime, whether by having a relaxing bath, listening to music or meditating. However, don't use television or electronic devices as part of your bedtime routine as research has suggested that screens can interfere with sleep.

- Create the right environment. Light, sound and temperature can all affect sleep and so use blackout blinds/curtains or an eye-mask if your room is too light, earplugs if it's too noisy and a fan/heater if it's too hot/cold. Make sure that your bed is comfortable and that your mattress is not too hard or soft.

- Relaxation/breathing exercises

- Deep muscle relaxation and breathing exercises may help you to nod off. However, if you are still tossing and turning after fifteen minutes then get up and try a relaxing activity (e.g. reading) before returning to bed when you are feeling drowsy again.

- Clear your mind

- Racing thoughts, rumination and anxiety can all interfere with sleep. Keep a pen and paper by the side of your bed and note down any thoughts and worries which can then be reviewed in the morning.

Food and drink

I'm not a nutritionist so I'm not going to suggest what you should or shouldn't be eating – it's more just a reminder about how food and drink can affect your mood. It is important to eat regularly as it turns out that being "hangry" is a real thing. Our blood sugar levels drop when we don't eat which causes irritability, weakness, loss of concentration and nausea. Additionally, low blood sugar levels trigger the release of stress-related hormones such as cortisol, adrenaline and neuropeptide.

We may also use food and drink in an unhealthy way when we are feeling stressed or overwhelmed. If we haven't slept well then, we may try to counteract this by drinking caffeine but as this is a stimulant then it can increase anxiety levels.   Similarly, after a long day at work we may turn to alcohol to relieve our stress but as this is a depressant it could actually lead us to feeling lower in mood.

Have a break

Taking a break is important in all areas of our lives, whether this is at work, home, or just taking time away from social media.   We can take breaks in all sorts of ways such as simply finding five minutes for ourselves, making sure that we have our lunch break, going on a relaxing weekend away or taking a two-week holiday.

Regular breaks reduce stress levels and can also lead to increased productivity, particularly as they boost creativity.   They also help with concentration and focus which can reduce mistakes or accidents. One technique which can help with taking breaks is the Pomodoro Method (developed by Francesco Cirillo in the late 1980s) whereby you take a 5-minute break after every 25 minutes of work.

It's not just at work that breaks are important but also in our personal lives.   Although it's good to spend time with others it's also important to make time for ourselves. This is particularly true when we are feeling emotionally drained.

Change your thinking

We can't always control what life throws at us, but we can change the way that we think about it, particularly if we realise that how we think, how we feel and how we act all interrelate.

A simple way of explaining this is through the ABC model which is used in Cognitive Behaviour Therapy:

A = the Actual event.

B = the Belief about the event

C = the Consequences (emotions and behaviour).

Imagine that you are walking down the street and see a neighbour across the road, but she doesn't acknowledge you (the Actual Event). If you think that she has deliberately snubbed, you (the Belief) then when you next meet her you may be annoyed and ignore her (the Consequence). Alternatively, if you think that she didn't see you (the Belief) then when you next meet her you have a conversation and ask her about it (the Consequence).

Our thoughts are therefore very influential in relation to how we feel and behave. However, it is useful to remember that thoughts are not facts and that they are also transitory. Practising "taking notice" as described above (at point 3) can help you to become more aware of your thoughts and to let go of them.

Be kind to yourself!

One of the most common topics I talk to clients about is practising self-care as "you can't pour from an empty cup". However, being kind to yourself is more than eating well and exercising as it is also about cultivating self-compassion.

You may have noticed that you have a very vocal inner critic which will say things to you like "You're useless", "Everyone thinks you're stupid" "You'll never succeed". Our self-talk often has a harsh tone to it and uses judgmental language such as "should". Instead practise talking to yourself in the same way you would speak to a friend as we often show more compassion towards others.

In Summary

There are many ways to look after your mental health and everyone's approach will be different. Choose the ideas that work for you and that you enjoy rather than what you think you should be doing. Activities are more likely to become part of your routine if you find them enjoyable or rewarding (so you might not enjoy exercise, but you may like how positive you feel afterwards). Implementing even just one of the ideas can have an impact, so how are you going to make your mental health a priority?

REFERENCES

Aked J. et al (2008) Five Ways to Wellbeing: A report presented to the Foresight Project on communicating the evidence base for improving people's well-being London: New Economics Foundation

Cantopher, T. (2012) Depressive Illness: The Curse of the Strong (3rd edn) London: Sheldon Press

Lawcare, Our Support Service (2019) Available online at www.lawcare.org.uk/about-us/key-statistics.

McManus, S., Meltzer, H., Brugha, T. S., Bebbington, P. E., & Jenkins, R. (2009). Adult psychiatric morbidity in England, 2007: results of a household survey. The NHS Information Centre for health and social care. Available online at digital.nhs.uk/data-and-information/publications/statistical/adult-psychiatric-morbidity-survey/adult-psychiatric-morbidity-in-england-2007-results-of-a-household-survey.

WHO (World Health Organisation) (2018) Mental health: strengthening our response. Available online at www.who.int/news-room/fact-sheets/detail/mental-health-strengthening-our-response.

3 RESILIENCE AND BOUNCING BACK BETTER

Introduction

I have long wondered how we become resilient. From what I hear many ask? From Failure. From rejection from jobs, applications, judicial applications, from friendships or lovers or simply how do you get up again when you fall? It's a tough one and I prefer to call it how do we Bounce forward in life and our careers.

In this chapter I have sought the assistance of my good friend and business psychologist *Rachel Ward Liley*. Thank you Rachel for your expertise and never ending friendship.

In this chapter we explore eight manageable ways.

Bouncing Forward (cultivating resilience and happiness) – 8 areas to explore...

As lockdowns start to ease, we have an opportunity to evaluate some of the changes we have experienced and to incorporate the best of these into our lives going forward. Resilience has been key to our efforts to adapt and it will serve us well when it comes to setting some new values to live by in the future. Now is a good time to reconsider our hedonistic obsessions with status, wealth and image and weigh them against the true happiness of human flourishing – what Aristotle labelled eudaemonia – for a more fulfilling experience.

Here are eight areas to explore:

1. Living in accordance with your values. Work out what is important to you and do the right thing as it is the right thing to do. Morals and ethics matter.

2. Having a positive attitude. Look for the silver lining in all situations; learn to hard-wire optimism into your system.

3. Looking after your mind. Settle your thoughts through regular meditation. This will help you appreciate every moment and not get too caught up in past and future worries over which you have no control.

4. Giving back. Remember that helping other people – even by random acts of kindness – will benefit others as well as yourself.

5. Recognising and managing your emotions. Stop, take a deep breath and observe honestly how you feel. Put your emotions to good use.

6. Looking after your body. Get sufficient sleep, regular exercise and eat healthy foods. This regime will give you energy and staying power.

7. Surrounding yourself with supportive people. Who do you spend time with, face-to-face and online? Are they your cheerleaders? Are you theirs? Do some editing. Reduce the time you spend with people that don't help and care for you.

8. Having a goal/s. Small or ambitious – it doesn't matter. Knowing where you want to go gives you a reason to get out of bed each day with a spring in your step.

And never forget that smiling always helps. That's one thing that even I can achieve!

Enjoy exploring and creating changes – for the good of everyone!

In Summary

Continue to explore and do what you can .

4
ADVICE FOR FUTURE LAWYERS
BEFORE YOU ENTER THE LAW

Many of my 27k listeners are students or those considering entering the law and the legal profession. The younger end. Maybe this is you. I thought it might be useful to offer some advice to future lawyers. I have so much hope because we have many young bright people wanting to enter the profession I love and who want change. Here I have outlined in brief some basic starting points to help with entering and then some simple advice that might help with interviews.

I am not an expert by any means. I do hope that in some *small way* these tips help. You know what they say about tips or advice you can either take it or leave it.

Q: In the legal profession what do we mean? What could you be in the law profession ?

<u>You could be:</u>

1. Barrister (like me)
2. Chartered Legal Executive
3. In-House solicitor/ barrister
4. Solicitor
5. Legal Apprentice
6. Academic Law Lecturer
7. Legal Author
8. Law Professor
9. Apprentice
10. Legal advisor in court

Your 'First Steps' Checklist

So if, you do decide that a career as a lawyer is for you, there are a few things you should be doing even before you start university. Here is a brief checklist to get you started.

- Talk to your careers adviser at school to go through your options.

- Research the different paths into law – university, chartered legal executive, paralegal, apprenticeship (read our new The Law Apprenticeships Guide) – and decide which is right for you.

- Get some practical work experience at a law firm, barristers' chambers or legal advice centre; it will help you to decide what suits you best and will also improve any applications you make later.

- Work hard at your academic studies. Excellent grades are essential!

- Talk to friends, parents, acquaintances – anyone with a connection to the legal profession; they may also be able to help you get some work experience.

- Think about the kinds of extracurricular things you can do to make yourself into a well-rounded candidate. Think sport, volunteering, drama, music.

- Sign up to LCN Weekly on LawCareers.Net, and Legal Cheek and even www.womeninthelawuk.com Free weekly emails and newsletters will deliver news and information about the profession, plus advice and reminders throughout the legal recruitment calendar, straight to your inbox.

- Read the business pages of the newspapers to improve your commercial awareness and get you starting to "think business".

Useful Organisations

Check out this list. Its just some of the organisations that you could look up and can help.

1. Lawcareers.net
2. Womeninthelawuk.com
3. Urban Lawyers
4. Rare Recruitment
5. Aspiring Solicitors
6. Legal Cheek
7. Nottingham Law School
8. Pathways to Law
9. Pupillage Podcast
10. Grays Inn (The Honourable Society of)
11. Middle Temple
12. Lincoln's Inn
13. Inner Temple
14. Follow some inspirational lawyers on Instagram such as Chrissie Wolfe, Chronicles of family lawyer, @essexbarrister @Dr Tunde Akewole MBE, On twitter follow @Phatsilk the brilliant Bernard
15. The bar Council
16. The Law society
17. InterLaw

Interview and Application Advice

Places at the top law firms (and chambers) for example are hard-won. Following these points will set you in good stead I hope. They are not definitive but at least a start when you don't know anyone in law. I wish I had some of these tips when I was going for so many interviews. I hope they help. Please don't feel you have to use them. They are just ideas you might want to consider. Some of them arise from errors I made and advice I wish I had been given.

1. Read carefully through the form before you start to complete it. Print off a copy and draft answers before submitting the form.

2. Put yourself in the shoes of the person who will assess you.

3. Am I clear about why I want this career?

4. Based on your research – what skills and abilities will I need to demonstrate that I can do this job?

5. What will make me stand out from the other 2,500 applicants?

6. The person reading your form will be reading and assessing many forms, so make sure your personality comes across, make the form engaging and interesting – hold the reader's attention.

7. Do not under-sell yourself. Some candidates feel they are "showing-off". If you talk about your experiences linked to what you know the recruiter is looking for, and you give examples of when YOU have used those skills, it will not come across as 'big-headed'.

8. Make sure you spell accurately and use correct grammar. You are applying for a job as a lawyer – written and oral communication is vital to being effective. If sending in a written version of the form, clear handwriting will make the reader's job easier.

9. Use any work placements (legal or non-legal) to demonstrate you understand about business, time management, communicating with people and meeting deadlines.

10. Use legal placements, law fairs, legal open days and information from universities (career advisers, law students, student law society events) to demonstrate your research info and understanding of the law and a legal career.

11. Use the information to back up statements on your form.

12. Don't use jargon.

13. Don't feed back quotes from the firm's own publicity – they have read it! It's you they are interested in and your reasons for choosing the law and possibly their firm – if it is their international practice you are interested in, say why, and what can you bring to the firm.

14. Keep a copy of your completed form – you will need it if you are called for an interview so you can refresh your memory about what you said.

Interviews can be nerve-wracking at any stage of ones career. Whether at QC stage or Judicial appointment or new area like lecturing. Even worst when you are at the start of your career.

Following this advice will help you give the best possible account of yourself

- Always prepare thoroughly – read up about the firm, check the website for current news, and the business and legal press.

- A well-conducted interview should be open exchange between you and the people conducting the interview – YOU should do most of the talking – about 80%.

- Think carefully about what the role involves (using your experience of placements, what you have read and the people you have spoken to) and then match up your skills in these areas. Be prepared to give examples at your interview about these skills that will make you effective in the role.

- Firms appreciate you are likely to be nervous, however, try to remain calm and look confident. Good eye contact and firm handshake at the start of the interview are important. Interviewers will be assessing how you may come across to clients – do you have the potential to inspire confidence in others – you would not instruct a lawyer who lacks this skill.

- Interviewers will give you time to answer questions. If you need time to think, ask for it. They are more interested in the content of your answer than the speed with which you deliver it!

- Be honest and be yourself, do not try to conform to what you think the interviewer may expect – you will probably be wrong. Instead, think about all the good things you want to get across about yourself.

- You should be prepared to ask a few questions yourself. You will be given the opportunity. Make sure they are pertinent, cover things you really want to know and are not answered by information readily available to you, e.g. on their website! For example, you may want more of an insight into the firm from a senior person's perspective – so you may want to know what they like about the firm and their job.

- Finally you are there because they like you. Be yourself. Be prepared and be yourself.

- If at first you don't succeed, then try again. Remember the I. Stephanie Boyce podcast interview with me.

5 FINANCIAL WELLBEING

Introduction

Financial wellbeing is crucial in law . It can affect ones mental health. I am passionate about mental health and wellbeing and financial health . I am grateful to Sarah Deacon, Manager from Wesleyan for sharing her views on financial management of women and some tips for all of us in an interview with me below. I have also attached some tips and thoughts we should all be thinking about out when it comes to our financial wellbeing.

Jane Portas from CII first introduced me to the report on women's finances.

Sarah Deacon, Manager, Wesleyan. Welseyan are the official partners with the Law Society of England and Wales and advice all their members on mortgages to partnerships. Wesleyan also advise doctors and teachers and other professions. Here I asked her why they support lawyers too.

Sarah Deacon

Who are you? Name and job title and firm and location.

Sarah Deacon, Lawyer Area Manager and Segment Leader, Wesleyan Financial Services, Home Based in Bedfordshire.

Where do you work?

I lead a team across England and Wales.

What is your link with lawyers and the law and women in the law UK?

My team at Wesleyan specialises in providing financial advice to those working in the legal profession. We are proud to have an ongoing relationship with Women in the Law UK to support members with financial wellbeing.

Why Law?

I originally started my career at Wesleyan working as a financial consultant looking after those working in general practice, I advanced my career by promotion to Area manager in our medical segment before moving across to lead the legal team. I have enjoyed working with all professions however do like working with Lawyers, I like the fact as a profession you are not afraid to challenge, happy to ask copious questions in order to get to the answer and like working at a very fast pace.

How did you get to where you are now?

I've worked in financial services since A 'Levels, it's a great industry to be part of, you can add real value to people's lives every day, you build great relationships, meet lots of people and help people to maintain financial security, protect themselves and their families.

Back in 2017 after 8 years of working within the medical divisions at Wesleyan an opportunity arose to lead the legal team and I jumped at the chance. I've not looked back.

I like leading and managing a team, working with them collectively and individually to reach their full potential, listening and learning, I don't pretend to know all the answers. I am human and I really care, about people, the industry, our clients. I am proud of what I do.

Who inspires you?

I don't have one person who inspires me, I find inspiration in others in many ways. I guess I am inspired by those who are confidant and successful but who aren't afraid to share and provide insight and feedback. Someone who is good at what they do, whatever that may be, that is inspiring.

What is a mentor? What is a sponsor? What is the distinction and Did you have one in your career? Why are they important?

I have had mentors yes, it is also important to have a good network of stakeholders/sponsors around you, those who challenge, provide feedback, support and care, those who listen and guide but also let you carve your own way and allow you to learn from your own experience.

Why do you support women in the law UK? What do you like about Women in the Law UK?

Individually I support Women in Law because it is headed up by the fantastic Sally Penni who is inspiring in her tenacity, hard work, personality and pure brilliance! However, this aside the network is a great place to be, both in terms of building on-going connections and business relationships but also for the self- development it provides. The learning and opportunity to talk, share and engage with others in a safe environment with dedicated experts. The work Sally has done to build an online forum of support during Covid 19 cannot go unnoticed. It has been fantastic.

Wesleyan is proud of its working relationship with Women in the Law UK, the opportunity it provides to support women to take ownership in making the right financial decisions and the right choice for them. Being able to discuss and ask questions with an expert who understands the legal profession to enhance financial wellbeing is of paramount importance. It is still something that many "put off" but financial wellbeing reviews and financial health checks should be at the top of our annual to do lists.

Are organisations like us still relevant and will they still be relevant? In 100 years?

Absolutely, and more so now since Covid. The ability to build connections across the country, the personal development it provides. These networks are vital and have been a great place for women to join and learn, share and support. It would be great for these networks to evolve over the next 100 years to be networks attended by men and women equally, however whilst gaps in social mobility, inclusion and diversity, gender and pensions pay gap, unconscious bias in the workplace, exists Women need to be able to connect and discuss. More men would better inform the change and speed it up.

Do you have a family?

I have a brilliant family, both immediate and through marriage. We are close and I have been very lucky. I don't have any direct children of my own. Although steal my nephews whenever possible as they certainly keep me grounded and in the moment. They soften me and I often need this. I have 2 dogs, a cat and aspirations for chickens if these count!

What do you think about diversity/ social mobility in our profession?

I find it disappointing that in 2020 we still must have these conversations; like financial services there is still much more the legal profession can do to diversify. It is getting better and there is a real clear appetite for change which is fantastic. Diversified teams make for much better interactions and outcomes.

What can each of us do to improve this in the profession?

Stand up and support each other, press for change and get involved

What or how can the men in the profession help improve gender diversity?

Get involved, Support, stand next to and include, challenge if they see something below standard.

What do you do for mental wellbeing? Work life balance

I run or walk and get outside. I do need time on my own and relish this. I love being outside, in all weathers, which is a good thing as having dogs assures you are outside come rain or shine!

I also keep a gratitude diary, read a lot, write a lot of to do lists and make sure I sleep. I am better when I am organised so can be selfish of my time if I need to get things done.

What is your favourite book and why?

I do read a lot of books and mainly fiction, something I can get lost in. Favourite book, probably those written by Sally Rooney. She has this amazing ability to cover the complexity of relationships in a way that you really feel it, the characters are relatable and real. She writes about life and that's important.

Who is your favourite fictional lawyer and why?

I grew up reading John Grisham, so I guess this would be my first taste of fictional lawyers, I recall all the hours and hard work, the sleeping in the office to get cases written up and ready and the real excitement at finding the one piece of the jigsaw that will just change the case.

Who is your favourite business leader?

I don't have a favourite, there are many business leaders doing amazing things from small to large firms and those running businesses from their own homes via social media. It would have to be adaptable and open to change, with fresh ideas and creative in approach and someone who is happy to listen.

Who is your favourite Male role model and why?

My dad. He has encouraged me to work hard, taught me to listen to both sides of the story and to be in receipt of all the facts before making any decisions. He has let me pave my own way and knew that to learn I had to have my own experiences, whilst also giving me the support I need should it not go as planned! I've been exceptionally lucky.

What are your hobbies?

Running, reading and sleeping in that order. I like to eat cake and drink tea so could probably say that's a hobby too. I love my animals, gardening and pre Covid, travelling to France for food, wine and a ramble around a brocante or empty attic sale – nothing better!

What do you do for wellbeing?

I go for a run and I know when I need to go; I can get quite tense and anxious if I don't get in a regular run!

What advice do you have for overcoming obstacles?

Maybe it wasn't the right time, but it will be. Pick yourself up, dust yourself down, take a breath, learn from your experience and you will do it better next time! My motto is "have courage and be kind!"

What obstacles have you had to overcome and how did you get over them?

Many, if you aren't running into obstacles how are you learning? The worst thing anyone can say to me is that I can't do something or tell me no. I've had quite a few no's, but ultimately this has only made me stronger, more resilient, taught me a lot about myself and ultimately made me a better, more understanding, patient person with real ambition!

Do you sit on any boards or committees? Are you a school governor?

I am not on any boards, but as I progress in my career this will be something I will want to do. I want to be able to utilise my experiences to best effect whilst learning from others.

What would you like to see in the next 100 years in terms of and for Women In The Law and Business?

More diversity within the workplace, better flexibility in working practices. It will be interesting to see a 4 day working week and more men taking shared parental leave!

Also, how important is financial wellbeing?

Having worked in financial services all my career I can hand on heart say making time for regular financial reviews to improve your financial wellbeing is of paramount importance. I've seen positive stories and sadly also negative ones. I've met people who have had to deal with bereavements where there have been no plans in place, people who have had to overcome serious illness and those who have been affected by long term incapacity without adequate income protection or family/mortgage protection and those who want to retire but can't as they don't have sufficient retirement income.

Of course, It's not all doom and gloom. Financial wellbeing for me is about making decisions that give you choice, to feel empowered in your decisions and clear on your plan. Of course, there are life challenges that may set these off course, but with good financial wellbeing decisions you can rest assured that you are in control. I believe financial wellbeing is as important as health and wellbeing.

You insure your pets, you MOT your car, you hopefully go for regular female gynae checks but when was the last time you sat down and ran through your own financial health check? It is such a good investment of your time and it definitely isn't boring.

What are the 3 top tips for any woman lawyer or lawyer for good financial wellbeing

Plan – Know from where you are starting, discuss your personal goals and make a plan and review it at least annually. What are your short, medium and long-term goals, both personally and in your career?

Protect - Our most important asset is ourselves, we insure our home, car, pets, sometimes even our mobiles and washing machines – have you sat down and considered insuring yourself. Protecting yourself is my 2nd top tip.

Review your existing arrangements and look at your budget. Is your mortgage on the best rate, are you spending money you don't need? How much are your debts really costing you? Could you make additional savings and if so, what are you saving for? Are your retirement plans in order? – do you know what you REALLY have in place. 3rd top tip - Have an annual health check to review.

Five things lawyers should be asking their financial consultant

Richard Ollive, Senior Financial Consultant at Wesleyan answers the five questions that lawyers should be asking their financial consultant in the face of COVID-19

Lawyers across the country have had to adapt to the changing work environment due to the coronavirus outbreak. From setting up home-based legal counsel operations to conducting court hearings over audio or video links to comply with social distancing guidelines, there's no doubt that the ongoing crisis has had a significant impact on the legal sector. On top of the concerns they have about how they best serve clients, the current pandemic may also be having an impact on their personal finances.

Reproduced with the kind permission of Richard Ollive, here are five questions that every lawyer should be asking their financial consultant when it comes to navigating through the current climate.

What should I do about protection cover?

The impact of coronavirus will have put the importance of protection front of mind, and you may be considering how you can ensure you have the right support in place.

As a first step, it's important that you understand what personal and professional protection you already hold, including any existing policies and employer benefits.

From here, you can then assess whether the solutions you have meet your current or anticipated needs, and determine where you may benefit from additional cover.

One area to consider is income – specifically whether you have a plan or a solution to help meet day-to-day costs, bills or outgoings like mortgage payments – in the event that you are unable to work.

Lawyers may be entitled to benefits including sick pay, within the scope of their benefits.

While the degree of sick pay and additional benefits packages will vary depending on whether a lawyer works in the public or private sector and differ from firm to firm, they may only provide support for a relatively short period of time. A solution like income protection could prove valuable, providing you with continued income to replace a proportion of your earnings if injury or illness prevents you from working.

Finally, in an effort to cut costs amid coronavirus pressures, some lawyers may be considering cancelling protection policies they currently hold.

When it comes to examining areas where cost-reductions can be made, protection should generally be marked as a 'no-go' area if it's possible to do so – particularly considering the current environment of ongoing uncertainty.

What should I be thinking about when it comes to mortgages?

Although the outbreak has caused significant disruption to the housing market, lenders are continuing to offer mortgages.

If you're looking to buy a property, you should first carefully consider the full range of mortgage options available to identify the right solution for your current, or future, circumstances. Here, your financial consultant will be a useful source of advice.

A low interest-rate environment makes now a good time to consider re-mortgaging – a process that could help you save money by securing a better mortgage deal or help you avoid facing potentially higher costs should your current deal be coming to an end.

Some lawyers, or their partners, may have been furloughed in recent weeks and will be concerned about how this will affect their ability to secure finance.

It's important to remember that it is still possible to secure a mortgage or carry out a re-mortgage application in these circumstances, with lenders available that will accept and assess mortgage applications using income received through the government-backed Coronavirus Job Retention Scheme (CJRS).

If you already have a mortgage offer agreed, it's advisable that you check with your lender to make sure that the offer is still valid, and take the time to review whether the level of borrowing you have agreed remains right for you. Should your financial circumstances have changed due to the outbreak, a previously agreed arrangement might no longer be suitable.

What does coronavirus mean for my investments?

Coronavirus has had a wide-ranging impact on investments.

If you don't need to access cash tied up in your investments immediately, it's recommended that you leave invested funds untouched, giving them a chance to recover some value when markets improve. As with any investment activity, it's important to remember that the value could go down as well as up, and that you may get out less than you put in.

If you have additional cash available, now could be a particularly good time to look at how you can make it work harder for you through investments.

Before investing, it's important that you consider how current market conditions align with your appetite for risk, and consider whether you can afford to commit your funds. Investing is generally carried out over periods of five years or more and may not be for you if you anticipate needing to access invested money in the immediate future.

Speak to your financial consultant before making any decisions to help understand the right course of action for you.

What does this mean for my pension? Should I access it now?

If you were planning to retire during the outbreak, or are looking to alter your retirement plans as a result of current conditions, it's important that you first speak to your financial adviser to help understand the implications of any decision, and to determine whether this is the right time to proceed.

In this climate, some lawyers – who are eligible to do so – may also be considering drawing down pension funds to support personal cashflow. It's essential that you consider the longer-term implications this could have.

Given current market performance, withdrawing funds now could mean getting less out than six months ago and potentially less than what you might receive in six months to come

Your circumstances, or those of your retirement investments, may have changed, and your financial adviser will be able to offer guidance on each available option.

What else should I be doing to support my finances?

Given the events of recent months, lawyers may now be exploring further ways that they can support their personal finances and prepare for any further disruption.

One option is to consider any payment holidays available from your lender that would temporarily reduce or suspend repayments.

If you haven't already done so, now could also be a good time to consider building an adequate 'emergency fund' to help weather any future financial headwinds.

We would recommend that this is large enough to meet a minimum of three months of net household income, or around £15,000, whichever is lower.

As with any financial decision, it's important to consider the longer-term implications that this could have for you – your financial adviser will be able to help you assess whether it's right for your individual circumstances. Should you need any further information visit www.wesleyan.co.uk or call 0800 980 2277.

WESLEYAN | *we are all about you*

6 FUTURE LEADERS IN LAW

I have been considered as a leader in law. Who knows by the time I write my next book I may well be a QC or Judge. Who knows. In the meantime, I am keen to showcase as many future leaders in law as possible. The next generation of leaders in my profession and in business. I have won many awards and each year I nominate hundreds of people for awards. I believe in paying it forward.

There now follows a small selection of future leaders from the list on first book and this book. Some are black and ethnic minorities. Some are white. All are future leaders in law. We need all types of leaders in the future. Some are from very traditional backgrounds into the law but it is what they are doing that counts. I believe you cannot be what you don't see. Here is a small selection of future leaders. I interviewed them about #blacklivesmatter, the next 100 years for Women in the Law UK and diversity. Here is what they thought.

Please let me know some more future leaders to include in Talking Law Vol III.

Yoelle Lalaye

Essay Winner 2019

Who are you?

My name is Yoelle Lalaye, I am currently a second year student at Xaverian Sixth Form College

What a levels and career route did you take?

I studied English Language, French and Law at A levels and I plan on studying Law at Uni

What is your link with the author?

From winning the essay competition in 2019, concerning the enforcement of the Sex Disqualification Act 1919, we were able to hold contact.

Why law?

Part of my desire to study law derived from the Windrush scandal which occurred in the year 2018. I found it disturbing how such injustice was condoned and how nothing had been implemented to prevent the deportation and detainment of the British/Caribbean descendants.

Who inspires you and why do they inspire you?

Barack Obama, as from a young age he knew what he wanted and how to get there. He defined success for himself and stayed focused.

What is a mentor? What is a sponsor? What is the distinction and Did you have one in your career?

I currently have a mentor. A mentor is Someone who supports you and helps you achieve your career aspirations (with minimal engagement), whereas a sponsor is more of an institution / or an « advocate » who has found potential in you and therefore is willing to provide the funds and help required. Although both roles are conducted by experts, sponsors tend to possess higher roles in their profession and so utilise their influence to assist whoever they've sponsored. - for example when training to become a solicitor/barrister, many students require financial aid.

Do you think gender equality can and will be achieved in your profession?

For it to be achieved in the law profession, it needs to be dismantled in society. Society has imposed this hierarchy on us, on people to an extent where it's hard to examine whether or not equality can really be established in the legal profession. Lord justice Sumption for example asserted that women lack patience, and that addressing the imbalance would "put off talented male lawyers". Until the foundation of the legal profession gets polished, then we can foresee gender equality. People are still obtaining roles in the House of Lords through heritage and not their ability to work in that sector. Those are the type of people who are enforcing laws and dealing with bails... to conclude the system is unfair 😳

Are organisations like us still relevant and will they still be relevant? In 100 years?

Yes, they are relevant. It's important to raise awareness and combat these injustices and disparities. It's 2020... why should females feel inferior? Hashtags also such as #METOO are as relevant also, seeming as nowadays everyone seems to be active on social media.

Do you have a family?

I currently live with my parents and my little brother.

What do you think about diversity/ social mobility in our profession?

There is a lack of diversity. Whilst it may seem it is improving, there still remains a huge gap. For example: the lack of BAME representatives amongst the Supreme Court Justices.

What can each of us do to improve this in the profession?

Figure out the cause- what causes this? Why aren't there many BAME individuals wanting to involve themselves in the law? This could be dealt with by possibly targeting the younger generation because the legal industry.. regarding the way it's displayed appears uninviting.

What or how can the men in the profession help improve gender diversity?

By not finding opportunities to discriminate or impose their "superiority" unto anyone. We are all equal. Know your place. They should not abuse their relationships with women in the working environment.

What do you do for your mental wellbeing and Work life balance?

I spend time working out and painting. I also take time to read my bible.

What is your favourite book and why?

My favourite book is "Becoming" by Michelle Obama. She informs us about her past as a black female, coming from a socioeconomically disadvantaged background. Her life as a lawyer, a student, a graduate, a black woman in a white society. I really like her book because it is relatable and her journey with Barak Obama is inspirational.

Who is your favourite fictional lawyer and why?

Lee Joon-gi in *Lawless Lawyers* because he fights to restore justice in a corrupted city called Kisung. Behind all the corruption appears to be a senior judge named Lee Hye Young who is recognised as a woman enriched with power and authority.

What are your hobbies?

Before this pandemic I spent most of my time at the gym, I also engaged in basketball and athletics. At times when I have nothing much to do, I bring out my canvas and oil paints or draw.

What do you do for wellbeing?

I'm a Christian so keeping a close relationship with God sustains me.

How did you get involved in fundraising?

Again before this pandemic I was involved in a youth funding group. We would help the youth in our community with funds. For example if they were very passionate in doing gymnastics, however they required £500 to advance, they would fill an application with a proposal of XYZ and we would check if they were eligible for such fund. We would also put together small fairs for the community to advertise our group.

What advice do you have for overcoming obstacles?

Well, if you see it as a wall just know you can climb over it, but it requires effort. How much effort are you willing to put in to climb over that wall. A reward stands on the other side only you are just a couple cms away from it

Any regrets?

Not being overly passionate about my dream to pursue a career in athletics. I still dream about it now but then I look at my age and think it's possibly a bit too late.

What quote inspires you or do you live by?

"I can do everything through Christ, who gives me strength."

What would you like to see in the next 100 years?

In terms of gender, race and diversity.

In your profession?

Hopefully it will not take 100 years to resolve the issue concerning the lack of ethnic minorities in the legal profession. I would like to see a change of class. In the legal profession there are a lot of privileged individuals mainly because becoming a lawyer is quite an investment.

Ijeoma Igbokwe

In House Solicitor

Who are you?

Ijeoma Igbokwe – in-house solicitor within the financial services industry, specialising in civil litigation and corporate law.

What is your background?

Daughter of Nigerian parents who settled in the UK in the early 1970's. I was born and raised in Liverpool, in a working class home, and attended a state school. My mother was very keen on education and wanted my siblings and I to take every opportunity to better ourselves. She had always wanted to be a lawyer, but had never had the opportunity to do so. She became a nurse as that was the best opportunity available to her at the time and had a rewarding career as a nurse until her retirement.

Why did you want to become to your Lawyer?

I was inspired by my mother who always encouraged me to reach for the stars and never placed a limitation on what I could achieve.

Did you have another career beforehand?

No

How do you think the legal sector will change after COVID-19?

I believe there'll a greater degree of adaptable and flexible working within the profession than has previously been available. This will naturally improve the work/life balances for people; particularly women who are more likely to be the primary carer at home or have to work part-time to balance their commitments. I also think this improved way of working will allow for firms and organisations to have access to a broader range of talent, nationwide, as location will no longer be a barrier to recruitment.

How can the legal sector be more diverse?

Unconscious bias training is there to educate people on the subtleties of bias. The focus of unconscious bias training is typically on helping individuals understand and recognise their own unconscious and intrinsic biases and suggesting behaviours to mitigate the preconceptions we are all prone to.

Anonymising CVs – using this method during the first round candidate selection process will help minimise the impact of unconscious bias and nepotism in candidate selection.

Value based recruitment – this could be incorporated into a firm/organisation's existing recruitment process. The benefits of which is to ensure that the individual values and behaviours of a proposed candidate aligns with the values of the firm/organisation.

Nepotism is prevalent in the legal sector (and other industries); as the phrase commonly goes, it's not what you know but who you know. This can serve to compound the issue of limited diversity within the legal sector as opportunities are afforded to those with family ties or social connections within the legal sector. For example, candidates from a working class background and/or who are the first generation of their family in the UK, are unlikely to have family ties or social connections to someone in a position of influence within the legal sector.

Representation matters – the lack of diversity in senior positions within the legal sector can give the impression that there are barriers to advancement and progression within the sector. The legal sector would do well to reflect and research on why organisations tend to have some diversity at junior levels, but as seniority increases and you move up the professional ladder the diversity falls away.

Improving diversity in Human Resources departments could also support with encouraging diversity in organisations.

Do Black Lives Matter?

Yes

What does that mean to you?

It means that my life does not hold less weight or value because of my skin colour. It means that I am treated equally and fairly; judged as an individual on the content of my character and not the colour of my skin or on the basis of negative stereotypes. It means not having to have a conversation with my future children on how the world may treat them differently because of their skin colour. It also means my history and education not being limited to a month/event in the year and/or being limited to slavery and nothing else.

What do you want to see after the Black Lives Matter movement?

I don't think there'll be an "after" the BLM movement, at least not in my lifetime. The movement has reignited conversations and actions that began decades ago. There have been many historical figures that have fought for equality and justice for all; essentially the BLM movement stands on the shoulders of the giants of the Civil Rights movement, both in the US and the UK. The BLM movement is taking that mantle forward with this generation. What I'd like to see, at least in the next 5 years, is a firm and real commitment to change across our government, justice system, organisations, schools, health service, etc; not just lip service and/or black squares on social media while it's trending.

What do you want to see in the next 100 years in terms of gender and race?

First and foremost, equality. I'd love to think that in 100 years people would look back and be astounded that we placed so much emphasis and were so divisive over race and gender. I'd like to think that in 100 years' time the conversations we're having today, and that are needed today, would no longer be necessary.

What do you do for wellbeing?

Spend time with friends and family; exercise; read; listen to music; and visit spas

What advice for kids at school and secondary school who want to become lawyers?

Explore all your options – there are so many routes to becoming a lawyer, and what is suited to you will depend on your circumstances. Don't limit yourself to the conventional route and don't let rejection phase you. You will get there; how you get there is the exciting part.

Who inspires you and why?

My mother – her tenacity, perseverance and unwavering focus in the face of adversity will forever be an inspiration to me. Whenever I feel like I'm struggling or I can't do something, I remind myself that she scaled and conquered far greater obstacles with grace.

Favourite fictional lawyer and why?

Jessica Pearson (from TV Series 'Suits') – she's the perfect balance of grace and strength. Her character is formidable, but remains true to herself and her values. I'd also love her wardrobe and handbag collection.

Nicola Jackson

LPC student

Who are you?

Nicola Jackson, first class British Airways hostess and LPC student.

Why law?

I have always harboured a desire to study law as I have a passion for helping people and I want to be able to make the law accessible to those who may find it intimidating should they ever have a need for it. Twenty years after my first degree I achieved my goal by studying the GDL and I am now studying the LPC. I was fortunate to meet Sally Penni, founder of Women in the Law through my sister.

Who inspires you?

All those who have had to fight for things in their lives; my mother, my maternal grandmother, and the myriad of people that I have encountered through my job and through friends.

What is a mentor? What is a sponsor? Did you have one in your career?

A mentor is a person who gives you advice and encourages you in your career progression. Someone with a wealth of experience who has the patience and generosity to give you some of their time and who believes in you. A sponsor is a person who may champion you in your chosen field, who may introduce and promote you to people who have the ability to help you either get a foot on the ladder or help with career progression further down the line. They are important in the sense that they do not want to see you fail and so inspire you to keep going even when you feel hopeless.

I am very fortunate to have met and benefitted from the wise words and encouragement of Sally Penni and also the wonderful women in the law members that she has introduced me to.

Why do you support Women in the Law UK? What do you like about it?

I love the fact that it is an extremely welcoming network and is open to all to join as members whether you are a student or at the top of your career. It brings diversity in its membership and provides advice and support in a wealth of topics. The members are really encouraging of others and genuinely want to support each other to achieve their individual and collective goals.
I support the organisation as I believe it to be a fantastic opportunity for women (and men) with an interest in the law to develop themselves both cerebrally and spiritually. When I eventually qualify, I hope to be able to give back the encouragement and support that I have found from the incredible people that I have met through the organisation.

Are organisations like WILUK still relevant and will they still be relevant in 100 years?

Absolutely! In such a challenging society and in a world of huge competition organisations such as Women in the Law UK are very relevant and necessary. People will always need advice and encouragement from their peers, and an organisation in which the members strive to help rather than compete is essential for community in the legal world.

Do you have a family?

In the traditional sense of the word I have a very close relationship with my mother and sister, and I am a favourite aunty to my two adorable nephews. I also class my friends as my family as we have always been there to support each other through both the happy times and the sad.

What do you think about diversity/social mobility in the profession?

I think that it has definitely improved in the past twenty years but there is still a long way to go before any child no matter what their background will consider a career in law without thinking that it is unavailable to them.

What can each of us do to improve this in the profession?

We can try to find ways of granting opportunities to those who do not have the traditional connections. To champion other attributes of students and career changers and to instil a culture of diversity in the sphere that we work in.

What or how can men in the profession help improve gender diversity?

Men should appreciate the attributes that women have that they themselves often do not, and focus on what women can bring to being a well rounded team who work together. That certain qualities such as soft skills actually enhance the overall experience for the clients. Generally working as a team will inevitably mean that each other's attributes rub off and everyone has a part to play.

What do you do for mental wellbeing? Work/life balance?

I try to escape from daily life for an hour a day (usually bedtime) into a good book. I strongly believe in some form of daily exercise even if that is just a short walk in the fresh air. I gain perspective on life from spending time with friends and family who only expect me to be me.

What is your favourite book and why?

I read so many books and have so many favourites but off the top of my head I would say "Rebecca" by Daphne du Maurier. The twisted story set against the wonderfully descriptive background of Cornwall. I always disappear into the pages and can almost feel like a real life observer of the tale of intense loyalty and devotion.

Favourite fictional lawyer and why?

I think that has to be Atticus in "To kill a Mockingbird" as that was the first book that I read that had the law as its story and I was enthralled by his integrity and determination to fight for justice for all despite the small town mentality in which he resided. His humility and his resilience in raising his children and teaching them the value of life.

Who is your favourite male role model and why?

I think that would have to be Barack Obama who managed to combine holding the highest office in the world whilst still being a fantastic father and husband. A man who was clearly devoted to his family, championed his wife, and had humility and integrity.

What are your hobbies?

Along with reading I love to cook, mainly with spices and have been lucky enough to attend cookery schools in Thailand and India. I love the mountains and try to ski a few times a year and also pop out for a week in the summer for walks and picnics.

What advice do you have for overcoming obstacles? What have you had to overcome?

I have encountered many obstacles both in my personal life and my work/study life and I think the answer for both is the same. When you get knocked down it is important to feel sad or despondent as that will be what inspires you to pick yourself up and be determined to move on. If you never experience failure, then you have no idea of how to improve. Determination, tenacity, and the support of good friends and family is essential for overcoming the trials and tribulations that you will experience in your life journey.

I also asked Nicola about herself as a future leader in law.

What is your background?

Born in 1974, I had a very happy childhood. Both my parents were teachers and so education was obviously important to them. After my parents divorced in my late teens my mother was determined that both my sister and I would not suffer educationally and so single handedly ensured that we were able to go to university, something that I will be forever grateful for. Whether she was disappointed that I chose to become cabin crew after university I'll never know as she has always been so supportive of me.

Why did you want to become a lawyer?

I always wanted to read law at university, but I did not achieve the A level grades required when I was 18. Twenty years later I managed to achieve that goal by studying the GDL in which I gained a distinction. As I got older I imagine that my reason for wanting to become a lawyer changed from when I was at school; I realised that many people are intimidated by the law, that lawyers sometimes appear to speak another language and so my goal has always been to make the law more accessible for those who need it. To be able to achieve the outcome that people are seeking whilst putting them at ease throughout the process.

Did you have another career beforehand?

I spent twenty four years flying long-haul for British Airways looking after passengers in the first and business class cabins. I absolutely loved the opportunities that I was granted by being a first class 'trolley dolly' and experienced things that many could only dream about; climbing Mount Fuji in Japan, wandering across the Golden Gate Bridge for lunch in Sausalito, watching the fireworks over Sydney Harbour from a yacht, getting to know NYC better than my home city, and my absolute favourite seeing the new millennium in at

Victoria Falls, Zimbabwe with three elephants and a bottle of champagne!

How do you think that the legal sector will change after Covid-19?

I imagine that there will be more opportunities to work remotely and lawyers will have to develop more technical skills.

How can the legal sector be more diverse?

By focussing more on the aptitude of new lawyers rather than the traditional academic approach. Historically the legal sector has been seen as one where the majority need to have achieved excellent grades and have a wealth of connections which may be out of reach for students from poor backgrounds. By encouraging career changers to bring their transferable skills and embracing applicants who do not fit the traditional mould.

Do black lives matter? What does that mean to you?

Of course black lives matter. It is incredibly important for society to steer away from prejudice and the judgment of people by the colour of their skin. I am fortunate to have been raised to appreciate every person for who they are rather than what they are and where they may come from. As a little girl I was cared for by my granny so that my mother could continue her career, my gran lived on a road where she was the only white lady and I never considered the people living by her as anything other than her neighbours thanks to the inclusivity that the street had.

What do you want to see after the black lives matter movement?

I would wish that not only the future generations but just as importantly the older and my generation reach a point where diversity is seen as a major positive, where we all can learn from each other's experiences and what people bring to the conversation. I would like to think that the subject of race is one that is discussed freely without any awkwardness. Most importantly I would like for my nephews to grow up into young men who feel that whoever they socialise with are accepted as individuals and no less important than them.

What do you want to see in the next 100 years in terms of gender and race?

I would like to see a world where gender and race do not play a part in the jobs and opportunities that people have. Where the percentage of people in partner roles accurately reflect the number of women and BAME employees in the sector and that all sectors of society have a diverse workforce who are achieving equal pay regardless of their race or gender.

What do you do for wellbeing?

I am actually quite good at switching off from daily life and losing myself in a good book. I prefer reading to watching films or television and love to escape into the pages of another world. I try to eat healthily and ensure that I manage some form of exercise every day.

What advice for kids at school would you give for those who want to become lawyers?

I would suggest that they initially work hard and seek as much support in their studies as possible. For those who may not have the academic aptitude to attain the required grades to read law at university I would advise them to never give up if that is their dream, instead to work for a while in another area to save the money for funding, and then to apply again as a mature student when dedication and aptitude is valued more highly than A-level grades.

Who inspires you?

My maternal grandmother has always been my inspiration. As a seamstress she encouraged my mother to fulfil her desire to become a teacher and then supported her return to the profession after she had her own children. She was not afraid of anyone and she treated everyone, no matter what their status, the same. When her house was served with a compulsory purchase order and she was offered a pittance for the home that she had lived in for seventy years she refused to move, instead she was the last woman standing in a road full of boarded up houses, only moving when she achieved four times the original offer. She was 88 at the time!

FUTURE LEADERS IN LAW
ONES TO WATCH LIST

Some future leaders to looks out for and follow in their work

1. Amanda Oluwapelumi Adeoala, HC at Family Law firm and part time Tribunal Judge,
2. Chrissie Wolfe, Solicitor, Irwin Mitchell LLP
3. Nicola Jackson LPS student
4. Gabrille Coates BTPC
5. Amlia Albu student
6. Kashmira Aukeer student
7. Ambiola Johnson Barrister
8. Alexandra Wilson , barrister @essexbarrister
9. Christian Weaver, Barrister garden court North
10. Natasha Shotunde
11. Michael Ettiene
12. Karen Kabweru-Namulemu
13. Mass Ndow-Nijie founder of Bridging the Bar
14. Akil hunte, Trainee solicitor at CMS founder of Skills for lawyers
15. Ciara Bartlam
16. Emily Landale
17. Mira Hammad
18. Elaine Banton 9 Bedford Row not so young but leader
19. Cordella Bart -Stewart
20. Chrissie Wolfe
21. Natsha Allen, (non lawyer) Irwin Mitchell LLP
22. Amanda Oluwapelumi Adeoala, HC at Family Law firm and part time Tribunal Judge,
23. Yaa dankwa Ampadu-Sackey
24. Ijeoma Igbokwe, Lawyer, head of colections at Hoist Finance
25. Harold Brako, Solicitor Addleshaw Goddard
26. ....INSERT YOUR NAME

7 SKILLS FOR FUTURE LAWYERS

WWW.WOMENINTHELAWUK.COM COVID 19 skills webinars.

During the pandemic, I carried on my work with women in the law trying to upskill educate and above all inspire, support connect. Covering topics and soft skills to students, established junior lawyers to senior lawyers. From wellbeing to nutrition to confidence and coping with imposter syndrome. Other areas covered included interviews with inspirational leaders called How I reached the Top and also Why Black lives Matter to young People. These are available to watch again on Youtube channel. Type in Womeninthelawuk on Youtube. Do watch and give us a like . I hope you find them useful. Until the date of writing this book these were over 109 webinars, podcasts, articles on various social media platforms.

Thank you to the hundreds of expert speakers who I hosted and cross examined on the subjects. We all learnt so much. Of course they are available to give training to the organisations you work for. Thank you.

Date	Event	Topic	Speaker
Friday, 13 March 2020	Postponed - Future Women in the Law Conference by Women in the Law UK		Andy Burnham, Mayor of Manchester
Thursday, 19 March 2020	POSTPONED ANNUAL DINNER CELEBRATING INTERNATIONAL WOMENS DAY		Baroness Hale, former President, UK Supreme Court

Friday, 20 March 2020	Friday Lunch and Learn	Social Media	Alex McCann
Tuesday, 24 March 2020	Tuesday Lunch and Learn	Managing personal wellbeing during lockdown	Kate Thorpe
Thursday, 26 March 2020	Thursday Lunch and Learn	Networking	Sue Tonks
Friday, 27 March 2020	Friday Lunch and Learn	How to be an Effective Communicator?	Susan Heaton Wright
Tuesday, 31 March 2020	Tuesday Lunch and Learn	Managing Neuro Diverse People in the Work Place	Rachel Morgan Trimmer
Friday, 3 April 2020	Friday Lunch and Learn	Wellbeing	Susan Carr
Tuesday, 7 April 2020	Tuesday Lunch and Learn	Wellbeing	Adriana Galimberti-Rennie
Thursday, 9 April 2020	Thursday Lunch and Learn	Financial Wellbeing	Sarah Deacon from Wesleyan
Friday, 10 April 2020	Friday Lunch and Learn	How to be more Resilient	Rachel Ward Lilley
Tuesday, 14 April 2020	Tuesday Lunch and Learn	Nutrition and exercise during uncertain times	Veera Stannard
Thursday, 16 April 2020	Thursday Lunch and Learn	How to Be A Good General Counsel	Kevin Withane
Friday, 17	Friday		SRA

April 2020	Lunch and Learn		
Tuesday, 21 April 2020	Tuesday Lunch and Learn	Imposter Syndrome	Vanessa Ugatti
Thursday, 23 April 2020	Thursday Lunch and Learn	Wellbeing During Lockdown	Maria Mander
Friday, 24 April 2020	Friday Lunch and Learn	Social Media	Alex McCann
Tuesday, 28 April 2020	Tuesday Lunch and Learn	Careers how to Become a Magistrate	Tricia Peters
Tuesday, 28 April 2020	"In Conversation with….."	How I reached the top	Mary Prior QC
Thursday, 30 April 2020	Thursday Lunch and Learn	How to get published	Nigel Booth
Thursday, 30 April 2020	"In Conversation with….."		Sally Penni
Friday, 1 May 2020	Friday Lunch and Learn	How to Manage your fear of Public Speaking	Susan Heaton-Wright
Tuesday, 5 May 2020	Tuesday Lunch and Learn	Happiness Coach	Hannah Beko
Thursday, 7 May 2020	Thursday Lunch and Learn	Networking	Sue Tonks
Friday, 8 May 2020	Friday Lunch and Learn	How to Look Cool on Zoom	Allie Crewe
Friday, 8	Friday	How to use	Eileen Donaghey

May 2020	Lunch and Learn	Instagram for Business	
Monday, 11 May 2020	Monday Lunch and Learn	How to get published	TheManWithTheBeard.com
Tuesday, 12 May 2020	Tuesday Lunch and Learn	"Fashion and Lock Down"	Harry Purewal
Wednesday, 13 May 2020	Wednesday Lunch and Learn	How I reached the top	Grieselda Togobo Forward Ladies
Thursday, 14 May 2020	Thursday Lunch and Learn	HowTo Communicate With Confidence	Luan De Burgh
Thursday, 14 May 2020	"In Conversation with....."		Tim Lambert
Friday, 15 May 2020	Friday Lunch and Learn	Confidence	Sarah Perris
Monday, 18 May 2020	Monday Lunch and Learn	How I reached the Top	Stacey Copeland Pro Boxer and Broadcaster
Tuesday, 19 May 2020	Tuesday Lunch and Learn	Developing Skills for a Future Lawyer	Suzanne Reece
Thursday, 21 May 2020	Thursday Lunch and Learn	How to energise and liberate your talent	Rachel Brushfield
Thursday, 21 May 2020	"In Conversation with....."	Authentic/Smart Influencing in the Legal Sector!	Donna Mcgrath
Friday, 22 May 2020	Friday Lunch and Learn	Wellbeing	Adriana-Galimberti-Rennie

Monday, 25 May 2020	Monday Lunch and Learn	Additional income streams to the law	Bethan Jepson
Tuesday, 26 May 2020	Tuesday Lunch and Learn	CV specialist	Rebecca Pay
Wednesday, 27 May 2020	Wednesday Lunch and Learn	How I reached the top	Emma Palmer
Wednesday, 27 May 2020	Wednesday Special	The Power of Change - Learning to be a Weirdo	Rachel Morgan Trimmer
Thursday, 28 May 2020	Thursday Lunch and Learn	Three advanced ways to get publicity during a pandemic	Carrie Eddins
Thursday, 28 May 2020	"In Conversation with....."	Happiness Coach	Hannah Beko
Friday, 29 May 2020	Friday Lunch and Learn	becoming a DDJ	Ruwena Khan
Friday, 29 May 2020	Book and Theatre Club	Book Club Convictions	Caroline England
Monday, 1 June 2020	Monday Lunch and Learn	disciplinaries during COVID 19	SRA
Tuesday, 2 June 2020	Tuesday Lunch and Learn	Leadership	Tim Lambert
Wednesday, 3 June 2020	Wednesday Lunch and Learn	Financial Wellbeing	Weslyen
Thursday,	Thursday	Networking	Kirsty James from

4 June 2020	Lunch and Learn		Colony Networking
Thursday, 4 June 2020	"In Conversation with….."	Good Posture and Pain	Suzette Pulman
Friday, 5 June 2020	Friday Lunch and Learn	Careers you and CV advice	Duanne Courmell
Tuesday, 9 June 2020	Tuesday Lunch and Learn	Imposter Syndrome	Kate Dodd
Wednesday, 10 June 2020	Wednesday Lunch and Learn	Out of a Crisis Comes Opportunity	Ella Overshot
Thursday, 11 June 2020	Thursday Lunch and Learn	Branding	Tanya Lloyd
Thursday, 11 June 2020	"In Conversation with….."	How to raise your profile and get more client	Stuart Anderson
Friday, 12 June 2020	Friday Lunch and Learn	Employment rights for women	Sarah Evans
Monday, 15 June 2020	Monday Lunch and Learn	PR and Advertising	Stuart Anderson
Tuesday, 16 June 2020	Tuesday Lunch and Learn	How to have more gravitas	Kevin Withane
Thursday, 18 June 2020	Thursday Lunch and Learn	My Journey from Solicitor	Phil Barnes
Thursday, 18 June 2020	"In Conversation with….."		Sally Penni
Friday, 19	Friday	Lawcare	Mary B. Jackson from

June 2020	Lunch and Learn		Lawcare
Friday, 19 June 2020	SPECIAL	Why Black Lives Matter	
Monday, 22 June 2020	How I Got to the Top		Karen Borden
Tuesday, 23 June 2020	Tuesday Lunch and Learn	from lawyer to other talents	Graham Hansen
Tuesday, 23 June 2020	How I Got to the Top		Sharon Amesu
Wednesday, 24 June 2020	Wednesday Lunch and Learn		Donna Mcgrath
Wednesday, 24 June 2020	Wednesday Special		Jodie Hill
Thursday, 25 June 2020	Thursday Lunch and Learn	How To Become A Judge	DJ Mark Angus Tribunal Judge
Thursday, 25 June 2020	"In Conversation with....."	COVID and recruitment	Duane Cormell
Friday, 26 June 2020	Friday Lunch and Learn	Prime your personal brand on camera and in person	Shola Kaye
Friday, 26 June 2020	Book and Theatre Club		Sally Penni Talking Law
Tuesday, 30 June 2020	Tuesday Lunch and Learn	Resilience	Rachel Ward Liley
Thursday, 2 July 2020	"In Conversation		

	with….."		
Friday, 3 July 2020	Friday Lunch and Learn	Branding	Janine Esbrand
Tuesday, 7 July 2020	Tuesday Lunch and Learn	Media Training, Crisis Communicatio ns and Presentations Skills	Catherine Across
Thursday, 9 July 2020	Thursday Lunch and Learn		Carol Gillespie
Thursday, 9 July 2020	"In Conversati on with….."		
Friday, 10 July 2020	Friday Lunch and Learn		
Tuesday, 14 July 2020	Tuesday Lunch and Learn		
Thursday, 16 July 2020	Thursday Lunch and Learn		
Thursday, 16 July 2020	"In Conversati on with….."		
Friday, 17 July 2020	Friday Lunch and Learn		
Tuesday, 21 July 2020	Tuesday Lunch and Learn		
Thursday, 23 July	Thursday Lunch and		

2020	Learn		
Thursday, 23 July 2020	"In Conversation with....."		
Friday, 24 July 2020	Friday Lunch and Learn		
Tuesday, 28 July 2020	Tuesday Lunch and Learn		
Thursday, 30 July 2020	Thursday Lunch and Learn		
Thursday, 30 July 2020	"In Conversation with....."		
Friday, 31 July 2020	Friday Lunch and Learn		
Friday, 31 July 2020	Book and Theatre Club	Caroline England, author	Women in the Law UK Book and Theatre Club
Tuesday, 25 August 2020	Birthday Q&A 1-2pm	Careers Advice	Sally Penni
Tuesday, 25 August 2020	Birthday Drinks 7-9pm	Q&A Building Allies	Christian Weaver and Ciara Bartlam
Friday, 4 September 2020	Book and Theatre Club	Chris Daw QC Justice on Trial	Women in the Law UK Book and Theatre Club
Friday, 25 September 2020	Book and Theatre Club	Sarah Vaughan, Anatomy of a Scandal	Women in the Law UK Book and Theatre Club
Thursday, 19	Annual Conference	With Joanna Hardy	

November 2020		Barrister	

8 CONCLUSIONS

I have enjoyed interviewing and talking about the law with my guests pre-Covid19 and during Covid19. These podcasts have attracted nearly 20K listeners. I hope that, like me, you have been inspired by them and they bring you joy.

I hope they showcase ordinary leaders in the law and they are a representation of the rich diversity in the law.

I also hope to interview many more guests. Whatever the future holds, I look forward to my own career progression, whether that is as a QC, TC, a Bencher and or as a Recorder. I hope to progress if anything to defy the narrative and the double deficit.

It is important, as Dexter Dias QC and his research in Cambridge and Harvard indicate, that minority lawyers should not self-select out.

On the next stage of my journey if I succeed then you succeed.

Talking Law Volume II is part of a trilogy of books. I look forward to the final book.

Now get thinking about yourself and fill in the boxes on the next few pages!

How can you improve your wellbeing?

What can you do to improve diversity in the law?
e.g. mentor, speak in schools, read in schools

Who inspires you?

What is your favourite book and why?

What do you want your legacy to be?

What are you grateful for?

What are your five-year goals?
(You can't score without a goal)

ABOUT THE AUTHOR

Sally Penni is a practising barrister with over 20years experience
She is an author, legal commentator, public speaker and trainer.
She is passionate about access to the profession as well as social
mobility. Sally has also written legal text books as well as professional
development books and a children's book. She was awarded the
MBE in the Queen's Birthday Honours List 2020 for services to
diversity, social mobility and the law.

Follow her on:

- *On Twitter @sallypenni1*
- *Through Linked In*
- *Instgram @sjsallypenni*
- *She blogs at www.sallypenni1.co.uk*
- *Talking Law Podcast is available free on iTunes or Spotify, free via
  www.womeninthelawuk.com click on podcast or Youtube*

Coming soon – more books from Sally Penni

A Sense of Purpose

Penni on Data Protection

Penni on Employment Rights for Women

Penni on the Triple C's: Confidence, Clarity and Connection, Advice on How To Have More Triple C's and Beat Your Imposter Syndrome

Rosie and the Unicorn (children's book)

Thank you for reading this book

This book would not have been possible without
Wesleyan

WESLEYAN | *we are all about you*

www.wesleyan.co.uk

Profits from the sales of this book go to the following six charities

Billable Hour

Lawcare

Royal Manchester Children's Hospital

Manchester University
NHS Foundation Trust

Barristers' Benevolent Association

FRU

Advocate

Connect with Women In the Law UK

The Talking Law Podcast

Listen for new episodes on iTunes and wherever you get your podcasts

Coming up:

Alison Lobb, solicitor and managing partner
Mary Prior QC
Anesta Weekes QC
Simon McCrum
Andrew Powell, barrister
Harold Brako, solicitor, Addleshaw Goddard
Felicity Gerry QC
Professor Leslie Thomas QC
Max Hardy, barrister
Sam Hillas QC
Courtney Griffiths QC

Printed in Great Britain
by Amazon